I0816169

GREAT NATURE WISCONSIN

A GUIDE FOR NATURE IMMERSION IN WISCONSIN

RANDY HOFFMAN
LAURA & CODY STINGLEY

Little Creek Press
5341 Sunny Ridge Road
Mineral Point, WI 53565

ORDERING INFORMATION
Quantity sales. Special discounts are available on quantity purchases by corporations, associations, and others. For details, contact info@littlecreekpress.com

Orders by US trade bookstores and wholesalers.
Please contact Little Creek Press or Ingram for details.

Printed in the United States of America

Cataloging-in-Publication Data
Names: Randolph (Randy) Hoffman, Laura Stingley, and Cody Stingley, authors
Title: Great Nature Wisconsin
Description: Mineral Point, WI Little Creek Press, 2024
Identifiers: LCCN: 2024912199 | ISBN: 978-1-955656-75-7
Classification: TRAVEL / Special Interest / Family

Book design by Little Creek Press

For
Amelia
and Kai

Table of Contents

PREFACE

During one of my talks, an audience member asked a question, and I fumbled to answer. I presented how I developed the idea for my book *When Things Happen: A Guide to Natural Events in Wisconsin*. The presentation format focused on the who, what, where, how, why, and when of nature. I asked, "What resources are available for the nature enthusiast?"

The who is us. Dozens of books and online resources tell us what's in nature. Similarly, many resources tell us how to experience nature, especially with children. I explained the many information sources on where to hike, bike, paddle, and experience Wisconsin's most remarkable scenery.

Much of the presentation zeroed in on the why question. Thoreau was in love with a pond. Muir captured the wilderness ethos. Leopold made us think about the philosophical and ethical values of the natural world.

More recently, Richard Louv's book, *The Nature Principle*, asks and answers the fundamental question: What would our lives be like if we had as much nature immersion as technology? Florence Williams' book, *The Nature Fix*, investigates the science behind nature's positive effects on the brain and health, and informs the framework of this book.

Audience members asked whether Wisconsin-focused books are available for those wanting to apply the nature pyramid to their families. I was at a loss. I could not recall any such publications.

Later that evening, my thoughts harkened to nature experiences with my family. Vivid memories of the awe we experienced and felt upon entering an old-growth redwood forest. We stood silently, heads pointing skyward, slowly circling, without saying a word for over a half hour. We conversed in hushed tones for the rest of our slow hike as if respecting nature's majesty.

Another memory sprang forth that evening. My wife and I were on a Boundary Waters wilderness canoe trip with four other couples. We and another couple were seasoned paddlers and knew of a prime camping location. The strong winds, however, changed our plans.

We headed toward the campsite when the winds capsized one of the trailing canoes. One paddler suffered leg contusions while trying to escape from the lake. Plans needed immediate change. Our preconceived joyous campsite thoughts have now transformed into care and empathy for others. EMTs were not on call. As a group, we administered medical care as best we could and prepared to spend the night in a mosquito-infested brushland.

Two examples of millions where nature can transform normality.

Nature immersion offers bountiful benefits for humanity. Well-documented benefits include adolescent identity formation, grief, trauma healing, personal introspection, problem-solving, improved cognition, contemplative places, etc.

The nature pyramid provides a template for achieving the values nature offers.

Daily, spend some time outdoors, smell the flowers, get your hands dirty, make snow angels, play games, etc.

Every week, spend a few hours outdoors hiking a neighborhood trail, fishing, watching birds, exploring a pond, etc. Plan a nature outing that focuses on exploring and learning.

Every month, spend a weekend in nature, and vary the activities according to everyone's personal experience. New adventurers can simply be camping at a local park. Experienced enthusiasts may tackle physical or mental challenges.

Annually, spend a vacation in the wild. Locations must match the needs and experiences of the visitors. Family-friendly places may have a campground with a nature trail and beach for swimming. Those seeking wilderness therapy may use the abundant acres available that provide dispersed camping and bushcraft opportunities.

Where are the remaining places to reap the benefits of nature immersion? This question provided the impetus for compiling this book. It focuses on annual, monthly, and a sampling of weekly nature immersion needs of the citizens of Wisconsin and visitors from other locations.

Randy Hoffman

How to Use This Book

We wrote this book for those who consider nature an essential part of their lives. Also, we hope that others will appreciate nature's important role in maximizing human performance.

This book contains our top 400 places for a weekend excursion, a weeklong vacation, and a sample of our favorite weekly visitation areas. It is not all-inclusive because knowledge of every resource available in the state is impossible. Besides this book, the reader should attain local knowledge of sites and garner information from trusted sources.

We created a resource to be as inclusive as possible but much less than a Wikipedia of nature immersion sites. With limitations on size, we have shortcuts to information that needs explanation.

The heading gives the site's title, although some more significant areas have many subsections that may have other local names. Following the title is a dollar symbol followed by a letter. This means fees are charged for entrance (E), camping (C), trail use (T), or a more descriptive notation, such as a fee for biking.

The critical component of the book is locational information. Using a Global Positioning System (GPS), the location is identified by latitude and longitude (lat-long). The pin is usually at the entrance road or parking area. Sometimes, the pin is in the interior of a wild or sizeable natural area. For almost all state wildlife areas, national forest areas, and county forests, the pin is only at one of several access locations. The reader may need other resources to find the best accessible location for their interest.

Next are a series of 16 icons showing the nature immersion qualities of the site.

TRAIL. The site has trails for hiking. Sometimes developed trails are available, such as in state parks, but are often more primitive, such as maintenance roads in state wildlife areas, hunter-walking trails in county forests, or cross-country ski trails when there is no snow.

PAVED OR HARD-PACKED TRAIL. These trails are more developed and accessible for those with mobility concerns. In the text of sites, we list these trails as accessible. They are also great places for families with younger children or those with little nature experience.

BEACH. This icon shows that the site has a place for sandy shoreline activities. In almost all instances, the beaches are on natural lakes. Recreating at such sites opens the water world for youngsters by providing avenues for exploring aquatic biology and splashing in the water.

FISHING. We highlight these areas as places for youth or novice anglers to get a taste of the sport, not to highlight high-quality fishing locations.

CANOE OR KAYAK. This icon identifies the availability of canoeing access. Canoeing experiences range from calm water to dangerous rapids. The reader must assess their mastery of paddling. Challenging water may require experienced guides.

CAMPING. We chose campsites with limited motorized camper units for more solitude. Most sites with this symbol are more rustic camping areas. The icon also shows locations for primitive camping, such as dispersed camping on county and national forests or sandbar camping along paddle routes.

MOUNTAIN BIKE TRAIL. The sites with this icon have designated mountain bike trails. The text will give the mileage if known.

PAVED OR HARD-PACKED BIKE TRAIL. These trails are accessible to a wide range of non-motorized bikes. Many of these trails also accommodate hikers and other users, such as inline skaters.

BOARDWALK. These areas have significant floating boardwalks, elevated boardwalks, or spurs to observation decks. Also included are cord walks on shifting dunes. We did not include trails with short sections of elevated structures that avoid wet areas or small bridges crossing streams.

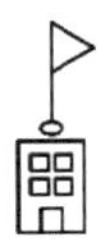

VISITOR CENTER. Sites harboring indoor centers for displays and other educational materials that may enhance the visitor's nature experience. These locations are significant as introductory centers to alleviate fears or trepidations among younger children and places to instill wonder.

STREAM OR RIVER. The value of water resources is an instant draw for enthusiasts. They are tremendous places for young, budding nature lovers to immerse themselves in the natural world.

WATERFALL OR RAPIDS. Another natural feature that acts as a focus for some adventures. While alluring, these features have inherent dangers associated with them. Serious injuries happen every year on slippery, unforgiving rocks.

LAKE. Similar to other water features in their ability to focus on nature experiences. The lakes featured in this book focus on undeveloped shorelines where the interplay of land and water can best be understood.

CLIFF OR ROCK OUTCROP. These features attract many outdoor lovers to these natural formations, with many wanting to climb them. Use caution within these areas. Keep the safety of yourself and your companions in mind as well as the safety of the natural world around you.

OBSERVATION TOWER OR DECK. These locations are a natural draw for overview and contemplation.

SNOWSHOE TRAIL. The icon shows there is an officially designated snowshoe trail. However, off-trail snowshoeing is available at most sites in the book.

The box of natural values found in the annual visitation sites gives the reader a quality ranking for general nature immersion principles. We added a gauge to give the reader a relative sense of our rankings. Many factors are considered when deciding your next family vacation. For those seeking areas to reap nature's benefits and needing a nature fix, these quality rankings can help with those decisions:

AREA			
	LOW	MEDIUM	HIGH
NATURAL DIVERSITY		✓	
PHYSICAL CHALLENGE			✓
ACCESS FRIENDLY		✓	
SERENITY AND SOLITUDE			✓
NIGHT SKIES			✓

NATURAL DIVERSITY shows the biological and geological diversity level found at the site with “high” indicating the most diversity. Ecological studies have shown that the most diverse places are the most resistant to long-term change. People in nature studies reveal the cognitive benefits of nature immersion as biological diversity increases. Benefits from a botanically rich forest are more significant than a forested city park with mowed bluegrass.

PHYSICAL CHALLENGE is excellent for adolescents, those experiencing grief, those recovering from trauma, individuals training for endurance activities, or anyone looking for a challenge. “Low” references easy hikes, level terrain, and calm water, whereas “high" indicates the inverse.

ACCESS FRIENDLY identifies areas that prioritize the needs of individuals with varying physical abilities. “High” reflects the ease of entry into the site, nature trails, more developed campgrounds, etc. The high-rated sites are ideal for families with younger children and those needing higher levels of accessibility.

SERENITY AND SOLITUDE show areas affected by noise. An example is camping at Mill Bluff State Park. The natural diversity is outstanding, but the campground is close to the interstate highway and its continuous noise.

NIGHT SKIES reflect light pollution. This will help you identify the best areas to retreat from this pollution and get lost in stargazing. Low to high identifies the least visibility to the best visibility for stargazing.

This box is color-coded to identify the site’s primary nature immersion feature rapidly. The colors and their associated values are further explained in the next section.

Next, the text details the property's nature connection values and amenities, as well as sources for more information. We list a primary information site, acknowledging that websites frequently change. We've recorded sites with the best potential for longevity. However, the reader may need to search for additional sources. We present URL addresses that are current as of 2024. If a link doesn't work, we suggest searching the site's name on Google.

Nature Principle Summary

The nature principle is backed by rigorous scientific studies that describe multiple ways nature immersion benefits human well-being. The many ways connecting to the natural world are fundamental and include balancing time spent on technology, enhancing physical and mental health, expanding the definition of community to include all living things, and purposefully developing an attachment to a region and its natural history.

We strongly support the notion that nature plays a significant role in human development. These intimate connections last from birth to death and can change during a lifetime. Any site can hold multiple benefits for users, but some sites provide more benefits for certain aspects of the nature principle.

We itemize these primary values by the site in the text to give the reader options regarding what sites meet their needs. needs. The words and phrases in the text are our choices for the nature rejuvenation values found at the sites. We acknowledge that the primary values described are subjective, and each reader needs to decide on a site's natural values.

Determining what values to describe combines our interpretation of the nature principle concepts and knowledge of the site characteristics. We matched them to our ability, but every site has intrinsic features. Fine-tuning nature's benefits may be impossible, and any nature is dramatically better than no nature.

COGNITIVE ENRICHMENT AREA. Improved cognition benefits thought processes, reasoning, perception, and awareness. The evidence regarding the benefits to brain health continues to grow. Several days in nature improve focused attention, cognitive flexibility, and improved memory. In addition, creative thinking parameters significantly increased in studies. There is a multitude of studies confirming nature's benefits, and we encourage readers to investigate further. We lump creativity, original thinking, inspiration, and innovative thinking into our definition of creative sites. We reserve this category for places with outstanding biodiversity and geodiversity. Research indicates that these highly complex sites maximize many of the cognition values described earlier.

FAMILY IMMERSION AREA. These areas are more accessible than others in the book. They have amenities for younger people and have fewer obstacles for families to navigate. In addition, they are great for helping adolescents form their identities, which is an essential part of building a lifelong unified sense of self. This process happens most rapidly during adolescence. The body's rapid transformation during puberty, increased activity in neural connectivity, and social interactions can create a lifelong trajectory of self-esteem. Knowing one's place in the technological and natural worlds can help develop an individual into a more rounded adult.

FOREST THERAPY AREA. These sites are wonderful for personal introspection, which combines the concepts of self-examination, contemplation, meditation, and spiritual reflection. This process involves silently talking to oneself and often involves analyzing personal actions taken or projected onto others. Such actions can lead to more mindful human beings.

The concept of awe also includes wonder, respect, and amazement. Definitions of awe include both dread and wonder. We focus on the wonder part of the definition and its value to humans. Awe can improve mood and self-satisfaction. Feelings of wonder can make us more humble, generous, and connected with others who have the same feelings. Studies have shown that people experiencing awe have reduced levels of inflammation and increased aspects of critical thinking.

PROBLEM-SOLVING AREA. While immersing oneself in nature, problem-solving can take on many forms that enhance cognition and self-value—the challenges of navigating around a deadfall while paddling, deciding where to place a dispersed wilderness camping site safe from bears, ticks, and mosquitoes, or using bushcraft to thrive without modern conveniences.

WILDERNESS THERAPY AREA most commonly refers to a combination of wilderness challenges and professional treatments to offer mental health benefits. In these therapy situations, they combine wilderness challenges with professional treatments. Our concept goes much beyond that narrow definition. We assert that we need spaces for the mind to recover from technology. Spending a week away from instantaneous information at our fingertips becomes akin to technological withdrawal. Such outings give context and perspective to our tech dependence.

In addition, the application of two more nature principles can occur within any of the above areas. Restorative sites refer to locations where the concept of restoring nature and you happens. Many people feel discomfort, angst, and fear when confronted with nature immersion. An ideal way for a safe and worry-free introduction to the nature experience is to join a restoration project, a citizen science project, or attend an organized field trip. These venues have experienced leaders and most often have others with similar concerns, which makes for great bonding.

Forest bathing, or *shinrin-yoku,* is gaining immense popularity in parts of the country. In essence, the practice focuses on living in the present. The main requirement is to immerse one's senses in the natural sights and sounds. Trappings of our technological world must be left behind during sessions. Benefits of the practice include lowered blood pressure, heart rate, and cortisol.

Forest bathing, which can occur anywhere in nature and not specifically in forests, is a subset of the vast benefits of employing a lifestyle utilizing the nature pyramid. While a part of the nature pyramid, it is more of a daily activity beyond this book's locational scope. But any site we identified in the book can be used for forest bathing.

Northern Wisconsin Nature Immersion Vacation Sites

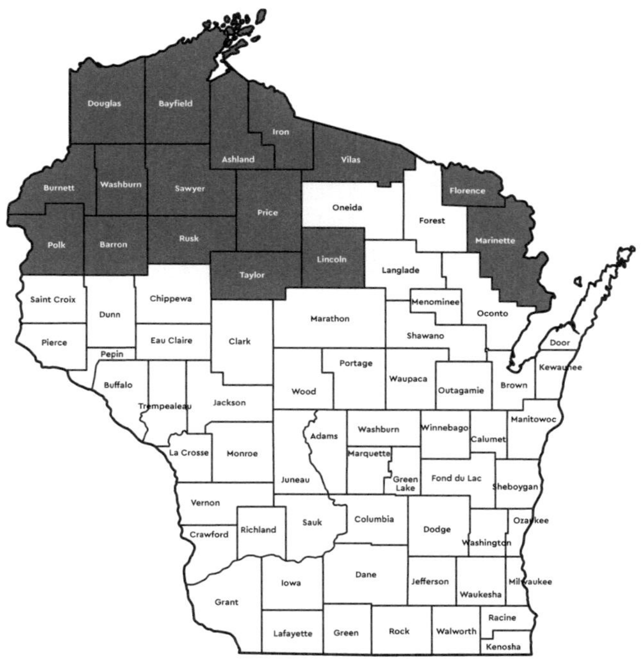

Apostle Islands National Lakeshore

Including Several State Natural Areas (SNA)

COGNITIVE ENRICHMENT AREA			
	LOW	MEDIUM	HIGH
NATURAL DIVERSITY			✓
PHYSICAL CHALLENGE		✓	
ACCESS FRIENDLY			✓
SERENITY, SOLITUDE			✓
NIGHT SKIES			✓

- TRAIL
- PAVED OR HARD-PACKED TRAIL
- BEACH
- CANOE OR KAYAK
- CAMPING
- BOARDWALK
- LAKE
- CLIFF OR ROCK OUTCROP
- SNOWSHOE TRAIL

Apostles Islands National Lakeshore is a terrific place to immerse in the natural world. Rugged sandstone shores softened in places by sand spits and tombolo beaches have inspired artists and poets for generations. Visitors, especially those who camp on the islands, have nature at hand to craft any individual's creativity. All one needs to do is go.

Every one of the 21 islands, and even the mainland portion, has places for solitude, contemplation, and inspiration. Creative areas are on every island. Several islands have incredible biological diversity that can promote cognitive enrichment. Below is a sample of these areas, which are co-designated Apostle Islands Maritime Forests State Natural Areas:

- Devil's Island is remote and accessible by watercraft only. It is the northernmost of the islands with yellow birch, white cedar, and balsam fir being the primary tree species. The 263-acre island features many boreal plant species.
- Sand Island is best accessed from Little Sand Bay. A short boat trip across the channel leads to many trails and sparse canopy of huge (to 40 inches) white pine.
- The 202-acre Outer Island unit covers the northern tip of the island. This tract never saw a lumberman's ax and is a great example of a virgin northern mesic forest. Forty-four-inch DBH hemlock dominates the stand, aged at over 400 years, and is perhaps the most significant Lake Superior shore stand. The site also features clay bank seeps, and ephemeral ponds.
- The Apostle Islands Yew Forest SNA lies on four islands. These tracts feature dense growths of Canada yew, some reaching twenty feet high. Raspberry Island is the most accessible and has an extensive trail system.
- Stockton Island is the easiest to visit. Daily ferry service transports campers and day visitors to the island. Most visitors head for the extensive sandy beaches, but hearty nature enthusiasts can spend a lengthy time hiking the trails or decompressing.

Sitting on a sandstone outcrop or a sand spit at night, listening to the waves and sky watching, is an unforgettable experience. Several county and private campgrounds are nearby.

Access to the National Lakeshore is mostly via watercraft. A visit to the headquarters at 46.813314, -90.820354 before getting on the water may be required. For more information, visit the Park Service website, https://www.nps.gov/apis/index.htm, or the Wisconsin DNR SNA website, https://dnr.wisconsin.gov/topic/StateNaturalAreas.

Birchwood Lakes Primitive Area

and Washburn County Natural Areas

PROBLEM SOLVING AREA			
	LOW	MEDIUM	HIGH
NATURAL DIVERSITY		✓	
PHYSICAL CHALLENGE			✓
ACCESS FRIENDLY		✓	
SERENITY, SOLITUDE			✓
NIGHT SKIES			✓

All the sites lie within the Washburn County Forest boundaries. The primitive area perches on glacial geology features with rolling hills and scores of lakes. In addition, visits to large wetland areas provide wilderness users with varied natural diversity. Whether camping in the county forest, staying at nearby campgrounds or private lodging, walking trails, canoe trails, or overland hikes can provide solitude.

Two primitive canoe routes are within the Birchwood canoe unit, six miles north of Birchwood. Both routes are in a primitive area with little to no development, providing a unique opportunity for a quiet, backcountry experience. The canoe route areas lie within heavily forested, rolling topography with a high density of small glacial lakes. These lakes are land-locked, deep, soft-water lakes with steep banks and wooded shores. Bass and panfish are abundant. A canoe portage and trail system has been marked to guide canoeists.

Due to the diversity of natural challenges, the entire complex can be considered a Problem-Solving Area. Deep forests, large bogs, and numerous clear lakes give visitors ample opportunities for forest therapy.

The Washburn County Forest allows primitive camping with a permit for up to 14 days.

Two great wilderness places are the canoe trails. Sawmill Lake Canoe Portage Trail starts at Sawmill Lake, either at the campground or the boat landing. Nine short portage trails connect Sawmill, Fawn, Beartrap, Tadpole, Telstar, Mallard, Otter, and Deep Lakes. Loyhead Lake Canoe Portage Trail starts at the Loyhead Lake boat landing adjacent to the Birchwood Fire Lane.

Below is a base camp for a weeklong adventure:

- Sawmill Park Campground, with 25 sites, has a nature trail and opportunities to swim and fish. 45.755986, -91.560051.

Below are adventure areas to explore (see Washburn County Forest map for access):

- Crystal Swamp is an 800-acre black spruce bog. The site has a history of wildfires, resulting in an unusual vegetative pattern. 45.857272, -91.703887.
- Lost Lake Bog is over 1,000 acres in size and surrounds a 41-acre acid bog lake. The lake is 10 feet deep with very dark stained water. 46.042837, -91.669410.

These sites are remote with no development. All necessities must be supplied by the user and carried out after visits. For more information, visit the Washburn County Forest website, https://www.co.washburn.wi.us/departments/forestry/.

Blue Hills

Barron and Rusk Counties Natural Areas

PROBLEM SOLVING AREA			
	LOW	MEDIUM	HIGH
NATURAL DIVERSITY			✓
PHYSICAL CHALLENGE			✓
ACCESS FRIENDLY		✓	
SERENITY, SOLITUDE			✓
NIGHT SKIES		✓	

TRAIL

BEACH

FISHING

CANOE OR KAYAK

CAMPING

MOUNTAIN BIKE TRAIL

STREAM OR RIVER

LAKE

CLIFF OR ROCK OUTCROP

All the sites are within the boundaries of the Barron and Rusk County Forests. The 1.7-billion-year-old forested Blue Hills rise 600 feet above the landscape of northwestern Rusk and northeastern Barron Counties. Erosion-resistant red quartzite, topped with thin glacial deposits, comprises the base geology. This quartzite consists of the metamorphosed river and near-shore ocean sediment. In addition, a pipestone quarry cultural feature adds a human dimension to nature. This variety can provide the nature enthusiast with solitude.

Due to the diversity of natural challenges, the entire complex can be considered a Problem-Solving Area. Deep forest, headwater streams, and glacial geology features give the visitor ample opportunities for forest therapy. Several locations have rich ground layer vegetation.

The Rusk County Forest allows primitive camping with a permit for up to 14 days. Barron County Forest offers similar camping but prohibits camping during deer hunting season. These county forests provide opportunities for deep immersion into the forest. Rusk County offers an ideal location for a base camp at the Audie and Perch Lakes. 45.551266, -91.427239.

Below are adventure areas to explore (see Barron and Rusk Counties Forest map for access):

- Deer Creek Forest has 100 acres of the rich ground layer under mature hardwoods.
- Spring Creek Felsenmeer—the word *felsenmeer* means a sea of rocks. These 40 acres of jumbled granite around Spring Creek give the visitor a prime example of the term. Talus slopes on both sides of the vale drop to a fractured granite valley. Spring Creek flows through this jumble, sometimes emerging but often under the rocks.
- Lost Mans Lake is a potential meromictic lake, 1.9 surface acres and 38 feet deep, formed in a glacial cirque. This type of lake does not mix its water in spring and fall.
- Gundy's Canyon is a 30-foot-deep gorge with Rock Creek flowing through its center and a featured 20-foot waterfall.
- Pipestone Quarry National Historic Trail traverses a wooded ridgetop to old pipestone diggings. 45.487015, -91.591379.

These sites are remote with no development. All necessities must be supplied by the user and carried out after visits. Limitations on vegetation manipulation are in place. For more information, visit the Rusk County Forest website, https://ruskcounty.org/forestry, or the Barron County Forest website, https://www.barroncountywi.gov/index.asp?

Brule River State Forest

State Natural Areas

FAMILY IMMERSION AREA			
	LOW	MEDIUM	HIGH
NATURAL DIVERSITY			✓
PHYSICAL CHALLENGE			✓
ACCESS FRIENDLY		✓	
SERENITY, SOLITUDE			✓
NIGHT SKIES			✓

This state forest is linear, paralleling the Bois Brule River, but still has wild areas to explore. Staying in forest campgrounds or private lodging and visiting several state natural areas can provide the nature immersion many require. The sites listed harbor high-quality natural areas with outstanding biological diversity.

Due to the great diversity of natural features, the entire complex can be considered a Family Immersion Area. Deep forest, old-growth white cedars and pines, fast streams, and glacial geology features give the visitor ample opportunities for forest therapy. The forest has paddling opportunities and 60 miles of hunter-walking trails open for hiking.

Below are base camps for a weeklong adventure:

- Brule River Campground has 22 sites, with one accessible, and is open from mid-March to mid-November, with opportunities to fish and hike the nature trail. 46.539907, -91.589101.
- Copper Range has 17 sites. Fishing and canoeing are available. 46.610781, -91.581718.

Below are adventure areas to explore:

- Brule Glacial Spillway SNA covers 2,656 acres of conifer swamp and white cedar. Access is off County Highway P, Stone Chimney Road, and at Stone's Bridge. 46.417056, -91.716949.
- Motts Ravine SNA has 655 acres that feature a jack pine forest and pine-oak barrens. Access is off Motts Ravine Road. 46.432143, -91.614419.
- Brule River Boreal Forest SNA has 652 acres that feature a forest of white spruce and white pine on the steep terrace banks of the Brule River. Access is off Brule River Road. 46.719926, -91.600048.

Other SNAs are Bear Beach and Brule Smith Lake. The North Country Trail traverses the forest in many places, including a boardwalk into the glacial spillway cedar swamp. Paddling the upper sections is easy, but sections of the lower Brule require advanced skills.

These sites are remote with no development. All necessities must be supplied by the user and carried out after visits. For more information, visit the Brule River State Forest website, https://dnr.wisconsin.gov/topic/StateForests/bruleriver, or the Wisconsin DNR SNA website, https://dnr.wisconsin.gov/topic/StateNaturalAreas.

Crex Meadows and Fish Lake

Wildlife and Natural Areas

FOREST THERAPY AREA

	LOW	MEDIUM	HIGH
NATURAL DIVERSITY		✓	
PHYSICAL CHALLENGE		✓	
ACCESS FRIENDLY			✓
SERENITY, SOLITUDE		✓	
NIGHT SKIES		✓	

All the sites are within the boundaries of the Crex Meadows Wildlife Area and Fish Lake Wildlife Area. This portion of Burnett County is relatively flat, permitting extensive wetlands to persist among the gently rolling sandy uplands. These two wildlife areas contain vast impounded water, expansive wire-grass sedge meadows, and thousands of acres of pine-oak barrens. The combined properties encompass more than 34,000 acres. A series of internal roads easily access most places, and all but a 2,400-acre closed area is available for exploration.

Due to the great diversity of wildlife and plants, the entire complex can be considered a Forest Therapy Area. Lakes, shallow marshes, large sedge meadows, and barrens provide habitats for countless species interactions. The visitor has ample opportunities for mental stimulation. Families with younger children can use the extensive road system to introduce them to the splendor of nature.

Crex Meadows allows camping with a permit from September 1 to December 31. The nearby Burnett County Forest provides primitive camping on the land with a permit. Another option is the developed campgrounds in Governor Knowles State Forest.

Below are adventure areas open for hunting. Visitors must acknowledge the primacy of the hunting traditions while immersing in nature (visit the DNR websites for access information):

- Crex Meadows Wildlife Area covers more than 30,000 acres and features viewable wildlife. A nature center gives the visitor an overview of the meadows. Several access points are via internal roads. 45.795943, -92.679311.
- Reed Lake Meadow SNA covers 3,568 acres and harbors wire-grass sedge meadow, brush prairie, and oak savanna. Several rare birds and butterflies thrive in this unit. Access is via internal roads. 45.902659, -92.569775.
- Fish Lake Wildlife Area has 14,000 acres that feature expansive wire-grass sedge meadows, barrens, and prairie habitat, plus a nature trail into a 40-acre red pine forest featuring many old trees. Access is from several upland parking areas. 45.731591, -92.782377.

These sites are remote with no development. All necessities must be supplied by the user and carried out after visits. For more information, visit the Wisconsin DNR wildlife website, https://dnr.wisconsin.gov/topic/Lands/WildlifeAreas/alpha.html, or the Wisconsin DNR SNA website, https://dnr.wisconsin.gov/topic/StateNaturalAreas.

Douglas County Wildlife Areas

and County Natural Areas

PROBLEM SOLVING AREA			
	LOW	MEDIUM	HIGH
NATURAL DIVERSITY			✓
PHYSICAL CHALLENGE			✓
ACCESS FRIENDLY		✓	
SERENITY, SOLITUDE			✓
NIGHT SKIES		✓	

- TRAIL
- BEACH
- FISHING
- CANOE OR KAYAK
- CAMPING
- MOUNTAIN BIKE TRAIL
- STREAM OR RIVER
- LAKE
- CLIFF OR ROCK OUTCROP

All the sites lie within the boundaries of the Douglas County Forest. This portion of the county forest has a minuscule human population. It offers the visitor an incredibly wild experience. These bog-dominated lands lie on the continental divide. Many bogs have water flowing to the Great Lakes and the Mississippi River basin. The glacial geology feature is primarily flat with slight elevation changes. In addition, the sizeable adjacent upland acres harbor the largest gray wolf population in the state.

Due to the diversity of natural challenges, the entire complex can be considered a Problem-Solving Area. Deep forests, large bogs, and physical difficulties give the visitor ample opportunities for forest therapy and a true wilderness experience. A night punctuated by howling wolves and echoing calls of Saw-whet Owls can be a life-changing experience for tech-driven urbanites.

The Douglas County Forest permits dispersed camping with a permit. “Leave No Trace” camping ethics are encouraged. Only experienced wilderness campers or those guided by experienced wilderness campers should consider this activity.

Below are adventure areas to explore (see Douglas County Forest map or SNA website for access information):

- Black Lake Bog SNA is a 1,808-acre bog lake and open black spruce bog. The site continues into Minnesota. 46.371691, -92.284731.
- Belden Swamp SNA covers 1,795 acres and harbors the largest undisturbed open bog in the state. 46.362689. -92.185902.
- Ericson Creek Forest and Wetlands SNA covers 2,505 acres. All the wetland forest types of Douglas County are found at this site: 46.430407, -92.029138.
- Empire Swamp SNA occupies 1,570 acres of wetland. Forest, open bog, and northern sedge meadow are part of the SNA. 46.334132, -92.078968.

Upland sites between the bogs are managed forest land, which includes many stages of forest succession from recently harvested trees to mature patches of dense hardwoods. Abundant logging roads provide access to most interior bog locations.

These sites are remote with no development. All necessities must be supplied by the user and carried out after visits. For more information, visit the Douglas County Forest website, https://www.douglascountywi.org/211/Forestry-Parks-Recreation, or the Wisconsin DNR SNA website, https://dnr.wisconsin.gov/topic/StateNaturalAreas.

Flambeau River State Forest

Price and Sawyer Counties Natural Areas

PROBLEM SOLVING AREA			
	LOW	MEDIUM	HIGH
NATURAL DIVERSITY		✓	
PHYSICAL CHALLENGE		✓	
ACCESS FRIENDLY		✓	
SERENITY, SOLITUDE			✓
NIGHT SKIES			✓

- TRAIL
- BEACH
- FISHING
- CANOE OR KAYAK
- CAMPING
- MOUNTAIN BIKE TRAIL
- STREAM OR RIVER
- LAKE
- SNOWSHOE TRAIL

This portion of the state forest is less remote than other parts but still has wild areas to explore. Staying at nearby campgrounds or private lodging and visiting several state natural areas can provide the desired nature immersion. The sites listed harbor high-quality natural areas with outstanding biological diversity.

Due to the great diversity of natural features, the entire complex can be considered a Problem-Solving Area. Deep forest, old-growth hemlocks and pines, fast streams, and glacial geology features give the visitor ample opportunities for forest therapy and cognitive enrichment. The forest has 14 miles of ski trails open for hiking when the trails are snow free or not groomed.

Below are base camps for a weeklong adventure:

- The Lake of the Pines has 30 sites open from mid-April to mid-December, with opportunities to swim, fish, and hike the nature trail. 45.783996, -90.714642.
- Connors Lake has 29 sites with two accessible sites. Fishing, swimming, and a short nature trail are available. 45.740060, -90.744484.

Below are adventure areas to explore:

- Oxbo Pines SNA encompasses 287 acres of natural origin white and red pine forest. Access is off Dix Dox Road. 45.882058, -90.678893.
- Swamp Lake SNA covers 1,042 acres and features a wilderness lake and lowland conifers. Access is off Tower Hill Road. 45.791882, -90.701842.
- Hanson Lake Wetlands SNA covers 302 acres and features a mosaic of wetland communities. Access is off Payne Farm Road. 45.821319, -90.731899.
- Bass Lake Peatlands SNA encompasses 921 acres of open peatland with scattered trees. Access is from Tower Hill Road. 45.777397, -90.677600.

Orienteering opportunities abound. Interspersed with managed units, the dense forest provides outstanding challenges for those looking for this type of activity. Any person trying an orienteering challenge should notify the managers before starting. These sites are remote with no development. All necessities must be supplied by the user and carried out after visits. For more information, visit the Flambeau River State Forest website, https://dnr.wisconsin.gov/topic/StateForests/flambeauriver, or the Wisconsin DNR SNA website, https://dnr.wisconsin.gov/topic/StateNaturalAreas.

Flambeau River Paddle

and Natural Areas

PROBLEM SOLVING AREA			
	LOW	MEDIUM	HIGH
NATURAL DIVERSITY			✓
PHYSICAL CHALLENGE			✓
ACCESS FRIENDLY		✓	
SERENITY, SOLITUDE			✓
NIGHT SKIES			✓

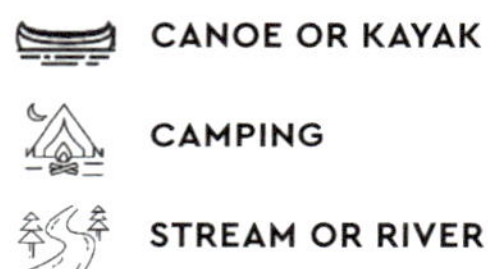

All the sites are contained within the boundaries of the Flambeau River State Forest and adjacent public lands. The north fork covers 77 miles, from the Crowley Dam to the Big Falls Flowage, and is free flowing. The 13-mile south fork is much wilder and should be paddled only by experienced whitewater adventurers. Quality natural areas are found near the river, with vast areas ripe for a wilderness experience. Most places require watercraft to access, but there are portions where visitors can walk in.

Due to the diversity of natural challenges, the entire complex is a Problem-Solving Area. Scenic riverway, mature pine and hemlock forest, expansive wetlands, and physical difficulties give the visitor ample opportunities for forest therapy.

Camping is allowed at 32 designated canoe access campsites with a one-night limit at each site. Permits are not required and are first come, first served. Many areas have land access for short-term experiences. "Leave No Trace" camping ethics are encouraged.

Below are adventure areas to explore (visit the Wisconsin DNR Park and SNA websites for access information):

- North Fork Pines SNA has 87 acres and features pines up to 30 inches in diameter. Access is overland from the riverside location. Walk north to the site. 45.843543, -90.668603.
- Flambeau River Hardwood Forest SNA has 266 acres and features the area that recovered from the 1977 derecho without timber salvage. 45.722259, -90.781776.
- Skinner Creek Hardwoods SNA covers 228 acres and features a rich ground layer under hardwoods approaching old-growth. 45.619639, -90.771696.
- Several old-growth hemlock stands are found along the passively managed corridor.
- Stopping at tributary streams, whether by paddling upstream or landing, then exploring the small stream ecosystems, can open a new understanding of the natural world. Abundant wildlife, especially black bear, are commonly seen.

By combining a paddle with time in the upland portion of the state forest, nature enthusiasts can lengthen their nature immersion experience. This forest is best suited for more experienced nature lovers. These sites are remote with no development. All necessities must be supplied by the user and carried out after visits. For more information, visit the Flambeau River State Forest website, https://dnr.wisconsin.gov/topic/StateForests/flambeauriver/info, or the Wisconsin DNR SNA website, https://dnr.wisconsin.gov/topic/StateNaturalAreas.

Governor Knowles State Forest

State Natural Areas

FAMILY IMMERSION AREA			
	LOW	MEDIUM	HIGH
NATURAL DIVERSITY		✓	
PHYSICAL CHALLENGE			✓
ACCESS FRIENDLY		✓	
SERENITY, SOLITUDE			✓
NIGHT SKIES			✓

This state forest is linear, paralleling the St. Croix River, but still has wild areas to explore. Staying in forest campgrounds or private lodging and visiting several state natural areas can provide the desired nature immersion. The sites listed harbor high-quality natural areas with outstanding biological diversity.

Due to the great diversity of natural features, the entire complex is a Family Immersion Area. Deep forest, open barrens, old-growth red pines, fast streams, and glacial geology features give the visitor ample opportunities for forest therapy. The forest has interpretive trails, nine primitive campsites, 40 miles of hiking trails, and access for canoeing on the St. Croix River.

This state forest follows a geological feature. A huge outwash plain of sand and gravel soils extends well into Minnesota. The melting of the last glacier created the St. Croix River, which cut through deposits, forming an immense terrace of dry sands at the top and wet forests near the river. The slopes have abundant springs and seeps, adding to the site's diversity.

Below are base camps for a weeklong adventure:

- St. Croix Family Campground has 30 rustic sites and is open year-round, with opportunities to fish and hike the nature trails. 45.766057, -92.777157.
- Sioux Portage has 60 sites. Hiking, fishing, and canoeing are available. 45.973882, -92.463033.

Below are adventure areas to explore:

- Brant Brook Pines and Hardwoods SNA has 498 acres and features old-growth red pines. Access is off Gile Road. 45.860496, -92.723513.
- Norway Point Bottomlands SNA has 4,022 acres and features five lowland communities and an interpretive trail into the white cedars. Access is at the end of Norway Point Road. 45.923528, -92.639614.
- St. Croix Seeps SNA covers 350 acres and features seeps and spring runs emanating from the steep terrace banks. Access is from Sunrise Ferry Hiking Trail. 45.681892, -92.873148.
- Kohler-Peet Barrens SNA covers 834 acres and harbors an open barrens landscape. Access is from County Highway F. 45.931326, -92.548301.

These sites are remote with no development. All necessities must be supplied by the user and carried out after visits. For more information, visit the Governor Knowles State Forest website, https://dnr.wisconsin.gov/topic/StateForests/govknowles, or the Wisconsin DNR SNA website, https://dnr.wisconsin.gov/topic/StateNaturalAreas.

Harrison Hills

and Lincoln County Natural Areas

FOREST THERAPY AREA			
	LOW	MEDIUM	HIGH
NATURAL DIVERSITY			✓
PHYSICAL CHALLENGE			✓
ACCESS FRIENDLY		✓	
SERENITY, SOLITUDE			✓
NIGHT SKIES		✓	

All the sites are within the boundaries of the Lincoln County Forest. The wooded Harrison Hills glacial geology features have steeply undulating hills and scores of lakes. In addition, visits to large wetland areas beyond the hills provide the wilderness user with varied natural diversity.

Due to the diversity of natural challenges, the entire complex is a Forest Therapy Area. Deep forests, large bogs, and numerous clear lakes give the visitor ample opportunities for forest therapy. Terminal moraine topography limits the extent of many natural features; therefore, the visitor can experience a tremendous variety of plants and animals over short distances.

The Lincoln County Forest allows primitive camping with a permit for up to 14 days. Littering and cutting or defacing timber is prohibited. There are two campsites along the Ice Age Trail segment where Ice Age camping rules apply.

More experienced wilderness users can find great quality lakes for exploration or shoreline solitude. Some of the best quality lakes are below:

- Coppes Lake is a soft water seepage lake with clear water and muck bottom plants.
- Pine Lake Sec. 20T34N-R8E is a hard water-drained lake with a bog wetland.
- Tahoe Lake is an exceptionally deep (about 54 feet) soft water seepage lake.
- High Lake is a deep, very soft water seepage lake with rosette plants.
- Turtle Lake has a shallow west basin filled with aquatic vegetation.

Below is a base camp for a weeklong adventure:

- Otter Lake Recreation Area Campground, with 25 sites, has a nature trail, a boardwalk, and opportunities to swim and fish. 45.443657, -89.548715.

Below are adventure areas to explore (see Lincoln County Forest map for access):

- Tomahawk Bog is a 1,300-acre black spruce bog. The east side has mineral-rich water forming a tamarack fen. 45.416732, -89.926550.
- Sparrow Bog is over 1,000 acres in size and has a domed center with stunted black spruce. 45.486878, -89.956521.

These sites are remote with no development. All necessities must be supplied by the user and carried out after visits. For more information, visit the Lincoln County Forest website, https://co.lincoln.wi.us/forestry-land-and-parks.

Namekagon River Paddle

Wildlife and Natural Areas

PROBLEM SOLVING AREA			
	LOW	MEDIUM	HIGH
NATURAL DIVERSITY			✓
PHYSICAL CHALLENGE			✓
ACCESS FRIENDLY		✓	
SERENITY, SOLITUDE			✓
NIGHT SKIES			✓

All the sites are within the boundaries of the St. Croix National Scenic Riverway and adjacent public lands. The river from the Namekagon Dam to the confluence with the St. Croix River is primarily free flowing. Two impoundments at Hayward and Trego can be bypassed or portaged. Wild sections border the river and contain vast areas ripe for a wilderness experience. This part of the St. Croix National Scenic Riverway encompasses more than 100 miles of free-flowing river. Most places require watercraft to access, but there are portions where visitors can walk in.

Due to the great diversity of natural challenges, the entire complex is a Problem-Solving Area. Scenic riverways, mature forests, expansive wetlands, pine barrens, and physical challenges give the visitor ample opportunities for forest therapy.

Camping is allowed for up to three days at any site. Permits are not required. Campsites must be in designated camping areas or public-owned campsites, and all human waste must be buried six inches below the surface. Many areas have land access for short-term experiences. "Leave No Trace" camping ethics are encouraged.

Below are adventure areas to explore (visit the Park Service and DNR websites for access information):

- Trego Nature Trail covers 2.8 miles and features hardwood forest and scenic river views. Access from NPS visitor center. 45.906348, -91.810108.
- Trego Lake Trail covers 3.6 miles with scenic views of the water. Access via watercraft or from River Road. 45.927934, -91.868328.
- Namekagon-Lac Courte Oreilles Portage Trail covers 0.8 miles of the historic portage. 45.560721, -91.295515.
- Namekagon Barrens Wildlife Area covers more than 6,400 acres and is accessible from many roads. 46.079545, -92.117071. Opportunities exist to reserve blinds for observation of Sharp-tailed Grouse mating displays.

At the confluence with the Totogatic River is a large floodplain forest with many southern plant species growing. The best forest is found by paddling upstream on the Totogatic River, about 1.2 miles. These sites are remote with no development. All necessities must be supplied by the user and carried out after visits. For more information, visit the St. Croix Riverway website, https://www.nps.gov/sacn/index.htm, or the Wisconsin DNR Wildlife website, https://dnr.wisconsin.gov/topic/Lands/WildlifeAreas/namekagon.html.

Northern Highland American Legion State Forest

and Turtle-Flambeau and Manitowish Natural Areas

COGNITIVE ENRICHMENT AREA			
	LOW	MEDIUM	HIGH
NATURAL DIVERSITY			✓
PHYSICAL CHALLENGE			✓
ACCESS FRIENDLY		✓	
SERENITY, SOLITUDE			✓
NIGHT SKIES		✓	

The huge Turtle-Flambeau Flowage, a state wilderness area, and several state natural areas provide deep immersion and wilderness camping opportunities. Access to most campsites is by water or backpacking. Camping is best found on islands, limiting exploration of many habitats, but other more biologically diverse areas are attainable via canoe or kayak.

The sites can provide outstanding cognitive enrichment and forest therapy.

Below are wilderness areas to explore:

- Turtle-Flambeau Flowage, 37,000 acres of land and water that is open year-round. These acres harbor over 13,000 acres of water, and the forest is predominately aspen, maple, and white birch. Patches of old-growth hemlock and white pine are found in protected spots. A person experiencing solitude may see Bald Eagles, Osprey, Common Loon, or Trumpeter Swans. Most camping is accessible only by water. Several access points are available (visit the forest website below). 46.091913, -90.169712.
- Manitowish Wild Resources, approximately 5,000 acres of closed canopy forest and wetlands bordering the Manitowish River. 46.114825, -90.043544. The primary feature of the area is old-growth white and red pines found within the Frog Lake and Pines SNA. 46.114825, -90.043544. A person can experience solitude in abundance at a campsite by the river.

Below are other SNAs to explore:

- DuPage Lake, 3,221 acres, features old-growth hemlock and white pine on scattered islands in a vast boggy wetland. 46.170429, -89.976808.
- Turtle-Flambeau Patterned Peatland, 5,460 acres, features sphagnum lawns, water tracks, and sedge ridges. This site is for expert wilderness travelers only. 46.044333, -90.098049.
- Springstead Muskeg encompasses the northernmost portion of an extensive undisturbed bog from Springstead Lake to Newman Lake. 46.002113, -90.118511.

These sites are remote with no development. All necessities must be supplied by the user and carried out after visits. For more information, visit the Wisconsin DNR website, https://dnr.wisconsin.gov/topic/lands/turtleflambeau. In addition, several state natural areas are close and available for cognitive enrichment. For more information, visit the Wisconsin DNR SNA website, https://dnr.wisconsin.gov/topic/StateNaturalAreas.

Northern Highland American Legion State Forest

Central Vilas County Natural Areas

COGNITIVE ENRICHMENT AREA			
	LOW	MEDIUM	HIGH
NATURAL DIVERSITY			✓
PHYSICAL CHALLENGE			✓
ACCESS FRIENDLY			✓
SERENITY, SOLITUDE		✓	
NIGHT SKIES		✓	

This portion of the state forest is more popular than other parts but still has wild areas to explore. Staying at nearby campgrounds or private lodging and visiting several state natural areas can provide the nature immersion needed for many. The sites listed harbor high-quality natural areas with outstanding biological diversity.

Due to the diversity of natural features, the entire complex is a Cognitive Enrichment Area. Deep forest, old-growth hemlocks and pines, clear lakes, and barrens give the visitor ample opportunities for nearly the full range of nature benefits. The Fallison Lake and Escanaba Lake Trails give visitors an understanding of the Northwoods' ecology, plus tremendous lake views.

Below are base camps for a weeklong adventure:

- North Trout Lake has 48 rustic sites and access to a nature boardwalk and a paved bike trail, with opportunities to swim and fish. 46.065608, -89.646428.
- Razorback Lake has 52 rustic sites available. The site features opportunities for swimming and fishing. 46.02387, -89.53220.

Below are adventure areas to explore:

- Bittersweet Lakes SNA has 1,070 acres of closed canopy forest, including old-growth hemlock and pine. Access is off Highway 70. 45.917232, -89.597741.
- Lake Laura Hardwoods SNA has 852 acres and features old-growth maple, yellow birch, basswood, and hemlock forest. Access from Deerfoot Road. 46.047475, -89.431812.
- Plum Lake Hemlocks SNA has 747 acres of upland hemlock-hardwood forest. Access is off Rearing Pond Road. Walk east to the site 46.022390, -89.504610.
- Johnson Lake Barrens and Springs SNA has 1,130 acres of pine barrens, jack pines, and several springs. Access is from Jute Lake Road. 46.149457, -89.503650.
- Other SNAs nearby are Lost Canoe Lake, Nixon Lake, and Lake Alva.

An extensive paved bike trail system exists that permits nature access for those with younger children, novice explorers, or people with mobility concerns. This trail system connects many communities north of Woodruff.

These sites are remote with no development. All necessities must be supplied by the user and carried out after visits. For more information, visit the Northern Highland American Legion State Forest website, https://dnr.wisconsin.gov/topic/StateForests/nhal, or the Wisconsin DNR SNA website, https://dnr.wisconsin.gov/topic/StateNaturalAreas.

North Country Trail

State Parks and Natural Areas

FAMILY IMMERSION AREA			
	LOW	MEDIUM	HIGH
NATURAL DIVERSITY			✓
PHYSICAL CHALLENGE			✓
ACCESS FRIENDLY			✓
SERENITY, SOLITUDE			✓
NIGHT SKIES			✓

All the sites are next to the North Country Trail, with the trail covering more than 200 miles in far northern Wisconsin, of which 134 miles are off-road. The most extended section of uninterrupted trail lies within the Chequamegon-Nicolet National Forest. Other sections traverse state parks, county forests, and private parcels. The Wisconsin portion of the trail sections includes scenic waterfalls, geologic outcrops with incredible vistas, lakeshores, towering old-growth forests, boardwalks into bogs, and even sand prairies.

Due to the great diversity of natural challenges, the entire trail system is a Family Immersion Area. Deep Northwoods forest, stream crossings, vistas, and physical challenges give visitors ample opportunities for solitude. Many sections of the trail system are close to other sites in this book. Families can take advantage of the proximity of sites to plan multi-day adventures. Especially significant is the opportunity for varied lodging, then utilizing the trail system for day excursions. The nature immersion values for younger people are incalculable.

The trail system has designated camp areas and allows primitive camping more than 100 feet away from the trail or lakeshore. Swimming and fishing opportunities exist if the user is okay with entering through natural vegetation. Many segments have access points for shorter-term visitation. "Leave No Trace" camping ethics are required.

The best sites are listed below:

- Copper Falls SNA lies within the state park, covers 746 acres, and features pine forests, waterfalls, and deep gorges. Users must have a park sticker. 46.351256, -90.643068.
- Lake Owen Hardwoods SNA covers 1,535 acres, harbors patches of old-growth hemlock hardwoods and red pine growing on thin soils over bedrock, and offers lakeshore features. Rare species include sightings of moose. Access is via Lake Owen Road. 46.304508, -91.208735.
- Nature enthusiasts should not miss the five miles of trail passing through the Douglas County Wildlife Area. During the late summer and fall, prairie flowers are at their showiest.46.17182, -91.49262.
- Pattison State Park's 1,400 acres feature an expansive forest, waterfalls, and deep gorges. Users are required to have a state park sticker. Access is from the park. 46.536934, -92.119967.

These sites are remote with no development. All necessities must be supplied by the user and carried out after visits. For more information, visit the North Country Trail website, https://northcountrytrail.org/the-trail/wisconsin/, Wisconsin Parks website, https://dnr.wisconsin.gov/topic/Parks, or the Wisconsin DNR SNA website, https://dnr.wisconsin.gov/topic/StateNaturalAreas.

Pine and Popple Rivers Paddle

and Natural Areas

PROBLEM SOLVING AREA			
	LOW	MEDIUM	HIGH
NATURAL DIVERSITY			✓
PHYSICAL CHALLENGE			✓
ACCESS FRIENDLY		✓	
SERENITY, SOLITUDE			✓
NIGHT SKIES			✓

All the sites are contained within the boundaries of the Pine and Popple Wild Rivers and adjacent public lands. The Pine River is free flowing 89 miles from the headwaters to the Pine Flowage. The 62-mile Popple River is free flowing the entire section from the sources to the confluence with the Pine. Quality natural areas are found near the river, with vast areas ripe for a wilderness experience. Most places require watercraft to access, but there are portions where visitors can walk in.

Due to the great diversity of natural challenges, the entire complex is a Problem-Solving Area. Scenic riverways, whitewater, mature cedar and hemlock forest, wetlands, and physical challenges give the visitor ample opportunities for forest therapy. The Pine and Popple Rivers Area has immense acres of forested land surrounding it. These adjacent forests are excellent locations to polish orienteering skills or reap the benefits of deep wilderness immersion. Camping in the same location for a few days and venturing into uninhabited land permits the nature seeker immense solitude.

Camping is limited on the state land, but primitive camping is permitted in the Chequamegon-Nicolet National Forest and the Florence County Forest. We Energies has four campsites on the Pine Flowage. Many areas have land access for short-term experiences. "Leave No Trace" camping ethics are encouraged.

Below are adventure areas to explore (visit the Wisconsin DNR Park and SNA websites for access information):

- Alvin Creek SNA is 1,048 acres and features expansive wetlands and old-growth hemlock forest. Access from Elliot Road. 45.963191, -88.852045. Walk south and east onto the site.
- Savage Lake SNA is 1,882 acres and features four wild lakes, mature hardwoods, and old-growth cedar and hemlock patches. Access from the Pine River or overland via Savage Lake Road. 45.880168, -88.455244.
- Popple River Corridor SNA is 235 acres and features old red and white pines. Access via the Popple River. 45.759428, -88.529557.

Canoeists should prepare for many rapids and several chute waterfalls. Many locations will need portages by those with less than expert skills.

These sites are remote with no development. All necessities must be supplied by the user and carried out after visits. For more information, visit the Pine and Popple Wild Rivers website, https://dnr.wisconsin.gov/topic/lands/pinepopple, or Wisconsin DNR SNA, https://dnr.wisconsin.gov/topic/StateNaturalAreas.

Spread Eagle Barrens

and Northern Marinette County Natural Areas

FOREST THERAPY AREA			
	LOW	MEDIUM	HIGH
NATURAL DIVERSITY			✓
PHYSICAL CHALLENGE			✓
ACCESS FRIENDLY			✓
SERENITY, SOLITUDE			✓
NIGHT SKIES			✓

All the sites are contained within the boundaries of the Spread Eagle Barrens SNA, 45.854872, -88.164777, and Marinette County Forest. Spread Eagle Barrens contains an extensive landscape of bracken grassland and barrens. Scattered jack pine, red pine, and Hill's oak form the sparse tree canopy. The sandy soils support an understory of sedges, bracken, and sweet fern. The wild Pine River flows through the center of the barrens. In adjacent Marinette County, more barrens, plus many bedrock features, sprinkle the landscape. This variety can provide the nature immersion needed for many.

Due to the diversity of biological features and natural challenges, the entire complex is a Cognitive Enrichment Area and a Wilderness Therapy Area. Open barrens, bedrock glades, and numerous waterfalls give visitors ample forest therapy opportunities.

For immersion into the barrens, the visitor must stay elsewhere and then visit the site during the daytime. Parking is available along many places adjacent to the road system, but camping is prohibited. The adjacent Florence County Forest permits primitive camping anywhere. The Marinette County Forest requires a permit. Florence County offers an ideal location for a base camp at Lake Emily Park with 18 campsites, beach, and fishing, 45.873760, -88.274791.

Below are adventure areas to explore (see Wisconsin DNR SNA maps and Marinette County Forest maps for access):

- Dunbar Barrens has 1,412 acres of open barrens with numerous prairie plants and Upland Sandpipers. 45.662531, -88.254969.
- Long Slide Falls is a series of waterfalls and cascades forming a complex turbulent watercourse. 45.686579, -87.930153.
- Spur Lake is 40 acres with alkaline water and rare plants and invertebrates.
- Spikehorn Canyon features bedrock glades and cliffs along Spikehorn Creek. Steep canyon walls allow cool air drainage, which provides habitat for more northerly species. There are no hiking trails into the canyon.

The Twin Lakes Headwaters Area features three bedrock glades and talus slopes harboring rare plants and animals. Purposefully, this site and the previous ones do not have GPS coordinates to allow readers to do their own research. These sites are remote with no development. All necessities must be supplied by the user and carried out after visits. For more information, visit the Marinette County Forest website, https://www.marinettecountywi.gov/departments/forestry-br/general-information/, or the Wisconsin DNR SNA website, https://dnr.wisconsin.gov/topic/StateNaturalAreas.

St. Croix River Paddle

Wildlife and Natural Areas

PROBLEM SOLVING AREA			
	LOW	MEDIUM	HIGH
NATURAL DIVERSITY			✓
PHYSICAL CHALLENGE			✓
ACCESS FRIENDLY		✓	
SERENITY, SOLITUDE			✓
NIGHT SKIES			✓

- TRAIL
- PAVED OR HARD-PACKED TRAIL
- BEACH
- CANOE OR KAYAK
- CAMPING
- MOUNTAIN BIKE TRAIL
- VISITOR CENTER
- STREAM OR RIVER
- CLIFF OR ROCK OUTCROP

All the sites are within the boundaries of the St. Croix National Scenic Riverway and adjacent public lands. The portion of the St. Croix River from the dam at Gordon to the flowage at St. Croix Falls is free flowing. Wild sections border the river and contain vast areas ripe for a wilderness experience. The St. Croix National Scenic Riverway encompasses more than 200 miles of free-flowing river. Most places require watercraft to access, but there are portions where visitors can walk in.

Due to the great diversity of natural challenges, the entire complex is a Problem-Solving Area. Scenic riverways, mature forests, expansive wetlands, pine barrens, and physical challenges give the visitor ample opportunities for forest therapy.

Camping is allowed for up to three days at any site. Permits are not required. Campsites must be in designated camping areas or state-owned campsites, and all human waste must be buried six inches below the surface. Many areas have land access for short-term experiences. "Leave No Trace" camping ethics are encouraged.

Below are adventure areas to explore (visit the Wisconsin DNR websites for access information):

- Big Island SNA covers 1,450 acres and features old pine forests, seeps, and barrens. Access is by watercraft or overland from the Highway 35 bridge. 46.074879, -92.246226.
- St. Croix State Park (MN) covers more than 33,000 acres and harbors the area's many natural and cultural features. Access is via watercraft or MN Highway 48 and Clayton County Highway 22. 45.960559, -92.609724.
- Trade River Forest and Wetlands SNA covers 909 acres and features a southern and northern forest, pine barrens, and expansive wetlands. 45.571150, -92.761811.
- Interstate Park (MN and WI) occupies more than 1,000 acres and is accessible from Taylors Falls and St. Croix Falls. Bedrock and geology features dominate the park's importance. 45.395914, -92.644486.

Several bedrock glades are found in the St. Croix Falls region. They have unique features that permit only a small fraction of plants and animals the ability to survive. Most of these glades are still in private ownership and are under threat from mining. However, a few glade owners value natural and geological history over money.

These sites are remote with no development. All necessities must be supplied by the user and carried out after visits. For more information, visit the St. Croix Riverway website, https://www.nps.gov/sacn/index.htm, MN and WI Parks or Wisconsin DNR SNA website, https://dnr.wisconsin.gov/topic/StateNaturalAreas.

Chequamegon-Nicolet Nature Immersion Vacation Sites

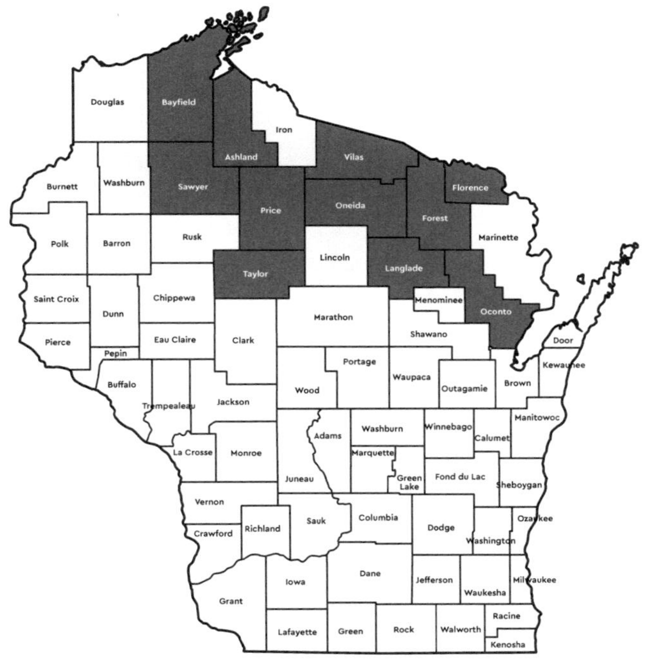

Chequamegon-Nicolet National Forest

Bayfield (southeast) Ashland County (central) Natural Areas

FAMILY IMMERSION AREA			
	LOW	MEDIUM	HIGH
NATURAL DIVERSITY			✓
PHYSICAL CHALLENGE			✓
ACCESS FRIENDLY		✓	
SERENITY, SOLITUDE		✓	
NIGHT SKIES		✓	

TRAIL
FISHING
CANOE OR KAYAK
CAMPING
STREAM OR RIVER
WATERFALL OR RAPIDS
LAKE
CLIFF OR ROCK OUTCROP

This portion of the national forest is remote, with small campgrounds and moderate development.

Staying at these remote or private campgrounds and visiting several nearby state natural areas can provide the nature immersion needed for many. The sites listed harbor high-quality natural areas with outstanding biological diversity. Between the natural areas are extensive areas of managed forest land with abundant bedrock features, giving the site a western feel. Roads are sparse, and cell coverage is limited, which helps attain wild immersion.

Due to the area's trails and other recreation development, the entire complex is a Family Immersion Area. An accessible trail to Morgan Falls provides opportunities to explore interior forest conditions, but the geology of the faults and waterfalls are more impressive. Accessible trails are available.

Below are base camps for a weeklong adventure:

- Beaver Lake, with 10 sites, has a spur trail access to the North Country Trail and opportunities to fish and hike other trails. 46.301521, -90.897395.
- Mineral Lake has eight sites, solitude, and shore fishing. 46.289983, -90.827802.

Below are adventure areas to explore:

- Brunsweiler River and Mineral Lake SNA cover 1,523 acres of closed canopy forest, including pockets of old-growth hemlock, a gorge, and cliffs. Access is off FR 187 (Mineral Lake Road near 46.305709, -90.834770.
- English Lake Hemlocks SNA is 155 acres and features old-growth hemlock. Access south of Best Road. 46.311549, -90.760333.
- St. Peter's Dome SNA covers 5,092 acres of upland hemlock-hardwood forest. The site harbors many natural features, including interior forest conditions, gorges, waterfalls, and bedrock glades. Access is best attained at the Morgan Falls Trailhead near 46.350642, -90.923733.
- North Country Trail Hardwoods SNA is 371 acres of interior sugar maple-basswood forest. Access is off FR 202 near 46.307810, -91.010449, and walk east 0.4 miles to SNA. Interior forest orienteering skills will be helpful at this site.

These sites are remote with no development. All necessities must be supplied by the user and carried out after visits. For more information, visit the Chequamegon-Nicolet National Forest website, https://www.fs.usda.gov/cnnf, or the Wisconsin DNR SNA website, https://dnr.wisconsin.gov/topic/StateNaturalAreas.

Chequamegon-Nicolet National Forest

Bayfield County Wilderness Areas

WILDERNESS THERAPY AREA			
	LOW	MEDIUM	HIGH
NATURAL DIVERSITY			✓
PHYSICAL CHALLENGE			✓
ACCESS FRIENDLY		✓	
SERENITY, SOLITUDE			✓
NIGHT SKIES			✓

These two designated wilderness areas provide deep immersion and wilderness camping opportunities. Seclusion or isolation can bring tremendous mental benefits for those seeking escape from the hectic urban world. Planning a week or more of wilderness camping provides challenges rarely encountered while scrolling through a phone. The explorer can leave with a newfound purpose.

Those needing more amenities can enjoy these areas by staying at nearby developed campsites and making forays into the wilderness. Whether deeply immersed or only penetrating the areas on day trips, the sites can provide outstanding wilderness therapy. Many trails are well-marked and allow families with younger children to enjoy the wilderness experience.

Below are wilderness areas to explore:

- Porcupine Lake Wilderness Area covers 4,446 acres of closed canopy forest. These acres harbor forests of hemlock, white pine, oak, and maple growing on rolling hills. A person can experience abundant solitude sitting on the shore of Porcupine Lake or Eighteen-Mile Spring Pond. The North Country Scenic Trail traverses the site. Several access points are available. 46.291091, -91.135200. For more information, visit https://www.fs.usda.gov/recarea/cnnf/recarea/?recid=27739.
- Rainbow Lake Wilderness Area covers 6,583 acres of closed canopy forest. The primary feature of the area is the numerous lakes. One can experience much solitude on these shores as the North Country Scenic Trail traverses the site. The Anderson Grade Trail and the Beaver Lake Trail penetrate deep into the wilderness. Several access points are available. 46.412971, -91.298005. For more information, visit https://www.fs.usda.gov/recarea/cnnf/recarea/?recid=27843.

Below are base camps for a weeklong adventure:

- Namekagon Lake is open from late April until the end of October. Close to the Porcupine Lake Wilderness, there's a trailhead to the Namekagon Nature Trail at the campsite, plus fishing and a beach. 46.244432, -91.085129.
- Perch Lake has 16 sites adjacent to the Rainbow Lake Wilderness. Swimming and shore fishing opportunities are at the camp, and there are opportunities for trout fishing nearby. The campground is open from Memorial Day through Labor Day. 46.404456, -91.269778.

These sites are remote with no development. All necessities must be supplied by the user and carried out after visits. For more information, visit the Chequamegon-Nicolet National Forest website, https://www.fs.usda.gov/cnnf, or the Wisconsin DNR SNA website, https://dnr.wisconsin.gov/topic/StateNaturalAreas.

Chequamegon-Nicolet National Forest

East Vilas County Wilderness and Natural Areas

WILDERNESS THERAPY AREA			
	LOW	MEDIUM	HIGH
NATURAL DIVERSITY			✓
PHYSICAL CHALLENGE			✓
ACCESS FRIENDLY		✓	
SERENITY, SOLITUDE			✓
NIGHT SKIES			✓

- TRAIL
- BEACH
- FISHING
- CANOE OR KAYAK
- CAMPING
- MOUNTAIN BIKE TRAIL
- STREAM OR RIVER
- LAKE
- SNOWSHOE TRAIL

Immersion into the wilderness or exploring several natural areas can provide solitude and wilderness camping opportunities. It can even be enjoyed by those needing more amenities by staying at nearby developed campsites. Whether deeply immersed or only penetrating the areas on day trips, the sites can provide outstanding wilderness therapy.

These seldom-visited sites are close at hand to a multitude of vacation spots in Vilas and Oneida Counties. People vacationing in these developed areas have tremendous chances to add wild area benefits to their cabin experiences. The lure of a lakeside cabin adds to the quality of life for many. Visiting this wilderness area can significantly add to the mental health benefits of a Northwoods cabin. Even short treks into solitude can be enlightening.

Below is a wilderness area to explore:

- Blackjack Springs Wilderness Area covers 5,800 acres of closed canopy forest, bogs, and headwaters streams. These acres harbor forests of mixed species; tracts of old-growth red pine and white spruce are especially significant. These hills are interspersed with areas of forested wetlands, including four large, crystal-clear spring ponds. A person can experience solitude in abundance. Several access points are available (visit the forest website below). 45.982698, -89.067262.
- A designated natural area lies within the wilderness area (Blackjack Springs, 1,398 acres). Two other natural areas are accessible from the developed campsites in the area. The Kentuck Lake SNA features a 0.7-mile swale harboring abundant, diverse plant life. Beaver Creek SNA contains 130-year-old red pine. For more information, visit the Wisconsin DNR website below.

Below are base camps for a weeklong adventure:

- Kentuck Lake has 31 sites open from late April until mid-October. There is a 2.5-mile trail connecting Spectacle Lake and a trail to the natural area, plus fishing and outstanding botany. 45.993183, -88.981290.
- Spectacle Lake has 34 sites open from late April to mid-October. A nature trail leads to Kentuck Lake. Swimming and shore fishing, 46.010380, -89.010233.

The wilderness site is remote with no development. All necessities must be supplied by the user and carried out after visits. For more information, visit the Chequamegon-Nicolet National Forest website, https://www.fs.usda.gov/cnnf, or the Wisconsin DNR SNA website, https://dnr.wisconsin.gov/topic/StateNaturalAreas.

Chequamegon-Nicolet National Forest

Florence County Wilderness and Natural Areas

WILDERNESS THERAPY AREA			
	LOW	MEDIUM	HIGH
NATURAL DIVERSITY			✓
PHYSICAL CHALLENGE			✓
ACCESS FRIENDLY	✓		
SERENITY, SOLITUDE			✓
NIGHT SKIES			✓

Immersion into the wilderness or exploring several natural areas can provide solitude, cognitive enrichment, and wilderness camping opportunities. Seclusion or isolation can bring tremendous mental health benefits for those seeking escape from the hectic urban world. They can even be enjoyed by those needing more amenities by staying at nearby developed campsites. Whether deeply immersed or only penetrating the areas on day trips, the sites can provide outstanding wilderness therapy.

Below is the best area to explore:

- Whisker Lake Wilderness Area encompasses 7,500 acres of closed canopy forest, beaver ponds, and a section of the Brule River. These acres harbor white pine and maple forests growing on rolling glacial hills. Large-diameter pines encompass the lakes. A person can experience solitude in abundance. Day trippers can experience the wilderness setting by walking the main trail into Whisker Lake or walking from the main trail north along Riley Creek to experience life at a beaver pond. Several access points are available. 45.954450, -88.466263. For more information, visit https://www.fs.usda.gov/recarea/cnnf/recarea/?recid=27895.
- Several designated natural areas lie just south of the wilderness area and are accessible from the developed campsites. The Kieper Creek SNA is a botanical paradise. Lauterman Lake SNA harbors old-growth maple with pockets of hemlock. Fox Maple Woods SNA is 40 acres of old-growth forest. South of the Pine River is Haley Creek Swamp with its old-growth white cedars and Savage Lake with a large undeveloped lake and forested bedrock outcrops. For more information, visit the Wisconsin DNR website below.

Below are base camps for a weeklong adventure:

- Lost Lake has 27 sites open from late April until mid-October. There is a one-mile trail through old-growth hemlocks, fishing, and a beach. Several nearby walk-in campsites are also available. 45.884814, -88.561889.
- The Lauterman National Recreation Area consists of a small campground with five walk-in/canoe-in campsites complete with tables, tent pads, fire rings, and wilderness-style toilets along Lauterman Lake. The campsites offer access to the Lauterman Lake National Recreational Trail for hiking, mountain biking, and skiing, 45.924428, -88.507660.

The wilderness site is remote with no development. All necessities must be supplied by the user and carried out after visits. For more information, visit the Chequamegon-Nicolet National Forest website, https://www.fs.usda.gov/cnnf. In addition, several state natural areas are close to the wilderness areas and are available for cognitive enrichment. For more information, visit the Wisconsin DNR SNA website, https://dnr.wisconsin.gov/topic/StateNaturalAreas.

Chequamegon-Nicolet National Forest

Forest County Wilderness and Natural Areas

WILDERNESS THERAPY AREA			
	LOW	MEDIUM	HIGH
NATURAL DIVERSITY			✓
PHYSICAL CHALLENGE			✓
ACCESS FRIENDLY	✓		
SERENITY, SOLITUDE			✓
NIGHT SKIES			✓

- TRAIL
- BEACH
- FISHING
- CANOE OR KAYAK
- CAMPING
- BOARDWALK
- STREAM OR RIVER
- LAKE
- SNOWSHOE TRAIL

Immersion into the vast wilderness area or exploring several natural areas can provide solitude and wilderness camping opportunities. They can even be enjoyed by those needing more amenities by staying at nearby developed campsites. Whether deeply immersed or only penetrating the areas on day trips, the sites can provide outstanding wilderness therapy.

These three blocks of wilderness offer the greatest wilderness challenge in the state. National forest roads provide the boundaries, but interior travel is challenging. Trails are primitive, and vast acres of bog make hiking nearly impossible in places. A feel of the Canadian boreal forest is at hand, with conifers lining streams and lakes, abundant boreal wildflowers, and birds, such as the Boreal Chickadee, searching for food among the spruce trees. Only experienced wilderness campers should stay in the vast interior.

Below is a great area to explore:

- Headwaters Wilderness Area encompasses 20,000 acres of closed canopy forest, bogs, and headwaters streams. These acres harbor forests of hemlock, white pine, and maple growing on gently rolling hills. These hills are interspersed with vast areas of forested wetlands. A person can experience solitude in abundance. Day trippers can experience the awe of the wilderness setting by walking into the Giant White Pine Grove or taking the boardwalk into the bog surrounding Shelp Lake. Several access points are available. 45.818904, -88.954564. For more information, visit https://www.fs.usda.gov/recarea/cnnf/recarea/?recid=27893.
- Several designated natural areas lie just north of the wilderness area and are accessible from the developed campsites. The Anvil Lake Trail SNA provides outstanding hiking opportunities. Echo Lake SNA harbors old-growth hemlocks. Franklin and Butternut Lakes SNA have 400-year-old trees. Pat Shay Lake SNA also harbors old-growth hemlocks. For more information, visit the Wisconsin DNR website below.

Below are base camps for a weeklong adventure:

- Luna-White Deer has 37 sites open from late April until mid-October. There is a four-mile trail around the lakes, fishing, and a beach. 45.899390, -88.962230.
- Franklin Lake has 77 sites open from late April to mid-October. A nature trail leads through 400-year-old trees and has a bog boardwalk, 45.931598, -88.993097.

The wilderness site is remote with no development. All necessities must be supplied by the user and carried out after visits. For more information, visit the Chequamegon-Nicolet National Forest website, https://www.fs.usda.gov/cnnf, or the Wisconsin DNR SNA website, https://dnr.wisconsin.gov/topic/StateNaturalAreas.

Chequamegon-Nicolet National Forest

Moquah Barrens

FOREST THERAPY AREA			
	LOW	MEDIUM	HIGH
NATURAL DIVERSITY			✓
PHYSICAL CHALLENGE			✓
ACCESS FRIENDLY		✓	
SERENITY, SOLITUDE			✓
NIGHT SKIES		✓	

- TRAIL
- BEACH
- FISHING
- CAMPING
- MOUNTAIN BIKE TRAIL
- LAKE
- SNOWSHOE TRAIL

This 22,000-acre barrens management area provides a unique opportunity for deep immersion into a large-scale barrens area. Primarily a day trip area, there's plenty of room to explore different aspects of the barrens natural community due to its size. Further enhancement can be found in peripheral area trails penetrating more forested landscape portions. The landscape can provide outstanding forest therapy.

Moquah Barrens is a managed landscape. Timber harvest and prescribed fire create and maintain the barrens aspect. Each year the forest service utilizes prescribed burns to rejuvenate between 2,000 and 5,000 acres of barrens habitat. This management is essential to preserving habitat for such species as Sharp-tailed Grouse, Upland Sandpipers, badgers, and abundant blueberry crops. The unique aspect of Moquah Barrens is the vastness of the barrens. No other site in Wisconsin has the landscape aspect of upland barrens. Other sites with large landscape features have many wetlands interspersed, but here, the wet areas are limited to small pothole wetlands.

In addition, the Valhalla Trail system and the Bayfield County Forest provide opportunities to explore the more rugged portions of the vast moraine glacial deposits. The Long Lake Recreation Area provides opportunities for more accessible trails and a beach for swimming.

The barrens have numerous roads (Ino Road, Forest Roads 242, 406, 407, 449, 505, and 819) traversing the landscape. A good starting point for exploration is the southeast corner of the barrens located at 46.606005, -91.203447.

Below are base camps for a weeklong adventure:

- Birch Grove Campground is open from late April until mid-October. Close to the Moquah Barrens and other trails and Bayfield County Forest, the camp is a prime base camp for a week's stay. Close at hand is the Long Lake Recreation Area, featuring a nature trail, fishing, and a beach. 46.684593, -91.060643.
- Wanoka Lake has 20 sites, is adjacent to ATV trails, and close to the Iron River. The camp is still relatively quiet and provides swimming and shore fishing opportunities. The campground is open from late April through mid-October. 46.542415, -91.283046.

These sites are remote with no development. All necessities must be supplied by the user and carried out after visits. For more information, visit the Chequamegon-Nicolet website, https://www.fs.usda.gov/cnnf, or the Bayfield County website, https://www.bayfieldcounty.wi.gov/.

Chequamegon-Nicolet National Forest

Oconto County Natural Areas

COGNITIVE ENRICHMENT AREA			
	LOW	MEDIUM	HIGH
NATURAL DIVERSITY			✓
PHYSICAL CHALLENGE		✓	
ACCESS FRIENDLY		✓	
SERENITY, SOLITUDE			✓
NIGHT SKIES			✓

This portion of the national forest is less remote than other parts but still has wild areas to explore. Staying at nearby campgrounds or private lodging and visiting several state natural areas can provide the nature immersion needed for many. The sites listed harbor high-quality natural areas with outstanding biological diversity.

Due to the diversity of natural features, the entire complex can be considered a Cognitive Enrichment Area. Deep forest, old-growth hemlocks and pines, fast streams, and bedrock features give the visitor ample opportunities for forest therapy. The Cathedral Pines hiking trail leads through the interior forest to an area of large old-growth pine and hemlock. A heron rookery has killed many pines, which are now providing large-diameter woody debris.

Below are base camps for a weeklong adventure:

- Bagley Rapids, with 30 sites, has access to riverside and rapids on the Black River, as well as opportunities to swim, fish, and hike other trails. 45.156837, -88.466574.
- Boulder Lake is more modern and has numerous sites, a beach, fishing opportunities, and a hiking trail with a boardwalk. 45.139645, -88.639163.
- Dozens of county and private campgrounds are in the area.

Below are adventure areas to explore:

- Cathedral Pines SNA has 1,874 acres of closed canopy forest, including old-growth hemlock and pine. Access is off FR 3299. 45.290465, -88.564548.
- Bonita Country SNA covers 1,176 acres, featuring lowland conifers and numerous bedrock outcrops. Access east of Bonita Road. 45.134372, -88.555358.
- Hagar Mountain SNA has 1,006 acres of upland forest and a large bedrock glade. Access is via foot trail off County Highway W. The trailhead is near 45.202018, -88.409816.
- Tar Dam Pines SNA has 847 acres of red and white pine forest interior. Access is east of Tar Dam Road near 45.260197, -88.391325.
- Diamond Roof is a sprawling natural area with a large irregular boundary. The primary feature is three streams flowing through dense forest. Flowing brook sounds and water riffles can be mesmerizing and much-appreciated therapy. 45.339461, -88.672039.

These sites are remote with no development. All necessities must be supplied by the user and carried out after visits. For more information, visit the Chequamegon-Nicolet National Forest website, https://www.fs.usda.gov/cnnf, or the Wisconsin DNR SNA website, https://dnr.wisconsin.gov/topic/StateNaturalAreas.

Chequamegon-Nicolet National Forest

Price (northeast) Vilas County (southwest) Natural Areas

COGNITIVE ENRICHMENT AREA	LOW	MEDIUM	HIGH
NATURAL DIVERSITY			✓
PHYSICAL CHALLENGE		✓	
ACCESS FRIENDLY		✓	
SERENITY, SOLITUDE			✓
NIGHT SKIES			✓

This portion of the national forest is remote, with small campgrounds and moderate development. Staying at these remote campgrounds or private sites and visiting several nearby state natural areas can provide the nature immersion needed for many. The sites listed harbor high-quality Cognitive Enrichment Areas with outstanding biological diversity. Access is limited to primitive trails.

These seldom-visited sites are close at hand to a multitude of vacation spots in Vilas County. People vacationing in these developed areas have tremendous chances to add enrichment benefits to their cabin experiences. The lure of a lakeside cabin adds to the quality of life for many. Visiting biologically rich areas can significantly add to the mental health benefits of a Northwoods cabin.

Below are base camps for a weeklong adventure:

- Twin Lakes has 17 sites and access to a trail system. It is open from late April to mid-October and offers fishing opportunities and hiking other trails. 45.954946, -90.072655.
- Emily Lake has 11 sites with swimming and shore fishing opportunities. It is open from late April to mid-October. 45.964314, -90.009918.
- Wabasso Lake has five walk-in sites open seasonally. 45.972464, -90.000772.

Below are adventure areas to explore:

- Doering Woods SNA has 284 acres of closed canopy hemlock and yellow birch forest, including pockets of old-growth white pine. Access is off FR 144, Shady Knoll Road, near 45.922363, -90.103967.
- Chippewa Trail SNA covers 897 acres featuring old-growth hemlock, white pine, and red pine. Access is off Chippewa Trail Road at FR 916. 45.932273, -89.994291.
- Headwaters Lakes SNA covers 2,893 acres of upland hemlock-hardwood forest. The site harbors softwater lakes. Access is best attained at FR 514. 445.971703, -90.003126.
- Tucker Lake Hemlocks SNA has 674 acres of old-growth hemlock and yellow birch. Access is off FR 142 near 45.953506, -90.039545, and walk south 0.2 miles to SNA.
- Memorial Grove SNA has 182 acres of old-growth hemlock. Access is off FR 143. Follow a trail into the grove. 45.891338, -90.055717.

All necessities must be supplied by the user and carried out after visits. For more information, visit the Chequamegon-Nicolet National Forest website, https://www.fs.usda.govcnnf, or the Wisconsin DNR SNA website, https://dnr.wisconsin.gov/topic/StateNaturalAreas.

Chequamegon-Nicolet National Forest

Sawyer and Ashland Counties (South) Natural Areas

COGNITIVE ENRICHMENT AREA			
	LOW	MEDIUM	HIGH
NATURAL DIVERSITY			✓
PHYSICAL CHALLENGE			✓
ACCESS FRIENDLY	✓		
SERENITY, SOLITUDE			✓
NIGHT SKIES			✓

This portion of the national forest is remote, with small campgrounds and limited development. Staying at these remote campgrounds and visiting several nearby state natural areas can provide the nature immersion needed for many. The sites listed harbor high-quality natural areas with outstanding biological diversity.

Due to the proximity of these areas, the entire complex can be considered a Deep Woods Cognitive Enrichment Area. Ancient knowledge of biological systems is readily at hand for the curious mind. Family-friendly trails are few, and the site's natural qualities should strongly discourage bushcraft activities.

These blocks of high-quality natural forest offer great places to understand the Northwoods' ecology. National Forest roads provide access, but interior travel is challenging. Trails are primitive, and vast acres of bog make hiking nearly impossible in places. A feel of the essential Northwoods is at hand, with conifers lining streams and lakes, abundant boreal wildflowers, and birds, such as the Gray Jay, searching for food among the bogs. Only experienced wilderness campers should try weeklong stays in the vast interior.

Below are base camps for a weeklong adventure:

- Black Lake with 29 sites and access to an interpretive trail, beach, and fishing. 45.983204, -90.935478.
- Moose Lake has 15 sites, a beach, and shore fishing opportunities. 46.015859, -91.021239.

Below are adventure areas to explore:

- Spring Brook Drumlins SNA has 3,162 acres of closed canopy forest. Access is off FR 161 near 45.965805, -90.705318.
- Upper Brunet River SNA covers 2,547 acres featuring old red and white pines. Access east of Highway GG at Swanson Creek. 45.956292, -90.844058.
- Moose River Cedar Hills SNA encompasses 601 acres of an upland cedar forest. Access is south of FR 164 near 46.020430, -90.985335.
- Snoose Creek SNA covers 1,099 acres of interior forest. Access is off FR 177 near 45.973381, -90.910271.

These sites are remote with no development. All necessities must be supplied by the user and carried out after visits. For more information, visit the Chequamegon-Nicolet National Forest website, https://www.fs.usda.gov/cnnf, or the Wisconsin DNR SNA website, https://dnr.wisconsin.gov/topic/StateNaturalAreas.

Chequamegon-Nicolet National Forest

Taylor County Natural Areas

PROBLEM SOLVING AREA			
	LOW	MEDIUM	HIGH
NATURAL DIVERSITY			✓
PHYSICAL CHALLENGE			✓
ACCESS FRIENDLY		✓	
SERENITY, SOLITUDE			✓
NIGHT SKIES			✓

This portion of the national forest is less remote than other forested parts but still has wild areas to explore. Staying at nearby campgrounds or private lodging and visiting several state natural areas can provide the nature immersion needed for many. The sites listed harbor high-quality natural areas with outstanding biological diversity.

Due to the diversity of natural features, the entire complex can be considered a Cognitive Enrichment Area. Deep forest, old-growth hemlocks and pines, fast streams, and glacial geology features give the visitor ample opportunities for forest therapy. The Ice Age Trail traverses much of the national forest to large old-growth pine and hemlock areas.

These blocks of high-quality natural forest offer great places to understand the transition zone from southern to northern forest. National forest roads provide access, but interior travel is challenging. Trails are primitive, except for the Ice Age Trail. Abundant glacial geology features, including an ice-walled lake plain, give the visitor an understanding of the diversity of the area.

Below are base camps for a weeklong adventure:

- Chippewa Recreation Area, with 78 modern sites, has access to a large flowage and opportunities to swim, fish, and hike other trails. 45.222922, -90.694674.
- Spearhead Point has 27 sites with docks, fishing, and swimming available. The site also is a trailhead for the Ice Age Trail. 45.328620, -90.448120.
- Dozens of federal, county, and private campgrounds are in the area.

Below are adventure areas to explore:

- Bear Creek Hemlocks SNA, with 967 acres of closed canopy forest, including old-growth hemlock and pine. Access is off FR 578. 45.277766 -90.722059.
- Lost Lake Esker SNA, with 1,264 acres featuring lowland conifers and an extensive esker. Access east of Sailor Creek Road. 45.276581, -90.557581.
- Mondeaux Hardwoods SNA has 2,826 acres of upland hemlock-hardwood forest. Access is via the Ice Age Trail. The trailhead is near 45.327006, -90.453554.
- Yellow River Ice-Walled Lake Plain SNA, with 722 acres of interior hardwood forest with a rich ground layer. Access is from FR 575. 45.250680, -90.643031.

These sites are remote with no development. All necessities must be supplied by the user and carried out after visits. For more information, visit the Chequamegon-Nicolet National Forest website, https://www.fs.usda.gov/cnnf, or the Wisconsin DNR SNA website, https://dnr.wisconsin.gov/topic/StateNaturalAreas.

Southern Wisconsin Nature Immersion Vacation Sites

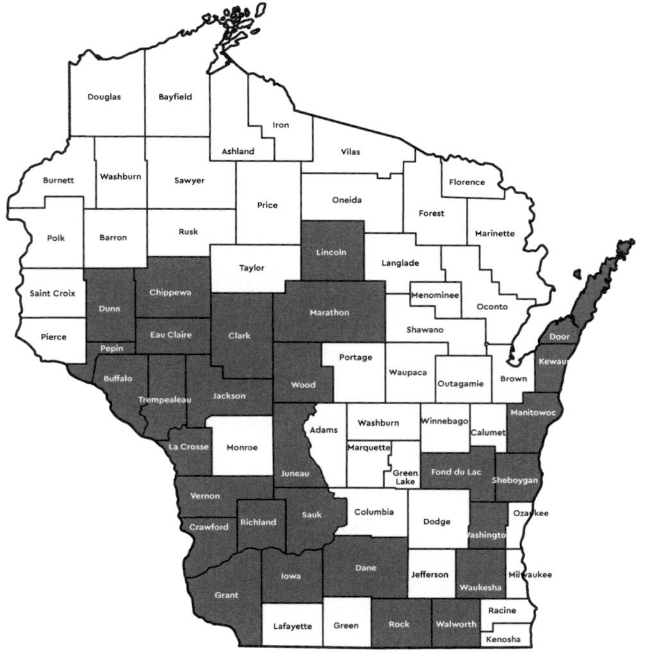

Baraboo Hills

Devil's Lake State Park and Nature Preserves

PROBLEM SOLVING AREA			
	LOW	MEDIUM	HIGH
NATURAL DIVERSITY			✓
PHYSICAL CHALLENGE			✓
ACCESS FRIENDLY			✓
SERENITY, SOLITUDE		✓	
NIGHT SKIES		✓	

This state park and nearby preserves are heavily visited, but many portions away from the lake are wild and seldom visited. Staying at the developed in-park campsites or nearby campgrounds, hiking the Ice Age Trail or other trails, or visiting the numerous nature reserves can provide the necessary nature immersion. The listed sites harbor high-quality natural areas with outstanding biological diversity.

The entire complex can be considered a Family Immersion Area. Deep forest, gorges, bedrock features, rare plants, and outstanding geology give the visitor ample opportunities for forest therapy. The preserves and park have many trails. The combined properties encompass thousands of acres of wild country. Natural areas are enclosed within the preserve boundaries and are open for wild exploration.

Below are base camps for a weeklong adventure:

- Devil's Lake State Park has 423 sites covering most camping options, with opportunities to fish, canoe, swim, and hike. 43.428493, -89.732308.
- White Mound County Park Campground has 46 sites. People seeking more solitude and wishing to visit western Baraboo Hills sites may choose this option. The park covers 1,100 acres and has many trails, swimming, and fishing opportunities. 43.360355, -90.094396.

The Baraboo Hills are close to more heavily populated southern Wisconsin cities. This fact alone requires different expectations versus visits to more remote northern sites. Solitude can be found, but it is harder to find. Anyone using the developed trail systems will most assuredly find numerous other nature enthusiasts seeking the same benefits. Off-trail wandering has challenges, from abundant slippery talus slopes to poison ivy and venomous snakes. Careful planning and caution are needed away from the developed areas of Devil's Lake, but curiosity can lead visitors to outstanding natural beauty and solitude.

Many locations are remote with no development. All necessities must be supplied by the user and carried out after visits. For more information, visit the Devil's Lake State Park website, https://dnr.wisconsin.gov/topic/parks/devilslake, or The Nature Conservancy website, https://www.nature.org/en-us/get-involved/how-to-help/places-we-protect/priority-area-the-baraboo-hills/.

Black River State Forest

State Natural Areas

FOREST THERAPY AREA			
	LOW	MEDIUM	HIGH
NATURAL DIVERSITY		✓	
PHYSICAL CHALLENGE		✓	
ACCESS FRIENDLY			✓
SERENITY, SOLITUDE		✓	
NIGHT SKIES			✓

This state forest is divided by the Interstate 94 corridor but still has wild areas well away from the road to explore. Staying at forest campgrounds or private lodging and visiting several state natural areas provides the nature immersion needed for many. The sites listed harbor high-quality natural areas with outstanding biological diversity.

Due to the great diversity of natural features, the entire complex is a Forest Therapy Area. Deep forest, old-growth white and red pines, sandstone bluffs, and glacial geology features give the visitor ample opportunities for forest therapy. The forest has 24 miles of trails open for hiking, including four nature trails.

Below are base camps for a weeklong adventure:

- East Fork Campground has 24 sites open from mid-April to mid-October, with opportunities to fish and hike the nature trail. 44.421432, -90.678731.
- Pigeon Creek Campground has 38 sites and is open year-round. Visitors can fish and swim at the beach. 44.214959, -90.616085.

Below are adventure areas to explore:

- Upper Black River SNA covers 1,562 acres of complex communities from the mesic forest through dry cliffs. Access is off Palm Road. 44.366626, -90.757046.
- Starlight Wetlands SNA covers 1,054 acres and features a mosaic of all major Wisconsin wetland types. Access is off County Highway O. Walk south into the areas. 44.206446, -90.559598.
- East Fork Black River SNA covers 513 acres and features a white and red pine forest and oaks growing on granite outcrops. Access from East Fork Campground. 44.420781, -90.671714.

As with many of the southern sites, solitude is harder to find. Noise from the interstate highway can travel miles, and the nearby Volk Field training site has regular flights over the forest. These limitations are not deal-breakers because the forest has great biological diversity. Cognitive enrichment is at hand in most of the forest. Rare plant communities and bugling elk add to the voracity of stimuli the visitor receives. A caution regarding deerflies needs saying. They can be intense in July and August.

These sites are remote with no development. All necessities must be supplied by the user and carried out after visits. For more information, visit the Black River State Forest website, https://dnr.wisconsin.gov/topic/StateForests/blackriver, or the Wisconsin DNR SNA website, https://dnr.wisconsin.gov/topic/StateNaturalAreas.

Chippewa Moraine

Chippewa County Forest Natural Areas

FAMILY IMMERSION AREA			
	LOW	MEDIUM	HIGH
NATURAL DIVERSITY			✓
PHYSICAL CHALLENGE			✓
ACCESS FRIENDLY	✓		
SERENITY, SOLITUDE			✓
NIGHT SKIES			✓

The combined properties of the Chippewa Moraine Reserve and the Chippewa County Forest occupy a significant portion of a terminal moraine. This glacial geology feature has steep rolling hills percolated with hundreds of lakes. Whether camping in the county forest, staying at nearby campgrounds or private lodging, walking trails or overland hikes provide the nature immersion needed for many. Sites harboring the highest quality natural areas are recognized.

Due to the great diversity of natural features, the entire complex is a Family Immersion Area. Deep forest, old-growth oaks and cedars, and numerous clear lakes give the visitor ample opportunities for forest therapy. Nature trails at the Ice Age Visitor Center or Brunet Island State Park give visitors an understanding of the area's ecology. The Chippewa County Forest allows permit-free camping anywhere in the forest for up to 14 days. Campers must not litter or alter natural vegetation.

Below is a base camp for a weeklong adventure:

- Brunet Island State Park, with 69 campsites, has access to an accessible nature trail and opportunities to swim and fish. A portion of the park is a designated state natural area, which features mature forest, including abundant hemlock. 45.179555, -91.162053.

Below are adventure areas to explore:

- Town Line Lake and Woods SNA covers 635 acres of closed canopy forest, including old red oaks. Access is off 255th Avenue. 45.210891, -91.376878.
- Tealey Creek Cedars is 120 acres and features old white cedar. Access from 290th Avenue. 45.262952, -91.288687.
- Chippewa Moraine Lakes SNA covers 306 acres with nine lakes and their surrounding uplands. For access information, visit the Wisconsin DNR SNA website below.
- The North of North Shattuck Lake covers 297 acres that includes a high-quality mature southern dry-mesic forest dominated by large red and white oaks. 45.227565, -91.425053.

These sites are remote with no development. All necessities must be supplied by the user and carried out after visits. For more information, visit the Chippewa Moraine State Recreation Area website, https://dnr.wisconsin.gov/topic/parks/chipmoraine, the Chippewa County Forest website, https://www.co.chippewa.wi.us/government/land-conservation-forest-management, or the Wisconsin DNR SNA website, https://dnr.wisconsin.gov/topic/StateNaturalAreas.

Door Peninsula

State Parks and State Natural Areas

COGNITIVE ENRICHMENT AREA			
	LOW	MEDIUM	HIGH
NATURAL DIVERSITY			✓
PHYSICAL CHALLENGE		✓	
ACCESS FRIENDLY		✓	
SERENITY, SOLITUDE			✓
NIGHT SKIES			✓

- TRAIL
- PAVED OR HARD-PACKED TRAIL
- BEACH
- CANOE OR KAYAK
- CAMPING
- MOUNTAIN BIKE TRAIL
- PAVED/HARD-PACKED BIKE TRAIL
- BOARDWALK
- LAKE
- CLIFF OR ROCK OUTCROP

The state parks and natural areas encompass the wildest portions of the heavily developed Door Peninsula. Staying at in-park campgrounds, hiking park trails, and visiting several state natural areas can provide abundant nature immersion opportunities. The sites listed harbor high-quality natural areas with outstanding biological diversity.

Due to the diversity of natural features, the entire complex is a Cognitive Enrichment Area. Deep forest, boreal wetlands, bedrock features, rare plants, and glacial geology features give the visitor ample opportunities for Family Immersion. The parks and natural areas have interpretive trails, hiking trails, beaches (bedrock and sand), and wave-sculpted cliffs. Visitors to the county, second homeowners, and residents can still find places of solitude and reflection.

Below are base camps for a weeklong adventure:

- Newport Park Campground has 17 backpack sites. This type of camping is popular. The visitor should reserve the sites well in advance. There are opportunities to fish, swim, and hike. 45.237731, -86.988639.
- Rock Island Campground has 40 walk-in sites. Hiking is the primary activity. The park is open from late May through Columbus Day. 45.409300, -86.829117.

Below are adventure areas to explore:

- Rock Island SNA features deep woods, rare plants, and cliffs. Fifty-seven percent of the island is an SNA. Access is via park ferry. 45.415867, -86.815309.
- Mink River Estuary SNA covers 2,118 acres and features the largest estuary in Door County. Access is from Newport Drive. 45.244659, -87.030020.
- Ridges Sanctuary SNA is 1,247 acres and features boreal forest and wetlands in a ridge and swale topography. An extensive boardwalk system makes this site accessible for mobility-limited people and younger children. Access is from County Highway Q. 45.074338, -87.119491.
- Other SNAs are Moonlight Bay Bedrock Beach, North Bay, Jackson Harbor Ridges, Ellison Bluff, Toft Point, Mud Lake, Europe Bay Woods, and White Cliff Fen.

These sites are remote with no development. All necessities must be supplied by the user and carried out after visits. For more information, visit the Wisconsin DNR Park website, https://dnr.wisconsin.gov/topic/parks/, or the Wisconsin DNR SNA website, https://dnr.wisconsin.gov/topic/StateNaturalAreas.

Eau Claire and Clark County Wildlife Areas

and State Natural Areas

FOREST THERAPY AREA			
	LOW	MEDIUM	HIGH
NATURAL DIVERSITY		✓	
PHYSICAL CHALLENGE			✓
ACCESS FRIENDLY			✓
SERENITY, SOLITUDE		✓	
NIGHT SKIES		✓	

- TRAIL
- BEACH
- CANOE OR KAYAK
- CAMPING
- MOUNTAIN BIKE TRAIL
- STREAM OR RIVER
- LAKE

All the sites are contained within the boundaries of the Eau Claire and Clark County Forests. These portions of the county forests have a low human population and offer the visitor an incredibly wild experience. The public lands are on the western edge of the great Wisconsin swamp, characterized by sandstone bluffs, rolling sandy uplands of pine-oak barrens, young forest, and scattered wetlands.

Sandstone mounds, river courses, and extensive wetlands break up the continuous forest canopy. The entire area is a mosaic of nature benefits for humans. Deep forests, large bogs, and physical challenges give the visitor ample opportunities for forest therapy.

Orienteering opportunities abound. Few places in southern Wisconsin can offer this type of activity at the landscape level. Interspersed with managed units, the dense forest provides outstanding challenges for those looking for this type of activity. Any person trying an orienteering challenge should notify the county forest managers before starting.

Both county forests allow dispersed camping with a permit for up to 14 days in Eau Claire County and 21 days in Clark County. "Leave No Trace" camping ethics are encouraged. Campers, however, cannot affect the growth of timber. Base camps for a week's outing include Coon Fork County Park in Eau Claire County. Its campground has 108 campsites. More primitive camping at either Levis Mound or Wildcat Park in Clark County offers wilderness experiences.

Below are adventure areas to explore:

- Coon Fork Barrens SNA is 580-acre jack pine-oak barrens with older white pine along the streams. 44.704781, -91.009801.
- North Fork Eau Claire River SNA covers 367 acres, features terraces and cliffs along the river, and harbors a mix of forest types. 44.75542, -90.96325.
- Blue Swamp SNA covers 560 acres. The site features a central poor fen and a northern wet forest. 44.802426, -90.872054.
- Other sites include South Fork Barrens, Windy Run Marsh, Bald Peak Marsh, Wildcat Mound, and the Levis Mound Recreation Area.

All necessities must be supplied by the user and carried out after visits. For more information, visit the Eau Claire County Forest website, https://www.co.eau-claire.wi.us/our-government, the Clark County Forest website, https://www.clarkcounty.wi.gov/forestry-parks, or the Wisconsin DNR SNA website, https://dnr.wisconsin.gov/topic/StateNaturalAreas.

Ice Age Trail

Family-Friendly Routes

PROBLEM SOLVING AREA			
	LOW	MEDIUM	HIGH
NATURAL DIVERSITY			✓
PHYSICAL CHALLENGE			✓
ACCESS FRIENDLY			✓
SERENITY, SOLITUDE		✓	
NIGHT SKIES		✓	

- TRAIL
- CAMPING
- BOARDWALK
- STREAM OR RIVER
- WATERFALL OR RAPIDS
- LAKE
- OBSERVATION TOWER OR DECK
- SNOWSHOE TRAIL

All the routes form segments of the more than 1,000 Ice Age trails in Wisconsin. The segments are considered family-friendly by the Ice Age Trail Alliance. The most extensive sections of uninterrupted trails lie within the public lands or segments purchased specifically as trail corridors. Portions of the trail pass through significant glacial geological features, incredible vistas, dense forests, open prairies, towering old-growth forests, and wetlands.

Due to the great diversity of hiking areas, the entire trail system is a Family Immersion Area. Deep forest, stream crossings, lakes, outstanding glacial features, vistas, and physical challenges give visitors ample opportunities for solitude and forest therapy.

The trail system has designated camp areas. "Leave No Trace" camping ethics are required. If you camp, be positive it is in an area designated for camping. Visitors should consider purchasing a guidebook with maps indicating precisely where such activity is allowed.

Below, family-friendly adventure areas abound (visit the sites' websites for access information):

- A northwest itinerary could include St. Croix Falls, Straight Lake, and McKenzie Creek segments. These sites have outstanding bedrock glades, deep forests, and wild lakes.
- A northeast itinerary could include Sturgeon Bay, Ahnapee State Trail, Point Beach, and Manitowoc Dunes segments. These sites feature the glacial effects of old lake levels. Alternating swells (former dunes) and swales (wetlands between the dunes) give the visitor an understanding of the site's great botanical diversity.
- An east-central itinerary could include LaBudde Creek, Parnell Esker, and Milwaukee River segments. These sites highlight depositional features such as kames, kettles, and eskers.
- A north-central itinerary could include segments at Grandfather Falls, Harrison Hills, Plover River, and Dells of the Eau Claire. Bedrock combined with terminal moraine deposits are at the surface in many places in these segments.
- A southeast itinerary could include Holy Hill, Glacial Blue Hills, Scuppernong Prairie, and Lapham Peak. The Kettle Moraine features prairie and savanna, giving visitors a feel for pre-European settlement in Wisconsin.
- A south-central itinerary could include segments at Storrs Lake, Devil's Staircase near Janesville, Montrose, and Verona prairies.

For more information, visit the Ice Age Trail website, https://dnr.wisconsin.gov/topic/parks/iceagetrail.

Jackson and Wood Counties Wildlife Areas

and County Natural Areas

PROBLEM SOLVING AREA			
	LOW	MEDIUM	HIGH
NATURAL DIVERSITY		✓	
PHYSICAL CHALLENGE			✓
ACCESS FRIENDLY	✓		
SERENITY, SOLITUDE			✓
NIGHT SKIES			✓

All the sites are contained within the boundaries of the Jackson and Wood County Forests. These places within the county forests have tiny human populations. It offers the visitor an incredibly wild experience. These public lands are part of the great Wisconsin swamp, characterized by extensive wetlands interspersed with drier pine-oak forest. Many bogs have water flowing to the east, towards the Wisconsin River, and to the west, towards the Black River. In addition, the acres harbor a growing reintroduced elk population.

Due to the diversity of natural challenges, the entire complex is a Problem-Solving Area. Deep forests, large bogs, and physical challenges give the visitor ample opportunities for Forest Therapy.

Both county forests allow dispersed camping with a permit. "Leave No Trace" camping ethics are encouraged. Only experienced wilderness campers or those guided by experienced wilderness campers should consider this activity.

Orienteering opportunities abound. Few places in southern Wisconsin still offer this type of activity at the landscape level. Interspersed with managed units, the dense forest provides outstanding challenges for those looking for this type of activity. Any person trying an orienteering challenge should notify the wildlife managers before starting.

Below are adventure areas to explore:

- Spaulding Fen SNA is a 479-acre wire-grass sedge meadow with a fringe of tamarack near the uplands. 44.327106, -90.442681.
- Deer Island SNA covers 2,121 acres and harbors a diverse mosaic of central Wisconsin wetland types. 44.303401, -90.376168.
- Bear Bluff SNA covers 186 acres. The site features the unique red maple-white pine swamp found only in central Wisconsin. 44.226508, -90.422205.
- Owl Creek Fen Savanna SNA occupies 814 acres of wetland. The acres include a unique savanna-like, open aspen forest. 44.388719, -90.089284.
- Other sites include Hiles Swamp, Jay Creek, and Martin's Marsh in Jackson County.

These sites are remote with no development. All necessities must be supplied by the user and carried out after visits. A caution regarding deerflies needs to be mentioned. They can be intense in July and August. For more information, visit the Jackson County Forest website, https://www.co.jackson.wi.us/index.asp, and the Wood County Forest website, or https://www.woodcountywi.gov/Departments/Parks/Forestry.aspx.

Kickapoo Valley Reserve

Wildcat Mountain State Park and State Natural Areas

COGNITIVE ENRICHMENT AREA			
	LOW	MEDIUM	HIGH
NATURAL DIVERSITY			✓
PHYSICAL CHALLENGE			✓
ACCESS FRIENDLY		✓	
SERENITY, SOLITUDE			✓
NIGHT SKIES			✓

- TRAIL
- FISHING
- CANOE OR KAYAK
- CAMPING
- MOUNTAIN BIKE TRAIL
- VISITOR CENTER
- STREAM OR RIVER
- WATERFALL OR RAPIDS
- CLIFF OR ROCK OUTCROP

This state reserve, a nearby state park, and natural areas encompass the wildest portion of the driftless area. Staying at remote campsites or in-park campgrounds, hiking reserve trails, canoeing the Kickapoo River, or visiting the state natural areas can provide the required nature immersion. The sites listed harbor high-quality natural areas with outstanding biological diversity.

Due to the diversity of natural features, the entire complex is a Cognitive Enrichment Area. Deep forest, floodplain, bedrock features and rare plants, and driftless area geology give the visitor ample opportunities for forest therapy. The reserve and park have many trails, including canoe trails. The combined properties encompass over 11,000 acres of wild country. Natural areas are enclosed within the reserve boundaries and are open for fantastic exploration.

Below are basecamps for a weeklong adventure:

- Kickapoo Valley Reserve has 26 remote sites on a first come, first served basis. Eight of the sites are canoe, walk-in access sites. There are opportunities to fish, canoe, and hike. Visit the reserve website for campsite locations.
- Wildcat Mountain State Park Campground has 46 sites, with 19 sites being cart-in. Hiking and canoeing are the primary activities, although compass orienteering courses are available for wilderness introduction. Visit Mt. Pisgah SNA within Wildcat Mountain State Park.

Below are adventure areas to explore:

- Kickapoo Valley Reserve SNA encompasses 3,600 acres that lie in two distinct reserve sites. They feature landscapes with diverse plant communities, several rare plants and animals, and archaeological and outstanding geological features. Meandering through both units is the scenic Kickapoo River, bordered by sheer, dripping cliffs and forested bluffs. Access is overland from reserve trails.

The Bell Center Wildlife Area, Tunnelville Cliffs SNA, and the Hogback Prairie SNA lie downstream from the reserve. Combined, they give the visitor a much different perspective on the Kickapoo Valley. These sites still have steep hillsides with bedrock features but harbor prairie and savanna communities. The Hogback is mostly prairie, with many rare species occupying a hill on a former meander of the river.

All necessities must be supplied by the user and carried out after visits. For more information, visit the Kickapoo Valley Reserve website, http://kvr.state.wi.us/Home, or the Wildcat Mountain State Park website, https://dnr.wisconsin.gov/topic/parks/wildcat.

Lower Black River

Wildlife and Natural Areas

FOREST THERAPY AREA			
	LOW	MEDIUM	HIGH
NATURAL DIVERSITY			✓
PHYSICAL CHALLENGE		✓	
ACCESS FRIENDLY	✓		
SERENITY, SOLITUDE		✓	
NIGHT SKIES		✓	

All the sites are contained within the boundaries of the Black River State Forest, North Bend Bottoms Wildlife Area, Van Loon Wildlife Area, and BLM islands. This portion of the Lower Black River from Black River Falls to the confluence with the Mississippi River is free flowing. An expansive floodplain borders the river and contains vast areas of backwaters suitable for a wilderness experience. The combined properties encompass more than 6,000 acres. Most places require watercraft to access, but there are portions where visitors can walk in.

Due to the diversity of natural challenges, the entire complex is a Forest Therapy Area. Deep floodplain forests, backwater sloughs, oak barrens, dry prairies, and physical challenges give the visitor ample opportunities for forest therapy.

The Van Loon Wildlife Area allows dispersed camping with a permit; elsewhere, camping is permitted on BLM-owned islands and sandbars. Many areas are accessed by land for short-term experiences. "Leave No Trace" camping ethics are encouraged. No developed trails exist on these sites.

Most recreationists use the river for fishing, boating, and stopping at sandy beaches to swim and picnic. While these activities get the user into nature, often, the tremendous benefits of venturing into the hinterland are never attempted. Excursion into the adjoining forest can accelerate the immersion experience. The floodplain forests, savannas, and prairies are a treasure trove of biological diversity. Along the Black River are sandstone cliffs with waterfalls, high sandy banks filled with Bank Swallow nests, wet seep areas with rare plants, and soaring Red-shouldered Hawks.

Below are adventure areas to explore (visit the DNR website for access information):

- Van Loon Floodplain Forest SNA covers 317 acres and features a floodplain forest on a large delta before entering the Mississippi River. The northern portion has oak barrens and floodplain prairies. 43.994269, -91.326763.
- Van Loon Floodplain Savanna SNA covers 1,574 acres and harbors a floodplain savanna ripe with prairie plants. Access is via watercraft. 44.051076, -91.311488.
- Black River Savanna SNA covers 566 acres and features expansive barrens, prairie habitat, and several small lakes. Access is from the water via upland parking areas. 44.082163, -91.078981.

For more information, visit the Wisconsin DNR wildlife website, https://dnr.wisconsin.gov/topic/Lands/WildlifeAreas/alpha.html.

Lower Chippewa River

Wildlife and Natural Areas

PROBLEM SOLVING AREA			
	LOW	MEDIUM	HIGH
NATURAL DIVERSITY			✓
PHYSICAL CHALLENGE			✓
ACCESS FRIENDLY		✓	
SERENITY, SOLITUDE		✓	
NIGHT SKIES		✓	

PAVED OR HARD-PACKED TRAIL
BEACH
FISHING
CANOE OR KAYAK
CAMPING
MOUNTAIN BIKE TRAIL
PAVED/HARD-PACKED BIKE TRAIL
STREAM OR RIVER

All the sites are contained within the boundaries of the Lower Chippewa River SNA, Dunnville Wildlife Area, and Tiffany Wildlife Area. This portion of the Lower Chippewa River from Eau Claire to the confluence with the Mississippi River is free flowing. An expansive floodplain borders the river and contains vast areas of backwaters suitable for a wilderness experience. The combined properties encompass more than 23,000 acres. Most places require watercraft to access, but there are places where visitors can walk in.

Due to the diversity of natural challenges, the entire complex is a Problem-Solving Area. Deep floodplain forests, backwater sloughs, oak barrens, dry prairies, and physical challenges give the visitor ample opportunities for forest therapy.

The Tiffany Wildlife Area allows dispersed camping with a permit; elsewhere, camping is permitted on state-owned islands and sandbars. Many areas are accessed by land for short-term experiences. "Leave No Trace" camping ethics are encouraged.

Most recreationists use the river for fishing, boating, and stopping at sandy beaches to swim and picnic. While these activities get the user into nature, often, the tremendous benefits of venturing into the hinterland are never attempted. The floodplain forests, savannas, and prairies are a treasure trove of biological diversity. Along the Chippewa River, there are sandy prairies with cacti and lizards, clear lakes filled with wild rice, and many freshwater mussels. A camping vacation on a sandbar with forays into the forest can be extraordinary.

Below are adventure areas to explore (visit the DNR websites for access information):

- Tiffany Bottoms Wildlife Area covers 14,000 acres and features a floodplain forest on the largest delta in the upper Midwest. The northern portion has oak barrens and floodplain prairies. 44.437208, -92.071634.
- Nine Mile Island SNA covers 1,592 acres and harbors a habitat similar to Tiffany. Access is via watercraft. 44.678415, -91.902070.
- Dunnville Wildlife Area covers 5,707 acres and features expansive barrens and prairie habitat, plus several small lakes at the intersection of two popular state trails. Access is from several upland parking areas. 44.708930, -91.870844.
- Lower Chippewa River SNA occupies 3,537 acres in several units. Floodplain forests, oak barrens, and small lakes provide diversity. 44.713779, -91.842638.

For more information, visit the Wisconsin DNR wildlife website, https://dnr.wisconsin.gov/topic/Lands/WildlifeAreas/alpha.html, or the Wisconsin DNR SNA website, https://dnr.wisconsin.gov/topic/StateNaturalAreas.

Lower Wisconsin Riverway

Paddle Plus Wildlife and Natural Areas

PROBLEM SOLVING AREA			
	LOW	MEDIUM	HIGH
NATURAL DIVERSITY			✓
PHYSICAL CHALLENGE			✓
ACCESS FRIENDLY		✓	
SERENITY, SOLITUDE		✓	
NIGHT SKIES		✓	

All the sites are contained within the boundaries of the Lower Wisconsin State Riverway. The portion of the Lower Wisconsin River from the Prairie du Sac dam to the Mississippi River confluence is free flowing. An expansive floodplain borders the river and contains vast areas of backwaters suitable for a wilderness experience. The Lower Wisconsin State Riverway encompasses more than 95,000 acres of public and private land. Most places require watercraft to access, but there are places where visitors can walk in.

Due to the great diversity of natural challenges, the entire complex is a Problem-Solving Area. Deep floodplain forests, backwater sloughs, oak barrens, dry-mesic prairies, and physical challenges give the visitor ample opportunities for forest therapy.

Camping is allowed for up to three days at any site. Permits are not required. Campsites must be on sandbars or state-owned islands, and all human waste must be buried six inches below the surface. Many areas are accessed by land for short-term experiences. “Leave No Trace” camping ethics are encouraged.

Most recreationists use the river for fishing, boating, and stopping at sandy beaches to swim and picnic. While these activities get the user into nature, often, the tremendous benefits of venturing into the hinterland are never attempted. A week of sandbar camping with excursions into the adjoining forest can accelerate the immersion experience. Along the Wisconsin River, there are sandy prairies with cacti and lizards, large tracts of floodplain forest with breeding Prothonotary Warblers, and abundant freshwater mussels.

Below are adventure areas to explore (visit the DNR website for access information):

- Avoca Prairie and Savanna SNA covers 2,208 acres and features the largest floodplain prairie east of the Mississippi River. The northern portion is savanna. 43.193416, -90.291313.
- Richwood Bottoms SNA covers 926 acres, harboring a large grove of swamp white oak and open wetlands. Access is via watercraft or over land. 43.178646, -90.652005.
- Wauzeka Bottoms SNA occupies 879 acres and features an expansive floodplain forest and huge beaver ponds. Access is via watercraft. 43.081429, -90.854185.
- Gotham Jack Pine Barrens SNA occupies 412 acres accessible from the uplands or watercraft. An unusual barrens community featuring jack pine is found here. Extensive sand blows harbor rare species. 43.201800, -90.256020.

All necessities must be supplied by the user and carried out after visits. For more information, visit the Wisconsin DNR Lower Wisconsin website, https://dnr.wisconsin.gov/topic/lands/lowerwisconsin.

Meadow Valley Wildlife Area

and State Natural Areas

PROBLEM SOLVING AREA			
	LOW	MEDIUM	HIGH
NATURAL DIVERSITY		✓	
PHYSICAL CHALLENGE			✓
ACCESS FRIENDLY	✓		
SERENITY, SOLITUDE			✓
NIGHT SKIES			✓

All the sites are within the boundaries of the 58,000-acre Meadow Valley Wildlife Area. This property abuts the Necedah National Wildlife Refuge, forming an immense wild area in central Wisconsin. It offers the visitor an incredibly fantastic experience. These public lands are part of the great Wisconsin swamp and are characterized by extensive wetlands interspersed with dry sand ridges. Former drainage ditches are now plugged, creating large expanses of wetlands and providing habitat for Whooping Cranes.

Due to the great diversity of natural challenges, the entire complex is a Problem-Solving Area. Deep forests, extensive wetlands, and physical challenges give the visitor ample opportunities for forest therapy.

The wildlife area permits camping at nine designated sites during the spring turkey season and from September 1 through December 31. "Leave No Trace" camping ethics are encouraged. Only experienced wilderness campers or those guided by experienced wilderness campers should consider this activity.

Orienteering opportunities abound. Few places in southern Wisconsin still offer this type of activity at the landscape level. Interspersed with managed units, the dense forest provides outstanding challenges for those looking for this type of activity. Any person trying an orienteering challenge should notify the wildlife managers before starting.

Below are adventure areas to explore:

- Suk Cerney Peatlands SNA is a 3,610-acre mosaic of wetlands mixed with barrens and dry forests. 44.081916, -90.232690.
- Kingston Pines SNA covers 535 acres and harbors a mature white and red pine forest mixed with oaks. 44.200731, -90.304407.
- Hog Island Tamaracks covers 462 acres in three units. The site features a tamarack and black spruce forest harboring northern bird species. 44.30758, -90.30771.
- Meadow Valley Barrens SNA occupies 631 acres of oak barrens with scattered jack and red pines. 44.100371, -90.271062.
- Other sites include the 21,000-acre Wood County Wildlife Area. 44.306985, -90.285058.

All necessities must be supplied by the user and carried out after visits. A caution regarding deerflies needs to be mentioned. They can be intense in July and August. For more information, visit the Meadow Valley Wildlife Area website, https://dnr.wisconsin.gov/topic/Lands/Wildlife Areas/meadowvalley.html.

Northern Unit Kettle Moraine State Forest

State Natural Areas

FAMILY IMMERSION AREA

	LOW	MEDIUM	HIGH
NATURAL DIVERSITY		✓	
PHYSICAL CHALLENGE		✓	
ACCESS FRIENDLY			✓
SERENITY, SOLITUDE		✓	
NIGHT SKIES	✓		

This state forest is linear, paralleling the glacial feature, and is close to population centers but still has wild areas to explore. Staying in forest campgrounds and visiting several state natural areas can provide outstanding nature immersion. The sites listed harbor high-quality natural areas with outstanding diversity.

Due to the great diversity of natural features, the entire complex is a

Family Immersion Area. Deep forest, bogs, mature red oaks, the Milwaukee River, and glacial geology features give the visitor ample opportunities for forest therapy. The forest has interpretive trails, 31 miles of the Ice Age Trail, and 42 miles of hiking trails, plus access to canoeing on the Milwaukee River.

Below are base camps for a weeklong adventure:

- Mauthe Lake Campground has 135 sites and is open year-round, with opportunities to swim, fish, and hike the nature trail. 43.601306, -88.177110.
- Long Lake has 200 sites, with hiking, swimming, fishing, and canoeing. 43.664034, -88.164445.

Below are adventure areas to explore:

- Spruce Lake Bog SNA covers 145 acres and features a boardwalk into a black spruce bog and rare plants. Access is off Airport Road. 43.666797, -88.196948.
- Milwaukee River and Swamp SNA covers 828 acres and features several wooded lowland communities and the river. Access from Mauthe Lake. 43.594072, -88.176831.
- Kettle Moraine Red Oaks SNA covers 242 acres and features old red oaks and steep moraines. Access is from County Highway A. 43.761078, -88.080033.
- Crooked Lake Wetlands is 88 acres and features a complex of southern Wisconsin wetland communities. Access is from County Highway SS. 43.618505, -88.158115.
- Other SNAs are Spring Lake, Milwaukee River Tamarack Lowlands, Haskell Noyes Memorial Woods, Butler Lake, Kettle Hole Woods, and Kewaskum Maple-Oak Woods.

This site is close to more heavily populated southern Wisconsin cities. This fact alone requires different expectations versus visits to more remote northern sites. Solitude can be found, but it is harder to find. Anyone using the developed trail systems will most assuredly find numerous other nature enthusiasts seeking the same benefits. Careful planning can lead visitors to outstanding natural beauty and solitude.

For more information, visit the Kettle Moraine North State Forest website, https://dnr.wisconsin.gov/topic/parks/kmn, or the Wisconsin DNR SNA website, https://dnr.wisconsin.gov/topic/StateNaturalAreas.

Point Beach State Forest

Manitowoc County

FAMILY IMMERSION AREA			
	LOW	MEDIUM	HIGH
NATURAL DIVERSITY			✓
PHYSICAL CHALLENGE		✓	
ACCESS FRIENDLY			✓
SERENITY, SOLITUDE			✓
NIGHT SKIES			✓

Point Beach State Forest is an excellent place to immerse in the natural world. Whether staying at the campground or in one of the rustic cabins, nature is always at hand. This Family Immersion Area is well-suited for families with young children.

The property has the most significant stretch of public beach along Lake Michigan, with rare opportunities to experience the beach and dunes without hordes of people. Six miles of beach and dunes provide potential serene settings for contemplation or exploration. Sitting on a dune at night, listening to the waves and sky watching, is an unforgettable experience.

The dunes continue landward from the open areas, but they are soon forested and alternate between forested ridges and wetland swales. This ridge and swale natural community is only found along the shores of the Great Lakes. More than 17 miles of trails allow easy access to this natural setting. These trails provide a human-nature connection to outstanding biological diversity, which in turn helps with cognitive processes.

Several trails are hard-packed, providing easy access for those needing such amenities. Campgrounds with restrooms offer a place to call home for your nature immersion. The indoor camps are great for group activities that benefit from nature immersion. Accessible wilderness is a challenge for mobility-limited individuals, but Point Beach offers one of the best places in the state for nature immersion experiences.

This site is close to more heavily populated southern Wisconsin cities. This fact alone requires different expectations versus visits to more remote northern sites. Solitude can be found, but it is harder to find. Anyone using the developed trail systems will most assuredly find numerous other nature enthusiasts seeking the same benefits. Careful planning can lead visitors to outstanding natural beauty and solitude.

Although not ideal as a site to get away from humanity, it is probably the best place in the state to introduce young children or novice nature explorers to the wonders of nature immersion. The close proximity to population centers and the relatively inexpensive costs of visiting give first-time nature seekers ample reasons to try. The interior offers the best cognition benefits, but if the bugs get too bad, head for the beach. Long strolls with numerous stops to explore curiosities can generate a long-term passion for nature.

The office is 5.6 miles north of Two Rivers city center via 22nd Street and County Highway O. 44.211814, -87.510095. A park sticker is needed for entry. For more information, visit the Point Beach State Forest website, https://dnr.wisconsin.gov/topic/parks/pointbeach.

Southern Unit Kettle Moraine State Forest

State Natural Areas

FAMILY IMMERSION AREA			
	LOW	MEDIUM	HIGH
NATURAL DIVERSITY		✓	
PHYSICAL CHALLENGE		✓	
ACCESS FRIENDLY			✓
SERENITY, SOLITUDE		✓	
NIGHT SKIES	✓		

- TRAIL
- PAVED OR HARD-PACKED TRAIL
- BEACH
- CAMPING
- MOUNTAIN BIKE TRAIL
- PAVED/HARD-PACKED BIKE TRAIL
- VISITOR CENTER
- STREAM OR RIVER
- OBSERVATION TOWER OR DECK

This state forest is linear, paralleling the glacial feature, and is close to population centers but still has wild areas to explore. Staying in forest campgrounds and visiting several state natural areas provide outstanding nature immersion. The sites listed harbor high-quality natural areas with outstanding biological diversity.

Due to the great diversity of natural features, the entire complex is a Family Immersion Area. Deep forest, open savannas, the largest lowland prairie east of the Mississippi River, and glacial geology features give the visitor ample opportunities for forest therapy. The forest has interpretive trails, 30 miles of the Ice Age Trail, and 42 miles of hiking trails.

Below are base camps for a weeklong adventure:

- Ottawa Lake Campground has 100 sites and is open year-round, with opportunities to fish, swim, and hike the nature trail. 42.936541, -88.473955.
- Pinewoods Campground has 101 sites. Hiking is the primary activity, with some camping loops enforcing a 24-hour-a-day quiet zone for solitude. Open mid-May to mid-October. 42.959755, -88.440969.
- Whitewater Lake Campground has 63 primitive sites, open from mid-May to mid-October. 42.784161, -88.697115.

Below are adventure areas to explore:

- Kettle Moraine Low Prairie SNA covers 250 acres and features prairie and fen. Access is off Stark Road. 42.911597, -88.473901.
- Kettle Moraine Oak Opening SNA covers 632 acres and features active management to re-establish an oak opening. Access is from Young Road. 42.841988, -88.603972. Nearby is Bald Bluff, with its dry prairie and historical legacies going back to the Black Hawk War.
- Young Prairie SNA covers 806 acres and features patches of native wet-mesic prairie and fen. Access is from Young Road. 42.840257, -88.636601.

This site is close to more heavily populated southern Wisconsin cities. This fact alone requires different expectations versus visits to more remote northern sites. Solitude can be found, but it is harder to find. Anyone using the developed trail systems will most assuredly find numerous other nature enthusiasts seeking the same benefits. Careful planning can lead visitors to outstanding natural beauty and solitude.

For more information, visit the Southern Unit Kettle Moraine State Forest website, https://dnr.wisconsin.gov/topic/parks/kms.

Upper Mississippi River National Wildlife and Fish Refuge

Wildlife and Natural Areas

PROBLEM SOLVING AREA			
	LOW	MEDIUM	HIGH
NATURAL DIVERSITY			✓
PHYSICAL CHALLENGE		✓	
ACCESS FRIENDLY			✓
SERENITY, SOLITUDE			✓
NIGHT SKIES	✓		

- TRAIL
- PAVED OR HARD-PACKED TRAIL
- BEACH
- FISHING
- CANOE OR KAYAK
- CAMPING
- STREAM OR RIVER

All the sites are within the boundaries of the Upper Mississippi River National Wildlife and Fish Refuge or adjacent wildlife and natural areas. This portion of the Mississippi River is primarily impounded for commodity transportation but contains vast areas of backwaters suitable for a wilderness experience. The refuge and other public land lie in four states and occupy 240,000 acres. Most places require watercraft to access, but there are portions where visitors can walk in.

Due to the great diversity of natural challenges, the entire complex is a Forest Therapy Area. Deep floodplain forests, backwater sloughs, and physical difficulties give the visitor ample opportunities for forest therapy.

The refuge permits dispersed camping for up to 14 days within a month. The exceptions are no camping in closed or no hunting areas during waterfowl season. Many areas have canoe trails for short-term experiences. "Leave No Trace" camping ethics are encouraged.

Below are adventure areas to explore:

- Nelson-Trevino Bottoms SNA is a 3,608-acre floodplain forest on the largest delta in the upper Midwest. The maze of sloughs is best used by experienced wilderness visitors. 44.415884, -92.052902.
- Whitman Dam Wildlife Area covers 2,253 acres and harbors a large, nearly undisturbed floodplain forest. 44.175682, -91.799712.
- Kellogg-Weaver Dunes and McCarthy Lake Wildlife Management Area (Minnesota) feature upland dunes with prairie plants and animals. Use restrictions apply. The adjacent wildlife area has abundant marsh species. 44.251842, -91.933517.
- Rush Creek SNA occupies 2,869 acres of bluff prairie and deep oak forests, providing outstanding river corridor views. 43.373240, -91.137534.

Most recreationists use the river for fishing, boating, and stopping at sandy beaches to swim and picnic. While these activities get the user into nature, often, the tremendous benefits of venturing into the hinterland are never attempted. Excursion into the adjoining forest can accelerate the immersion experience. The floodplain forests, savannas, and prairies are a treasure trove of biological diversity.

These sites are remote with no development. All necessities must be supplied by the user and carried out after visits. For more information, visit the Upper Mississippi River Refuge website, https://www.fws.gov/refuge/upper_mississippi_river/.

Wyalusing State Park Area

State Natural Areas

FAMILY IMMERSION AREA			
	LOW	MEDIUM	HIGH
NATURAL DIVERSITY			✓
PHYSICAL CHALLENGE			✓
ACCESS FRIENDLY		✓	
SERENITY, SOLITUDE		✓	
NIGHT SKIES		✓	

TRAIL
PAVED OR HARD-PACKED TRAIL
CANOE OR KAYAK
CAMPING
MOUNTAIN BIKE TRAIL
PAVED/HARD-PACKED BIKE TRAIL
VISITOR CENTER
STREAM OR RIVER
CLIFF OR ROCK OUTCROP

This state park and nearby natural areas encompass the wildest portions near the confluence of the Wisconsin and Mississippi Rivers. Staying at in-park campgrounds, hiking park trails, and visiting several state natural areas can provide incredible nature immersion. The sites listed harbor high-quality natural areas with outstanding biological diversity.

Due to the great diversity of natural features, the entire complex is a Family Immersion Area. Deep forest, floodplain, bedrock features and rare plants, and driftless area geology give the visitor ample opportunities for forest therapy. The park has many trails, including canoe trails. The natural areas are trail free and open for wild exploration.

Below are base camps for a weeklong adventure:

- Wyalusing Ridge Campground has 55 sites. This location overlooking the Wisconsin River is popular, so visitors should reserve the sites well in advance. There are opportunities to fish and hike. 42.993508, -91.119209.
- Homestead Campground has 54 sites. Occupying abandoned fields, the campground is now forested with young trees. Hiking is the primary activity. The park is open year-round. 42.978147, -91.123001.

Below are adventure areas to explore:

- Wyalusing Hardwood Forest SNA has 403 acres that lie in the eastern portion of the park along a north-facing ridge. It features all southern Wisconsin forest communities. Access is overland from park trails. 42.990987, -91.102471.
- Millville Oak Woodlands SNA covers 1,267 acres and features southern Wisconsin's most extensive oak woodland. Exciting is the occurrence of the chinquapin oak at its northmost location. Access is from County Highway C. 43.048562, -90.897835.
- Kickapoo Wild Woods SNA covers 635 acres and features all southern forest types on south- and west-facing slopes. Access is from Onstine Hill Road. 43.111232, -90.887343.

Although not ideal as a site to get away from humanity, it is a great place to introduce young children or novice nature explorers to the wonders of nature immersion. The close proximity to population centers and the relatively inexpensive costs of visiting give first-time nature adventurers ample reasons to try. Hiking the trails or simply watching the sunset from the bluff-top can leave a lifetime impression on first-time nature seekers.

For more information, visit the Wyalusing State Park website, https://dnr.wisconsin.gov/topic/parks/wyalusing.

Out-of-State Nature Immersion Vacation Sites

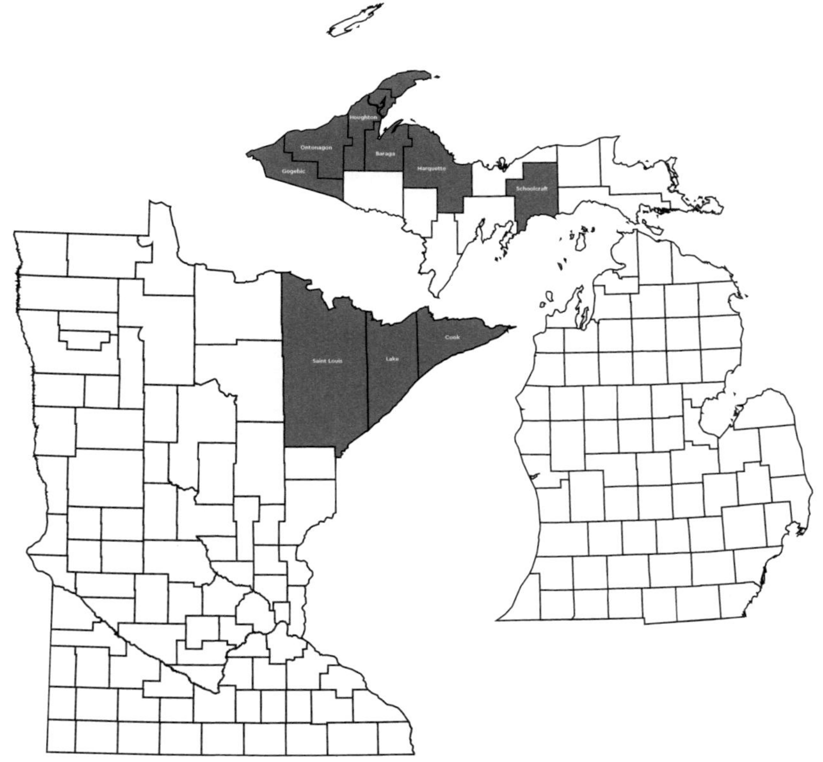

Boundary Waters Canoe Area Wilderness and Quetico Provincial Park

Minnesota and Ontario

WILDERNESS THERAPY AREA			
	LOW	MEDIUM	HIGH
NATURAL DIVERSITY			✓
PHYSICAL CHALLENGE			✓
ACCESS FRIENDLY		✓	
SERENITY, SOLITUDE			✓
NIGHT SKIES			✓

- FISHING
- CANOE OR KAYAK
- CAMPING
- STREAM OR RIVER
- WATERFALL OR RAPIDS
- LAKE
- CLIFF OR ROCK OUTCROP

The Boundary Waters is an international wilderness with almost equal parts in Minnesota and Ontario. In total, the wilderness encompasses more than two million acres. This wilderness area is a fantastic place to immerse oneself in the natural world. Every mental health benefit of a Wilderness Therapy Area adventure is achievable in the boundary waters. Nature envelopes the visitor.

The properties have over 3,000 bodies of water, including lakes, rivers, and streams; numerous small wetlands; abundant rock outcrops and waterfalls; and many acres of old-growth white and red pine forest. Late spring and early summer have at least 22 species of warblers singing from nearly every tree. The ethereal song of the Swainson's Thrush rings through the dense forest. Mid-summer has abundant orchid populations blooming in the dark recesses of the forest. Visitors may see timber wolves, black bears, moose, Great Gray Owls, and a few lucky adventurers have seen Canada lynx. The wilderness area provides serene settings for contemplation or exploration. Sitting on a lakeshore at night, listening to the night sounds, and sky-watching is an unforgettable experience.

Entering the wilderness can be a profound experience. It can bring out the best in a person, as it did with Sigurd Olsen. Or the adventure can be humbling, requiring reassessment of your core values. Any visitor must assess their personal limitations and adjust their expectations accordingly.

The wilderness is open year-round and attracts more than 250,000 visitors per year. Access points have quota systems in place to limit the number of users. Reservations are required for entry between May 1 and September 30. A Trip Planning Guide is recommended for anyone considering immersion in the wilderness. The Boundary Waters is a Dark Sky Sanctuary. Metal and glass containers are prohibited, and fees are required for entry.

The Superior National Forest Headquarters is in Duluth, Minnesota. For more information, visit the Superior National Forest website, https://www.fs.usda.gov/superior/or, the Quetico Provincial (Ontario) Park website, https://www.ontarioparks.com/park/quetico.

McCormick Wilderness Area

Michigan

WILDERNESS THERAPY AREA	LOW	MEDIUM	HIGH
NATURAL DIVERSITY			✓
PHYSICAL CHALLENGE			✓
ACCESS FRIENDLY	✓		
SERENITY, SOLITUDE			✓
NIGHT SKIES			✓

The McCormick Wilderness Area covers nearly 17,000 acres and is part of the million-acre Ottawa National Forest. This wilderness area is an excellent place to immerse in the natural world. Whether hiking the trail to the former McCormick grounds, the scenic Yellow Dog Falls, or backpacking to a remote campsite, nature is always at hand.

The property features the divide between the Lake Superior and Lake Michigan watersheds. Water falling in the central bogs could flow in either direction. Eighteen small lakes grace the wilderness. The surrounding forest has grown since the cutover in the early 1900s and is now more than 110 years old. Predominant species are hemlock, maple, birch, and basswood with patches of older white pine. Mid-summer has abundant orchid populations blooming in the darkest recesses of the forest. Visitors may see black bears, white-tailed deer, Bald Eagles, and a few lucky adventurers have seen moose. A deep forest camp with no trappings of civilization is an unforgettable experience.

The wilderness area is open year-round. Only two developed trails penetrate the wild. The White Lake Trail travels three miles to the former grounds of the McCormick estate. Three generations of McCormicks occupied the land accumulated by Cyrus McCormick, inventor of the reaper. The family willed the land to the Forest Service, so now the public can enjoy it.

The Yellow Dog Falls Trail is a 4.6-mile round trip to see the falls on the Yellow Dog River. Cascading rapids and waterfalls make this river unnavigable. Visitors are drawn to this wilderness section due to its incredibly wild character. Spray from the falls, abundant rare ferns, and the thundering water make for an unforgettable experience.

Dispersed camping is allowed within the wilderness for up to 16 days. Backpackers must carry everything needed in and out. Visitors should prepare for rugged and wet terrain. Metal and glass containers are prohibited.

Whitewater enthusiasts need to use caution. The Yellow Dog River is unnavigable, and the other rivers are meant for advanced experts only. Opportunities abound for hiking and solitude. The trails and natural features provide a human-nature connection to outstanding biological diversity, which in turn helps with cognitive processes.

The Ottawa National Forest Visitor Center is in Watersmeet, Michigan. Marquette, Michigan, is the closest community. 46.607532, -88.678511. Fees are not required.

Porcupine Mountains Wilderness State Park

Michigan

WILDERNESS THERAPY AREA	LOW	MEDIUM	HIGH
NATURAL DIVERSITY			✓
PHYSICAL CHALLENGE			✓
ACCESS FRIENDLY			✓
SERENITY, SOLITUDE			✓
NIGHT SKIES			✓

- TRAIL
- BEACH
- CAMPING
- MOUNTAIN BIKE TRAIL
- VISITOR CENTER
- STREAM OR RIVER
- WATERFALL OR RAPIDS
- LAKE
- CLIFF OR ROCK OUTCROP

The Porcupine Mountains Wilderness State Park covers more than 59,000 acres, of which 47,000 are legally dedicated wilderness. In the heart of the wilderness area is 35,000 acres of virgin old-growth timber. The park is a terrific place to immerse in the natural world. Whether staying at the campground, enjoying the scenic overlooks, pondering the two-billion-year-old rocks, beach combing on the sandy shores of Lake Superior, or backpacking to a remote campsite, nature is always at hand.

The property has 90 miles of trails, of which 23 miles are part of the North Country Trail system. Interior trails access numerous waterfalls and old virgin northern hemlock-hardwood forest never touched by sawyers. Late spring and early summer have at least 18 species of warblers singing from nearly every tree. Mid-summer has abundant wildflowers blooming in every corner of the forest. The wilderness area provides serene settings for contemplation or exploration. Sitting at a backcountry campsite or even a modern cabin, listening to the night sounds and sky-watching, is an unforgettable experience.

The park is open year-round, and campsites are highly prized. Reservations can be made up to six months in advance. Sixty-five backcountry campsites are available. Campsites are primitive, with a fire ring and wilderness latrine as the only amenities. Metal and glass containers are prohibited.

Adventure seekers requiring more amenities can use the 50 rustic sites at the Presque Isle Campground or reserve rustic cabins, yurts, outposts, or modern sites. People with mobility limitations have many options. Day-use visitors should stop at the park's contact stations for information. Users must obtain day-use and backpack permits for entrance. Opportunities abound for nature viewing, fishing, hiking, and swimming. The trails and natural features provide a human-nature connection to outstanding biological diversity, which in turn helps with cognitive processes.

The "Porkies" are unique amongst wilderness parks in that they have a portion accessible to people unable to hike into the interior. Hours of reflection can occur at the overlook of the Lake of the Clouds.

The Wilderness Visitor Center is three miles west of Silver City, Michigan. 46.813956, -89.622542. Fees are required for entry. For more information, visit the Porcupine Mountains Wilderness State Park website, https://www.michigan.org/property/porcupine-mountains-wilderness-state-park.

Seney National Wildlife Refuge and Wilderness Area

Michigan

WILDERNESS THERAPY AREA			
	LOW	MEDIUM	HIGH
NATURAL DIVERSITY			✓
PHYSICAL CHALLENGE		✓	
ACCESS FRIENDLY			✓
SERENITY, SOLITUDE			✓
NIGHT SKIES			✓

The Seney National Wildlife Refuge covers over 95,000 acres, of which 25,000 are designated wilderness areas. This refuge is an excellent place to immerse in the natural world. The Marshland Wildlife Drive and Fishing Loop auto trails provide mobility-challenged people unparalleled access to the refuge's interior. Long-day hikes or bike access is needed to visit the wilderness area.

The property features an immense wetland complex. In the early 1900s, the area was logged, and attempts were made to drain the wetlands. Farming ventures failed, and the forest recovered. Management as a waterfowl production area met with minimal success, but the water management regime was outstanding for Trumpeter Swans and Common Loons.

The western portion of the refuge is a wilderness area that features the Strangmoor Bog National Natural Landmark. Water falling in these bogs slowly moves, creating a patterned peatland with small tear-drop-shaped islands covered with pines. Pitcher plants and sundews abound in the national landmark. Visitors may see black bears, bobcats, fishers, otters, Bald Eagles. A few lucky adventurers have seen moose. The wilderness provides serene settings for cognitive enrichment, contemplation, or exploration.

The refuge is open year-round, but the Marshland auto trail is open from May 15 to October 20. Visitors can hike the 1.4-mile Pine Ridge Nature Trail or over 10 miles of designated trails. Access to the interior via hiking or biking the old unpaved roads is required to get deep into the refuge. The trails and natural features provide a human-nature connection to outstanding biological diversity, which in turn helps with cognitive processes.

Winter activities can lead the adventure well into the refuge when, in other seasons, the activity is prohibitive. Ten miles of groomed Nordic ski trails are available, but skiers may find the opportunity to break their own trail more intriguing. Skiers and snowshoers are welcome to venture anywhere on the refuge, except snowshoers are prohibited from using the groomed trails.

Camping and overnight visits are not permitted. One option for camping is the Mead Creek State Forest Campground. 46.180338, -85.986286. Private campgrounds are also found in the area. Backpackers must carry everything needed in and out. Visitors should prepare for remote and wet terrain. Boats and metal and glass containers are prohibited.

The Refuge Visitor Center is in Germfask, Michigan. 46.286553, -85.940662. Fees are not required for entry. For more information, visit the Seney National Wildlife Refuge website, https://www.fws.gov/refuge/Seney.

Sturgeon River Gorge Wilderness Area

Michigan

WILDERNESS THERAPY AREA			
	LOW	MEDIUM	HIGH
NATURAL DIVERSITY			✓
PHYSICAL CHALLENGE			✓
ACCESS FRIENDLY	✓		
SERENITY, SOLITUDE			✓
NIGHT SKIES			✓

The Sturgeon River Gorge Wilderness Area covers 14,729 acres and is part of the million-acre Ottawa National Forest. This wilderness area is an outstanding place to immerse in the natural world. Nature is always at hand, whether at the campground, hiking to scenic overlooks, or backpacking to a remote campsite.

The property features the 300-foot-deep Sturgeon River Gorge. Several rare plant species grow on the moist walls of the gorge. The surrounding forest has grown since the cutover in the early 1900s and is now more than 110 years old. A virgin 122-acre stand of hemlock is located within a research natural area. Predominant species are hemlock, maple, birch, and basswood with patches of older white pine. Mid-summer has abundant orchid populations blooming in the darkest recesses of the forest. The wilderness area provides serene settings for contemplation or exploration. A deep forest camp with no trappings of civilization is an unforgettable experience.

The wilderness area is open year-round. The Sturgeon River Campground has nine sites that can be used as a base for daytime penetrations into the wilderness. The North Country Trail traverses the perimeter of the wilderness area for eight miles. Only four developed trails penetrate the wild. Three—Sturgeon Falls, Bears Den Overlook, and Pine Bluff—are shorter trails for day hikers to see the gorge. The Sidnaw Creek Trail enters deep into the forest.

Dispersed camping is allowed within the wilderness for up to 16 days. Backpackers must carry everything needed in and out. Visitors should prepare for rugged and steep terrain. Metal and glass containers are prohibited.

The Sturgeon River Gorge Wilderness Area encompasses nearly 15,000 acres and offers a winter wonderland for snowshoe enthusiasts. There will surely be something for everyone on the beautiful snow-covered landscape. While no specific trails are designated for snowshoeing, a person can go virtually anywhere in the designated area with a compass and map. Snowshoers must exercise great caution if they attempt to cross the river. Fast currents keep the ice thin even in very cold winters.

Whitewater enthusiasts need to use caution. This river is meant for advanced experts only. Opportunities abound for hiking and solitude. The trails and natural features provide a human-nature connection to outstanding biological diversity, which in turn helps with cognitive processes.

The Ottawa National Forest Visitor Center is in Watersmeet, Michigan. Sidnaw, MI, is three miles south. 46.607532, -88.678511. Fees are not required for entry.

Sylvania Wilderness Area

Michigan

WILDERNESS THERAPY AREA			
	LOW	MEDIUM	HIGH
NATURAL DIVERSITY			✓
PHYSICAL CHALLENGE			✓
ACCESS FRIENDLY		✓	
SERENITY, SOLITUDE			✓
NIGHT SKIES			✓

Sylvania Wilderness Area covers 18,327 acres and is part of the million-acre Ottawa National Forest. This wilderness area is an outstanding place to immerse in the natural world. Nature is always at hand, whether at the campground, using the canoe trails, or backpacking to a remote campsite.

The property has 34 lakes, numerous small wetlands, and many acres of old-growth white pine, red pine, and hemlock forest. Late spring and early summer have at least 18 species of warblers singing from nearly every tree. Mid-summer has abundant orchid populations blooming in the dark recess of the forest. The wilderness area provides serene settings for contemplation or exploration. Sitting on a lakeshore at night, listening to the night sounds, and sky-watching is an unforgettable experience.

The site is open year-round, and campsites are highly prized. Reservations are required from May 15 through September 30. The rest of the year, they are on a first-come, first-served basis. Campsites are primitive, with a fire ring and wilderness latrine as the only amenities. Metal and glass containers are prohibited.

Adventure seekers requiring more amenities can use the 48 sites at Clark Lake Campground near the entrance. This camp offers more modern amenities and provides access to mobility-limited individuals. Day-use visitors should use this campground. Users must obtain day-use and backpack permits for entrance. Opportunities abound for canoeing, fishing, hiking, and swimming. The trails and natural features provide a human-nature connection to outstanding biological diversity, which in turn helps with cognitive processes.

Adjacent to the wilderness area is the Middle Branch of the Ontonagon Wild and Scenic River. This public property offers a different wilderness paddling option. Anglers find this branch the best trout fishing on the Ontonagon. Access is via canoe or inner tube.

The Sylvania Wilderness is very popular, because it has 26 miles of trails that penetrate through old-growth forests. In several places, the trails follow the shoreline of lakes. In winter, visitors find trails connecting to groomed trails outside the wilderness. Snowshoeing can occur anywhere in the wilderness. Winter users, especially, should be well aware of safety requirements.

The Ottawa National Forest Visitor Center is seven miles north in Watersmeet, Michigan. 46.24472, -89.31056. Fees are required for entry. For more information, visit the Ottawa National Forest website, https://www.fs.usda.gov/ottawa.

Weekend and Daylong Adventures

The Nature Pyramid stresses that a weekend devoted to nature should occur monthly. A pyramid is a simplified way to give recommendations. Food pyramids have been around for several decades, and they keep changing as more research identifies different nutritional values. Furthermore, advances in health studies have led to additional pyramid development. For example, we now have pyramids for sleep, exercise, and social-emotional learning, among others. In our book, we are focusing on the Nature Pyramid, sometimes called the Nature Connection Pyramid.

Following health recommendations can be a daunting task, further complicated by the number of pyramids. The purpose of creating these pyramids is to keep the information simple to attain better compliance. Our take on the Nature Pyramid is to answer a question. How much nature, different natural experiences, and different types of nature constitute a healthy lifestyle?

Spending time in nature is now recognized as a cornerstone of health. Diet, sleep, and exercise combined with nature immersion help develop high-performance individuals. Connections can be obvious. For example, the serotonin from sunlight reduces stress, which helps with sleep and regulates appetite. And the simple act of entering the natural world requires exercise.

Research shows abundant benefits for mental health. Stress levels lower, feelings of well-being are enhanced, people become more creative, and nature provides hidden connections.

The 12-weekend plan can be as simple as packing lunch, water bottles, sunscreen, and other necessary safety products and heading to your favorite natural area. Extensive studies show such adventures are on equal par with a healthy diet, physical activity, and education for a well-rounded person. These forays into nature are essential for mental health, creativity, and reasoning. Fortunate people are those with nature at hand. They can leave their backyards to attain nature's benefits. Most of us, however, live in urban and suburban areas and need to plan for nature immersion.

Changing habits can be one of the hardest things to do. Lives already packed with activities leave little time for other things. Setting priorities is a great challenge for families, individuals, or even groups. The hard realization that nature is essential should elevate nature connections to the same status as healthy food and exercise.

Initially, these outings must be fun, especially for families with younger children. Immersion plans must have a component of fun, such as building snow forts, exploring shallow streams, checking out the bugs on goldenrod flowers, etc. Extreme challenges early on can produce a reluctance to participate in the future.

Our plan considers that many families do not have the luxury of paying for multiple camping trips or hotel stays, especially in the winter. Daylong outings can achieve the same results and high-quality benefits as weekend trips. We also suggest visiting a diversity of sites with different natural features and amenities to provide a broader range of benefits for the visitor. Activities and adventures should be planned seasonally for greater experiences.

The following pages are places we suggest as starting points for nature's introduction. We have visited these locations and know they are essential to our families, but everyone has their tastes, and new places will soon be found.

This section is presented similarly to the Northern Wisconsin Immersion Vacation Sites section at the beginning of the book, with a few changes. First, they are presented by region and then alphabetically by county. Second, an accompanying map shows the GPS location in the county for navigation purposes. Third, the same series of icons is used to let the reader know what amenities are available for planning purposes. Finally, the descriptions of sites are in paragraph form to give the reader a feel for the sites.

The site title is followed by a dollar sign indicating if any activity requires a fee. The GPS locater is then identified, with a paragraph detailing the site's amenities, and afterward presents a website where the reader can obtain more information.

FIGURE 1: Statewide map of weekend (daylong) sites. We present this information to give the reader a spatial representation of the sites available for planning purposes.

Southeast Wisconsin

Jefferson County

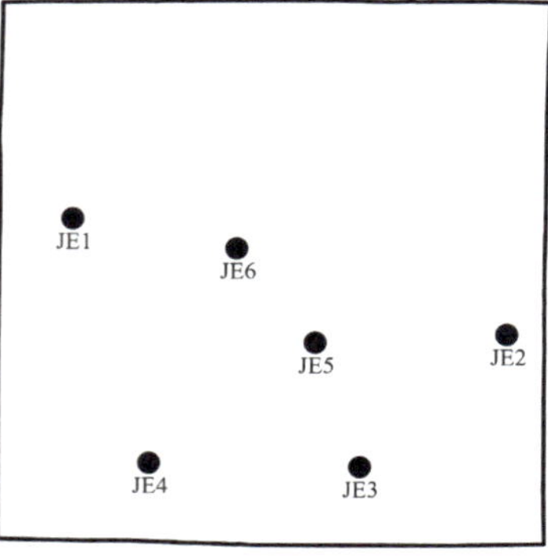

JE1 LAKE MILLS WILDLIFE AREA: 43.056224, -88.948849. This wildlife area covers 3,300 acres. Primary cover types are upland grassy fields, oak savanna restoration areas, wet prairie and sedge meadow, lake, and tamarack bog. The DNR manages the site using prescribed burning, invasive species treatments, and timber management. Amenities include opportunities for canoeing, hiking, and berry picking. Cognitive Enrichment Areas are tough to access, but the challenge provides more nature benefits. Overnight accommodations are absent. For more information, visit https://dnr.wisconsin.gov/topic/Lands/WildlifeAreas/lakemills.html.

JE2 ROME POND WILDLIFE AREA: 42.979789, -88.574225. The wildlife area covers 2,500 acres. Primary cover types are cattail marsh, upland grassy fields, oak-hickory forest, prairie restorations, and impoundments. The DNR manages the site using prescribed burning, invasive species treatments, and timber management. Amenities include opportunities for fishing, hiking, and berry picking. Cognitive Enrichment Areas are hard to access, but the challenge provides more nature benefits. Overnight accommodations are absent. For more information, visit https://dnr.wisconsin.gov/topic/Lands/WildlifeAreas/rome.html.

JE3 PRINCE'S POINT WILDLIFE AREA: 42.894032, -88.701217. This wildlife area covers 2,500 acres. Primary cover types are bottomland forest, open marsh, upland grassy fields, prairie restorations, and impoundments. The DNR manages the site using prescribed burning, invasive species treatments, and timber management. Amenities include opportunities for wildlife observation. Nature connections are plentiful, especially goal setting and problem-solving. Overnight accommodations are absent. For more information, visit https://dnr.wisconsin.gov/topic/Lands/WildlifeAreas/prince.html.

JE4 KOSHKONONG WILDLIFE AREA: 42.897388, -88.883457. This wildlife area covers 800 acres. Primary cover types are bottomland forests, deep marsh, and shrublands. The DNR manages the site using prescribed burning, invasive species treatments, and timber management. Amenities include opportunities for wildlife observation. Nature connections are plentiful, especially goal setting and problem-solving. Overnight accommodations are absent. For more information, visit https://dnr.wisconsin.gov/topic/Lands/WildlifeAreas/kosh.html.

JE5 JEFFERSON MARSH WILDLIFE AREA: 42.974997, -88.739545. This wildlife area covers 3,000 acres. Primary cover types are wet marshy fields, impoundments, oak savanna restoration areas, sedge meadows, and tamarack bog. The DNR manages the site using prescribed burning, invasive species treatments, and water management. Amenities include opportunities for wilderness immersion (in the 900-acre tamarack bog), hiking, and berry picking. Cognitive Enrichment Areas are difficult to access, but the challenge provides more nature benefits. Overnight accommodations are absent. For more information, visit https://dnr.wisconsin.gov/topic/Lands/WildlifeAreas/jefferson.html.

JE6 GLACIAL DRUMLIN TRAIL: $T. 43.036618, -88.807129. This 24-mile rail trail passes through many habitats in Jefferson County. The flat trail passes through wetlands, floodplain forests, prairie restorations, cross streams, and agricultural land. There is a 1.5-mile section where bikers must travel on public roads near Jefferson to connect the two sections. Cognitive Enrichment Areas are simple to access, and immersion into nature provides many benefits. Overnight accommodations are absent. For more information, visit https://dnr.wisconsin.gov/topic/parks/glacialdrumlin

JE7 DOROTHY CARNES COUNTY PARK AND NATURAL AREA: $E, C. 42.96282, -88.87291. This Jefferson County Park is approximately 512 acres, including a 400-acre natural area around Rose Lake. The primary features are a boggy lake, prairie restorations, and oak-hickory forests. The park is much more amenable to younger children and those needing accessibility than other Jefferson County sites. It has accessible trails and an observation deck. In addition, nature connections are abundant in remote areas, such as spiritual connections and personal introspection. The site can be an annual immersion site, especially for those with younger children. For more information, visit https://www.jeffersoncountywi.gov/departments/parks/.

Kenosha County

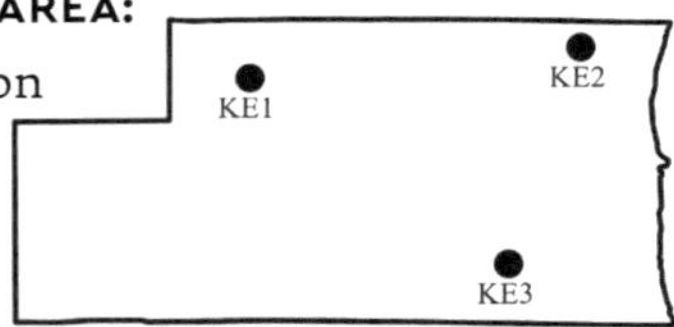

KE1 RICHARD BONG STATE RECREATION AREA: $E, C, T. 42.636299, -88.126126. This recreation area covers about 4,500 acres on the site of a planned air base. The primary features are examples of southeast Wisconsin natural communities—oak savanna restorations, upland forest, impoundments, prairie plantings, and lakes. The recreation area has 16 miles of hiking trails and eight miles of mountain bike trails. Campgrounds with more than 210 sites are open year-round but limited in winter and provide a base camp for hiking, fishing, and swimming. Nature connections, such as spiritual connections and personal introspection, are abundant. The site can be an annual immersion site, especially for those with younger children. For more information, visit https://dnr.wisconsin.gov/topic/parks/richardbong.

KE2 PETRIFYING SPRINGS COUNTY PARK AND NATURAL AREA: $E. 42.654150, -87.874202. This Kenosha County park is approximately 360 acres, including an old-growth hardwood forest. The primary natural features are an oak-hickory forest, stream, and prairie plantings. The park is much more amenable to younger children and those needing accessibility than many southeastern Wisconsin sites. It has accessible trails, an observation deck, and remote areas. Nature connections, such as spiritual connections and personal introspection, are abundant. The site can be an annual immersion site, especially for those with younger children. For more information, visit https://www.kenoshacounty.org/1652/Petrifying-Springs-Park.

KE3 PRAIRIE SPRINGS TOWN PARK AND DES PLAINES RIVER CONSERVANCY: $E. 42.528325, -87.928126. This Pleasant Prairie park and conservancy area covers approximately 750 acres, including a bottomland hardwood forest. The primary natural features are a wet prairie, sedge meadow, wetlands, stream, and prairie plantings. The park is much more amenable to younger children and those needing accessibility than many southeastern Wisconsin sites. It has accessible trails, a beach, and remote areas. Nature connections, such as spiritual connections and personal introspection, are abundant. The site can be an annual immersion site, especially for those with younger children. For more information, visit https://pleasantprairiewi.gov/.

Milwaukee County

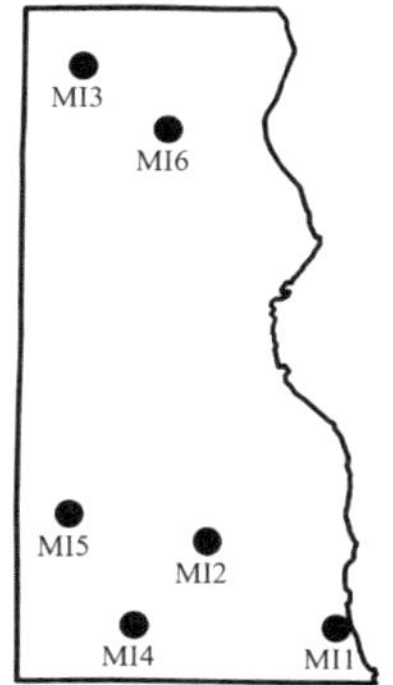

The nature immersion areas listed in Milwaukee County are smaller than in most other counties. However, they have added significance because of the county's population density. County parks cover more than 9,000 acres, each of which can benefit from personal introspection, contemplation, meditation, and reflection. Outings provided by places such as the Urban Ecology Center or Urban Canoe Trails can significantly help the citizens.

MI1 BENDER COUNTY PARK: 42.871423, -87.853142. Along the shores of Lake Michigan, this park lies on a high bank overlooking the lake. Primary cover types in this 303-acre park are southern hardwood forests, grasslands, and wetlands. Opportunities are present for nature observation, hiking, and snowshoeing. The Cognitive Enrichment Areas are simple to access, and natural immersion provides many benefits. Overnight accommodations are absent. For more information, visit https://county.milwaukee.gov/EN/Parks/Explore/Find-a-Park.

MI2 FALK COUNTY PARK: 42.916116, -87.940716. Located off Rawson Avenue, this park features conservation land. Primary cover types in this 265-acre park are southern hardwood forest, wet forest, grasslands, and wetlands. Opportunities are present for nature observation, hiking, and snowshoeing. The Cognitive Enrichment Areas are easy to access, and natural immersion provides many benefits. Overnight accommodations are absent. For more information, visit https://county.milwaukee.gov/EN/Parks/Explore/Find-a-Park.

MI3 LITTLE MENOMONEE RIVER PARKWAY: 43.163041, -88.024801. Along the Little Menomonee River, this park features conservation land. Primary cover types in this 868-acre park are southern hardwood forest, wet forest, wetlands, and river. Opportunities are present for nature observation, hiking, and snowshoeing. The Cognitive Enrichment Areas are easy to access, and natural immersion provides many benefits. Overnight accommodations are absent. For more information, visit https://county.milwaukee.gov/EN/Parks/Explore/Find-a-Park.

MI4 ROOT RIVER PARKWAY: 42.873153, -87.990782. Along the Root River, this park features conservation land. Primary cover types in this 3,931-acre parkway are the southern hardwood forest, wet forest, wetlands, and river. Opportunities are present for nature observation, hiking, and snowshoeing. The Cognitive Enrichment Areas are easy to access, and natural immersion provides many benefits. Overnight accommodations are absent. For more information, visit https://county.milwaukee.gov/EN/Parks/Explore/Find-a-Park.

MI5 WHITNALL COUNTY PARK AND WEHR NATURE CENTER: 42.930210, -88.034615. Located off College Avenue, this park features conservation land. Primary cover types in this 626-acre park are southern hardwood forest, wet forest, grasslands, streams, and lake. Opportunities are present for nature observation, hiking, and snowshoeing. The Cognitive Enrichment Areas are easy to access, and natural immersion provides many benefits. Overnight accommodations are absent. For more information, visit https://county.milwaukee.gov/EN/Parks/Explore/Find-a-Park.

MI6 HAVENWOODS STATE FOREST AND NATURE CENTER: 43.129792, -87.967307. Located off Hopkins Street, this state forest features conservation land. Primary cover types in this 237-acre state property are southern hardwood forest, wet forest, grasslands, streams, and wetlands. Opportunities are present for nature observation, hiking, and snowshoeing. The Cognitive Enrichment Areas are easy to access, and natural immersion provides many benefits. Overnight accommodations are absent. For more information, visit https://dnr.wisconsin.gov/topic/parks/havenwoods.

Ozaukee County

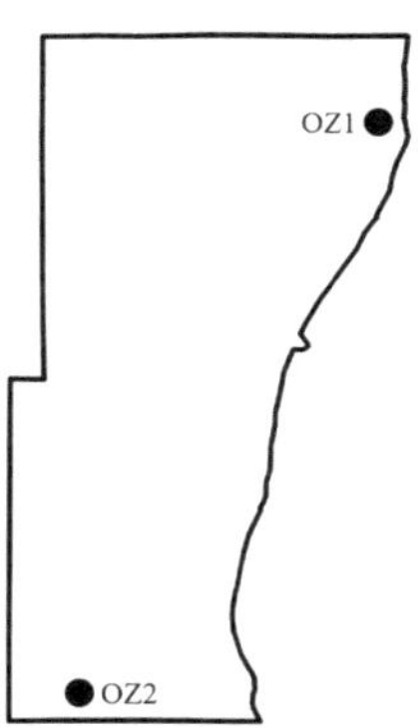

OZ1 HARRINGTON BEACH STATE PARK: $E, C. 43.499340, -87.811895. This state park encompasses almost 715 acres, of which 20 acres is the beach. The primary features are an outstanding example of lakeside forests, wetlands, dunes, and beaches. The miles of trails include a nature trail and accessible trail access to the quarry lake. Over 70 campsites are available. Nature connections, such as spiritual connections and personal introspection, are abundant. The site can be an annual immersion site, especially for those with younger children. For more information, visit https://dnr.wisconsin.gov/topic/parks/harringtonbeach.

OZ2 MEQUON NATURE PRESERVE: 43.206978, -88.015802. This private conservation organization project protects 510 acres of land. The primary features are hardwood and wetland forest types, open wetlands, and marsh. The preserve has miles of hiking trails, a boardwalk, and observation decks overlooking the marsh. Nature connections, such as spiritual connections and personal introspection, are abundant. The site can be an annual immersion site, especially for those with younger children. For more information, visit https://mequonnaturepreserve.org/#1.

Racine County

RA1 TICHIGAN WILDLIFE AREA: 42.822992, -88.234579. This wildlife area covers 1,562 acres on the west shores of Tichigan Lake. Primary cover types are wet sedge meadows, fen, marsh, shrubs, and oak woodland.

The DNR manages the site using prescribed burning, invasive species treatments, and timber management. Amenities are few, which makes the site desirable for Wilderness Therapy. Overnight accommodations are absent. For more information, visit https://dnr.wisconsin.gov/topic/Lands/WildlifeAreas/tichigan.html.

RA2 HONEY CREEK WILDLIFE AREA: 42.72739, -88.27793. This wildlife area encompasses about 1,500 acres in western Racine County. Primary cover types are wet sedge meadows, fen, marsh, shrubs, lakes, and oak woodland. The DNR manages the site using prescribed burning, invasive species treatments, and timber management. Amenities are few, which makes the site desirable for wilderness therapy. Overnight accommodations are absent. For more information, visit https://dnr.wisconsin.gov/topic/Lands/WildlifeAreas/honeycreek.html.

Walworth County

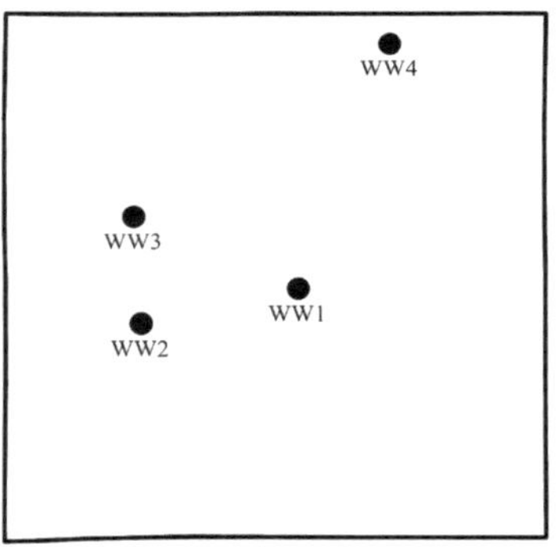

WW1 WHITE RIVER COUNTY TRAIL: $T. 42.660107, -88.521758. In Walworth County, the rail trail passes through several habitats. The flat trail crosses wetlands, penetrates woodlots, crosses streams, and features several places where native plants flourish. The county manages the site, removing invasive species and keeping the lane open. Amenities include opportunities for biking, hiking (no fees for hiking), and access to portions of the county previously unavailable. Spiritual connections and personal introspection areas are easy to access. Overnight accommodations are absent. For more information, visit https://www.co.walworth.wi.us/835/White-River-Trail.

WW2 TURTLE CREEK PADDLE (DELEVAN TO COUNTY HIGHWAY C): 42.637238, -88.658025. This eight-mile paddle is a leisurely family paddle with few obstructions and mild rapids. Downstream sections from the county line into Rock County are also possibilities. Primary cover types along the river are wet meadows, hardwoods, wet brushland, and fens. Amenities include opportunities for birdwatching and relaxation. Stretches of river flow through peaceful solitude. Overnight accommodations are absent. For more information, visit https://wisconsinrivers.org/wp-content/uploads/2019/08/Southeastern-Rivers-FINAL.pdf.

WW3 TURTLE VALLEY WILDLIFE AREA: 42.708737, -88.665406. The wildlife area covers about 1,900 acres. Primary cover types are upland grassy fields, marsh, prairie restorations, and nine flowages. The DNR manages the site by prescribed burning, brush removal techniques, and invasive species removal. Amenities include opportunities for hiking on the berms, birdwatching, and berry picking. The solitude and cognitive improvement challenges are at hand, and the challenge provides more nature benefits. Overnight accommodations are absent. For more information, visit https://dnr.wisconsin.gov/topic/Lands/WildlifeAreas/turtlevalley.

WW4 LULU LAKE CONSERVANCY AND STATE NATURAL AREA: 42.822909, -88.443273. These combined conservancy and state properties cover more than 1,800 acres. The primary features are glacial topography, oak savanna, native prairie and fen, hardwood forest, wetlands, stream, and deep clear lake. The state natural and conservancy areas preserve access for many without other nature immersion opportunities. State Natural Areas do not permit overnight camping. Nature connections, such as spiritual connections and personal introspection, are abundant. For more information, visit https://dnr.wisconsin.gov/topic/StateNaturalAreas.

Washington County

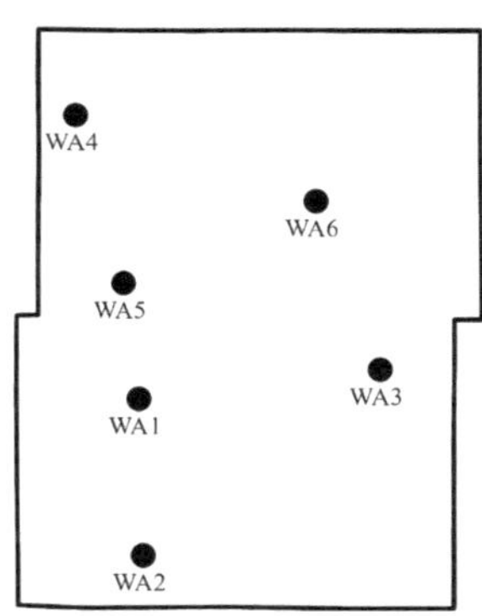

WA1 PIKE LAKE UNIT KETTLE MORAINE STATE FOREST: $E, C. 43.320436, -88.319589. This state forest unit encompasses 678 acres, of which 461 is a lake. The primary features are kettle moraine topography, woods, and beaches. The three miles of trails include a nature trail and an accessible boardwalk. Over 30 campsites are available. Nature connections, such as spiritual connections and personal introspection, are abundant. The site can be an annual immersion site, especially for those with younger children. For more information, visit https://dnr.wisconsin.gov/topic/parks/pikelake.

WA2 LOEW LAKE UNIT KETTLE MORAINE STATE FOREST: 43.224978, -88.315957. This state forest unit encompasses almost 1,000 acres, of which 23 is the lake. The primary features are kettle moraine topography, woods, lake, stream, and fen. The four miles of trails are part of the Ice Age Trail system. Overnight camping is not available. Nature connections, such as spiritual connections and personal introspection, are abundant. The site can be an annual Cognitive Enrichment Area, especially for those with younger children. For more information, visit https://dnr.wisconsin.gov/topic/parks/loewlake.

WA3 JACKSON MARSH WILDLIFE AREA: 43.337793, -88.122554. This 2,600-acre wildlife area is popular with many in Washington County. Primary cover types are bottomland hardwoods, upland planted prairie, sedge meadows, a white cedar swamp, cattail marshes, and brushland. The DNR manages the site using prescribed burning and timber management techniques to maintain cover types. Amenities include opportunities for nature immersion. The solitude and personal challenges are at hand, and the challenge provides more nature benefits. Overnight accommodations are absent. For more information, visit https://dnr.wisconsin.gov/topic/Lands/WildlifeAreas/jackson.html.

WA4 THERESA MARSH WILDLIFE AREA: 43.493114, -88.371189. This nearly 5,500-acre wildlife area is a popular destination for Washington County residents. Primary cover types are bottomland hardwoods, upland planted prairie, sedge meadow, cattail marsh, several impoundments, streams, and brushland. The DNR manages the site using prescribed burning and water management techniques to maintain productive wetlands. Amenities include opportunities for nature immersion. The solitude and personal challenges are at hand, and the challenge provides more nature benefits. Overnight accommodations are absent. For more information, visit https://dnr.wisconsin.gov/topic/Lands/WildlifeAreas/theresa.html.

WA5 ALLENTON MARSH WILDLIFE AREA: 43.390380, -88.331010. This nearly 1,100-acre wildlife area has little visitation outside hunting season. Primary cover types are bottomland hardwoods and upland planted prairie, sedge meadow, cattail marsh, and brushland. The DNR manages the site using prescribed burning and timber management techniques to maintain cover types. Amenities include opportunities for nature immersion. The solitude and personal challenges are at hand, and the challenge provides more nature benefits. Overnight accommodations are absent. For more information, visit https://dnr.wisconsin.gov/topic/Lands/WildlifeAreas/allenton.html.

WA6 LAC LAWRANN CONSERVANCY AND ROYAL OAKS PARK: 43.439588, -88.176031. These combined county and state properties cover more than 170 acres. While small, they perform a vital need for the county's citizens. The primary features are glacial topography, hardwood forest, wetlands, prairie restoration, and marsh. The park and conservancy area preserves access for many without other nature immersion opportunities. The conservancy does not permit overnight camping. Nature connections, such as spiritual connections and personal introspection, are abundant. For more information, visit https://laclawrann.org/.

Waukesha County

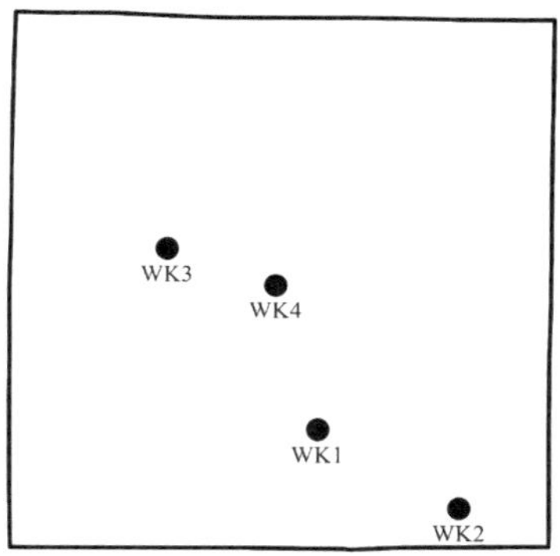

WK1 VERNON WILDLIFE AREA: 42.923010, -88.271762. This state wildlife area covers approximately 4,100 acres. The primary features are wet forest, brushland, marsh, woodlots, prairie planting, a small fen, and impoundments. The wildlife area provides access to a vast interior marsh. Overnight accommodations are absent. Nature connections, such as spiritual connections and personal introspection, are abundant. For more information, visit https://dnr.wisconsin.gov/topic/Lands/WildlifeAreas/vernon.html.

WK2 BIG MUSKEGO LAKE WILDLIFE AREA: 42.868745, -88.148563. This state wildlife area covers a few hundred acres around the 2,200-acre lake. The primary feature is the large shallow lake surrounded by cattail marsh. Uplands have small patches of oak savanna, planted prairie, and brushland. The wildlife area provides access to a vast shallow lake, although boat launches on the east side of the lake offer better watercraft access. Overnight accommodations are absent. Nature connections, such as spiritual connections and personal introspection, are abundant. For more information, visit https://dnr.wisconsin.gov/topic/Lands/WildlifeAreas/bigmuskego.html.

WK3 LAPHAM PEAK UNIT KETTLE MORAINE STATE FOREST: $E. 43.040951, -88.404164. This state forest unit covers 1,000 acres of kettle moraine topography. The primary feature is the dense forest on the rugged land. Primary cover types are oak forest, savanna, planted prairie, and brushland. The forest has many trails, including an accessible trail. They limit overnight accommodations to one backpack campsite. Nature connections, such as spiritual connections and personal introspection, are abundant. For more information, visit https://dnr.wisconsin.gov/topic/parks/laphampeak.

WK4 RETZER NATURE CENTER: 43.017277, -88.308036. This county park encompasses nearly 450 acres. The primary features represent almost every natural community in Waukesha County. The trails include a nature trail, an accessible fen boardwalk, and educational posts. Overnight camping is not available. Nature connections, such as spiritual connections and personal introspection, are abundant. The site can be an annual immersion site, especially for those with younger children. For more information, visit https://www.waukeshacounty.gov/retzernaturecenter.

South Central Wisconsin

Columbia County

CO1 FRENCH CREEK WILDLIFE AREA: 43.610892, -89.391319. This state wildlife area encompasses 3,500 acres. Primary cover types are wetlands (including high-quality calcareous fens and sedge meadows), restored prairie, conifer swamps, and grasslands. The DNR manages the site for various wildlife, especially waterfowl, by using prescribed burning and other techniques to manage the grasslands and timber harvest to manage the forest. Amenities include opportunities to experience different habitats for birdwatching, exploring, and berry picking. Nature connections are plentiful, especially for cognitive improvement. Overnight accommodations are absent. For more information, visit https://dnr.wisconsin.gov/topic/Lands/WildlifeAreas/frenchcreek.html.

CO2 SWAN LAKE WILDLIFE AREA: 43.518419, -89.406822. Swan Lake Wildlife Area covers almost 2,500 acres. Primary cover types are wetlands (including high-quality sedge meadows), restored prairie, conifer swamps, and grasslands. The DNR manages the site for water quality in the Fox River and re-establishes original vegetation for various wildlife, especially waterfowl, by using prescribed burning and other techniques to manage the grasslands and timber harvest to manage the forest. Amenities include opportunities to experience different habitats for birdwatching, exploring, and berry picking. Nature connections are plentiful, especially for wilderness therapy. Overnight accommodations are absent. For more information, visit https://dnr.wisconsin.gov/topic/Lands/WildlifeAreas/swanlake.html.

CO3 PINE ISLAND WILDLIFE AREA: 43.540868, -89.565732. This state wildlife area encompasses almost 5,500 acres. Primary cover types are wetlands, over 1,000 acres of open prairie, floodplain oak savanna, and floodplain forest. The site was initially managed for Canada geese but is now managed for various wildlife, especially several rare species, using prescribed burning and other techniques to manage the grasslands and timber harvest to manage the forest. Amenities include opportunities to experience different habitats for birdwatching, exploring, and berry picking. The interstate highway is adjacent, which diminishes values for those seeking solitude, but other nature connections are plentiful. Overnight accommodations are absent. For more information, visit https://dnr.wisconsin.gov/topic/Lands/WildlifeAreas/pineisland.html.

CO4 PETER HELLAND WILDLIFE AREA: 43.529676, -89.192130. The Pete Helland Wildlife Area covers almost 3,500 acres. Primary cover types are wetlands (including high-quality wet prairie and sedge meadows), restored prairie, and woodlands. The DNR manages the site for water quality in Duck Creek and re-establishes original vegetation for various wildlife, especially waterfowl, by using prescribed burning and other techniques. Amenities include opportunities to experience different habitats for birdwatching, exploring, and berry picking. Nature connections are plentiful, especially for wilderness therapy. Overnight accommodations are absent. For more information, visit https://dnr.wisconsin.gov/topic/Lands/WildlifeAreas/peterhelland.html.

CO5 MUD LAKE WILDLIFE AREA: 43.414708, -89.287179. Mud Lake (Columbia) Wildlife Area covers almost 2,300 acres. Primary cover types are wetlands, an oak opening/woodland restoration, restored prairie, forest, and grasslands. The DNR manages the site by re-establishing original vegetation for various wildlife, especially waterfowl, using prescribed burning and other techniques to manage the savanna and grasslands and timber harvest to manage the forest. Amenities include opportunities to experience different habitats for birdwatching, exploring, and berry picking. Nature connections are plentiful, especially for cognitive improvement. Overnight accommodations are absent. For more information, visit https://dnr.wisconsin.gov/topic/Lands/WildlifeAreas/mudlake.html.

CO6 LODI MARSH WILDLIFE AREA: 43.282270, -89.547150. This wildlife area encompasses almost 1,200 acres. Primary cover types are wetlands (including high-quality springs and sedge meadows), restored prairie, and woodlands. The DNR manages the site for water quality in Lodi Creek and re-establishes original vegetation for various wildlife, especially waterfowl, by using prescribed burning and other techniques to manage the grasslands and timber harvest to manage the forest. Amenities include a 2.5-mile section of the Ice Age Trail. Nature connections are plentiful, especially for wilderness therapy. Overnight accommodations are absent. For more information, visit https://dnr.wisconsin.gov/topic/Lands/WildlifeAreas/lodimarsh.html.

CO7 ROCKY RUN FISHERY AREA: 43.459340, -89.324505. This state fishery area covers almost 720 acres. Primary cover types are wetlands (including high-quality springs), high-quality oak savanna, restored prairie, and woodlands. The DNR manages the site for water quality in Rocky Run Creek, provides fishing opportunities, and re-establishes original vegetation for various wildlife, especially waterfowl, by using prescribed burning and other techniques to manage the grasslands and savanna. Amenities include immersion into a quality oak savanna. Nature connections are plentiful, especially for cognitive improvement. Overnight accommodations are absent. For more information, visit https://dnr.wisconsin.gov/topic/Lands/FisheriesAreas/2135rockyruncreek.html.

CO8 GRASSY LAKE WILDLIFE AREA: 43.425470, -89.161207. This state wildlife area encompasses almost 700 acres. Primary cover types are wetlands (including high-quality shallow marsh), restored prairie, restored savanna, and woodlands. The DNR manages the site for water quality in Grassy Lake to provide hunting opportunities and re-establishes original vegetation for various wildlife, especially waterfowl, by using prescribed burning and other techniques to manage the grasslands and savanna. Amenities include immersion into a quality shallow marsh. Nature connections are plentiful, especially for cognitive improvement. Overnight accommodations are absent. For more information, visit https://dnr.wisconsin.gov/topic/Lands/WildlifeAreas/grassylake2.html.

CO9 LOST LAKE STATE NATURAL AREA: 43.477576, -89.524815. This state natural area encompasses approximately 169 acres. Primary cover types are mature oak forest approaching old-growth, bedrock glades, and the four-acre Lost Lake. The SNA Program manages water quality in Lost Lake, provides research opportunities, and re-establishes the bedrock glade community for various wildlife by using prescribed burning and other techniques to manage the glade community. Amenities include immersion into a quality oak forest. Nature connections are plentiful, especially for those seeking solitude. Overnight accommodations are absent. For more information, visit https://www.devilslakewisconsin.com/wisconsin-parks-trails-natural-areas/lost-lake-state-natural-area/.

Dane County

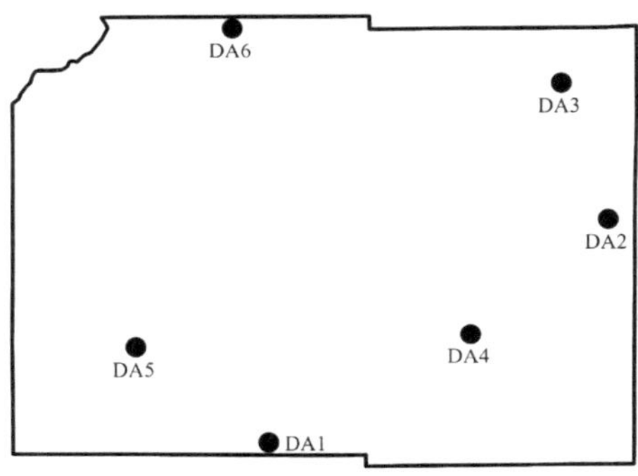

DA1 BROOKLYN WILDLIFE AREA: 42.870299, -89.499122. This state wildlife area encompasses 2,600 acres. Primary cover types are oak ridges, restored prairie, sedge meadows, and wetlands. The DNR manages the site by using prescribed burning and timber management. Amenities include opportunities for birdwatching, hiking, and berry picking. Nature connections are plentiful, especially concentrations of rare breeding birds. Overnight accommodations are absent. For more information, visit https://dnr.wisconsin.gov/topic/Lands/WildlifeAreas/brooklyn.html.

DA2 GOOSE LAKE WILDLIFE AREA: 43.092549, -89.047041. Goose Lake Wildlife Area is an almost 2,300-acre property comprising open grassland, mixed upland hardwoods, open marsh and floating sedge meadow, shrub-carr, and a tamarack bog. The DNR manages the site by using prescribed burning and timber management. Amenities include opportunities for exploring geological drumlins, hiking, and berry picking. Nature connections are plentiful, but solitude is problematic with the noise from the adjacent interstate highway. Overnight accommodations are absent. For more information, visit https://dnr.wisconsin.gov/topic/Lands/WildlifeAreas/goose.html.

DA3 DEANSVILLE WILDLIFE AREA: 43.227878, -89.109601. This state wildlife area covers more than 1,900 acres. Primary cover types are upland grassy fields, mixed hardwood upland forest, open fen, sedge meadow, shrub-carr, and brushy areas. The DNR manages the site by using prescribed burning and timber management. Amenities include opportunities for birdwatching, hiking, and berry picking. Cognitive Enrichment Areas are tough to access, but the challenge provides more nature benefits. Overnight accommodations are absent. For more information, visit https://dnr.wisconsin.gov/topic/Lands/WildlifeAreas/deansville.html.

DA4 LAKE KEGONSA STATE PARK: $E, C. 42.976093, -89.230445. Lake Kegonsa State Park is a nearly 350-acre park with a campground, swimming beach, and hiking and biking trails. Winter activities at the park include snowshoeing and cross-country ski trails. Cover types include hardwood forests, restored prairies, wetlands, and the shoreline of Lake Kegonsa. Amenities include opportunities to experience nature and different habitats. Nature connections are plentiful, especially for creativity and wonder. Overnight accommodations are present on-site, with 96 campsites. The park is open year-round. For more information, visit https://dnr.wisconsin.gov/topic/parks/lakekegonsa.

DA5 DONALD COUNTY PARK: 42.962810, -89.676199. This Dane County park covers 775 acres and features many outdoor activities. Winter activities at the park include snowshoeing and cross-country ski trails. Cover types include oak forests, restored savannas and prairies, streams, springs, and rock outcrops. Amenities include opportunities to experience nature and different habitats. Nature connections are plentiful, especially for creativity and wonder. Overnight accommodations are absent. The park is open year-round. For more information, visit https://www.danecountyparks.com/park/Donald.

Dodge County

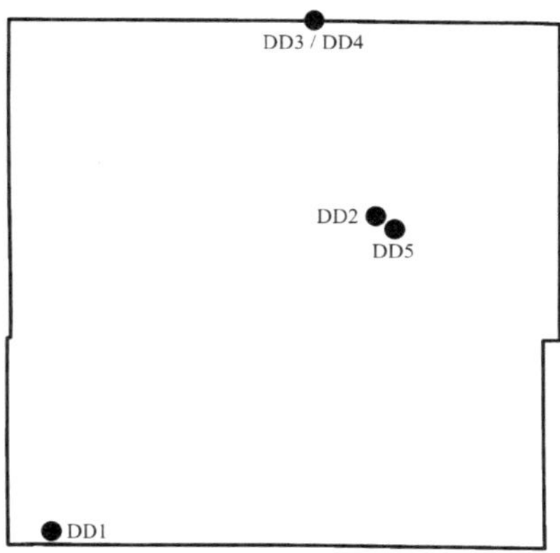

DD1 WATERLOO-MUD LAKE WILDLIFE AREA: 43.203991, -88.960368. Two units of this state wildlife area cover more than 4,500 acres. Primary cover types are upland grassy fields, oak savanna restoration areas, open fen and sedge meadows, wet prairie, and quartzite outcrops. The DNR manages the site by using prescribed burning and timber management. Amenities include opportunities for canoeing, hiking, and berry picking. Cognitive Enrichment Areas are hard to access, but the challenge provides more nature benefits. Overnight accommodations are absent. For more information, visit https://dnr.wisconsin.gov/topic/Lands/WildlifeAreas/waterloo.html.

DD2 HORICON MARSH WILDLIFE AREA: 43.472438, -88.600904. The southern third of the vast Horicon Marsh is a state wildlife area covering approximately 11,000 acres. Primary cover types are extensive cattail marsh, upland grassy fields, and islands of hardwoods. The DNR manages the site by using prescribed burning and timber management. Amenities include opportunities for canoeing, hiking, and an accessible boardwalk to an observation deck. Cognitive Enrichment Areas are simple, but immersion into nature provides many benefits. Overnight accommodations are absent. For more information, visit https://dnr.wisconsin.gov/topic/Lands/WildlifeAreas/horicon.

DD3 HORICON MARSH NATIONAL WILDLIFE REFUGE: 43.632973, -88.671452. The northern two-thirds of the vast Horicon Marsh is a national wildlife refuge covering approximately 22,000 acres. Primary cover types are extensive cattail marsh, upland grassy fields, and islands of hardwoods. The U.S. Fish and Wildlife Service (USF&WS) manages the site using prescribed burning, water level manipulation, and cattail management.

Amenities include opportunities for hiking and an accessible floating boardwalk to a marsh observation deck. Cognitive Enrichment Areas are accessible, but immersion into nature provides many benefits. Overnight accommodations are absent. For more information, visit https://www.fws.gov/refuge/horicon/.

DD4 WILD GOOSE TRAIL: 43.633320, -88.673079. This 34-mile rail trail parallels the west side of the world-famous Horicon Marsh, a national wildlife refuge. It's relatively flat and passes through wetlands, crosses streams, and has an area of native deep soil prairie next to the trail. The DNR manages the site by using prescribed burning. Amenities include opportunities for biking and access to the Horicon Marsh. Cognitive Enrichment Areas are easy to access, but immersion into nature provides many benefits. Overnight accommodations are absent. For more information, visit https://dnr.wisconsin.gov/topic/parks/wildgoose.

DD5 DODGE COUNTY LEDGE PARK: $C. 43.461769, -88.581512. This small Dodge County park is 82 acres and is perched on the Niagara Escarpment, a natural rock ledge, providing a habitat different from the nearby Horicon Marsh. Hiking trails meander along the ledge, allowing visitors to experience exciting rock formations. Amenities include opportunities to experience nature and different habitats. Nature connections are plentiful, especially for creativity and wonder. Camping accommodations are present with 41 sites. The park is open year-round. For more information, visit https://www.co.dodge.wi.gov/.

Green County

GN1 ALBANY WILDLIFE AREA: 42.728316, -89.453214. This wildlife area covers more than 1,400 acres. Primary cover types are upland grassy fields, oak savanna restoration areas, marsh and sedge meadows, floodplain forests, and prairie restorations. The DNR manages the site by using prescribed burning, treating invasive species, and timber management. Amenities include opportunities for canoeing, hiking, and berry picking. Places of solitude, reflection, and wonder are possible, and the challenge provides more nature benefits. Overnight accommodations are absent. For more information, visit https://dnr.wisconsin.gov/topic/Lands/WildlifeAreas/albany.html.

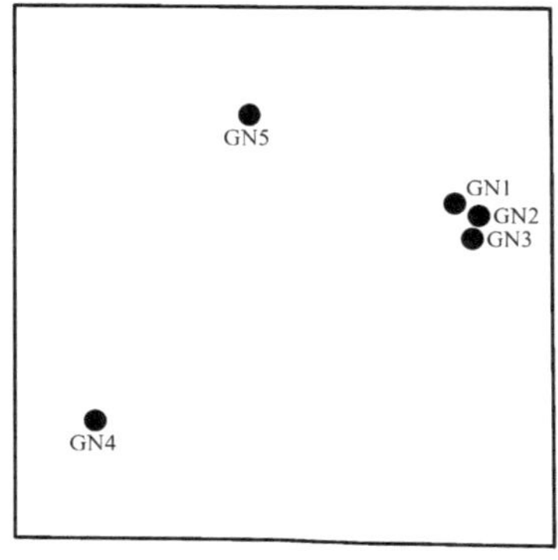

GN2 SUGAR RIVER STATE TRAIL: $T. 42.715650, -89.432647. In Green County, the rail trail passes through many habitats, including wetlands, floodplain forests, and prairie restorations. It crosses a stream and has patches of native deep soil prairie next to the trail. The DNR manages the site by using prescribed burning and removing invasive species. Amenities include opportunities for biking and access to portions of the Albany Wildlife Area. Cognitive Enrichment Areas are simple to access, and immersion into nature provides many benefits. Overnight accommodations are absent. For more information, visit https://dnr.wisconsin.gov/topic/parks/sugarriver.

GN3 SUGAR RIVER PADDLE: 42.707000, -89.437994. Several sections of the Sugar River are available for paddling. From the dam at Albany south to Brodhead is a nice paddle, as is the section from Brodhead to Avon. Upstream options are also available. These paddles have different amenities. Primary cover types along the river are agricultural areas, wooded floodplains, and marshes. Paddlers have opportunities for birdwatching, turtle-watching, and viewing floodplain forests. Stretches of river flow through incredible solitude. Overnight accommodations are present if sandbars are exposed. For more information, visit https://milespaddled.com/sugar-river-paddle-guide/.

GN4 CADIZ SPRINGS STATE RECREATION AREA: $E. 42.584063, -89.767381. This recreation area features two lakes, a swimming beach, nature trails, and hiking. Winter activities at the park include snowshoeing and cross-country ski trails. Cover types include hardwood forests, restored prairies, wetlands, springs, and streams. Amenities include opportunities to experience nature and different habitats. Nature connections are plentiful, especially for creativity and wonder. Overnight accommodations are absent. The park is open year-round. For more information, visit https://dnr.wisconsin.gov/topic/parks/cadizsprings.

GN5 NEW GLARUS WOODS STATE PARK: $E, C. 42.786741, -89.632713. This state park covers 435 acres and features dense hardwood forests, and 5.5

miles of hiking trails. Winter activities at the park include snowshoeing and cross-country skiing. Cover types include hardwood forests with many old oak trees and small restored prairies. Amenities include opportunities to experience nature in a deep forest setting. Nature connections are plentiful, especially for creativity and wonder. Overnight accommodations are present, with 18 drive-in campsites and 14 walk-to sites. The park is open year-round. For more information, visit https://dnr.wisconsin.gov/topic/parks/ngwoods.

Green Lake County

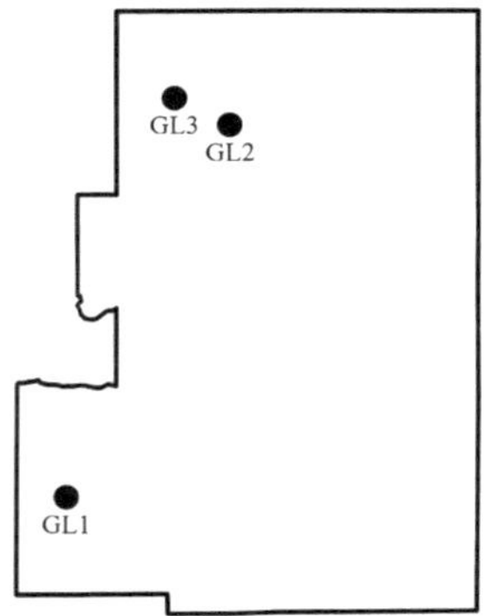

GL1 GRAND RIVER MARSH WILDLIFE AREA: 43.698910, -89.206735. This wildlife area covers 7,000 acres in Green Lake and Marquette Counties. Primary cover types are upland grassy fields, oak savanna restoration areas, open fen and sedge meadow, wet prairie, and a large impoundment. The DNR manages the site by using prescribed burning and timber management. Amenities include opportunities for canoeing, hiking, and berry picking. Cognitive Enrichment Areas are tough to access, but the challenge provides more nature benefits. Overnight accommodations are absent. For more information, visit https://dnr.wisconsin.gov/topic/Lands/WildlifeAreas/grandriver.html.

GL2 WHITE RIVER MARSH WILDLIFE AREA: 43.917378, -89.080137. This vast state wildlife area encompasses approximately 12,000 acres. Primary cover types are extensive sedge meadows, cattail marsh, wet prairies, upland grassy fields, and islands of bottomland hardwoods. The DNR manages the site by using prescribed burning and timber management. Amenities include opportunities for canoeing, fishing, and hiking off-trail. Cognitive Enrichment Areas are hard to access, but immersion into nature provides many benefits. Some portions of the site are closed during the bird nesting season. Overnight accommodations are absent. For more information, visit https://dnr.wisconsin.gov/topic/Lands/WildlifeAreas/whiteriver.html.

GL3 WHITE RIVER PADDLE: 43.933173, -89.123291. Takeout is only about a two-hour paddle from the County Highway D bridge to White River Road if that's all you do. Several places with high-quality wet prairie and even tamarack bogs relatively close to the river are upstream from Highway D and ripe for deep immersion in nature. Primary cover types along the river are reed canary grass and floodplain forest. A visit to the Wisconsin State Natural Areas website, https://dnr.wisconsin.gov/topic/StateNaturalAreas, gives location information on the best natural communities. Stretches of river flow through incredible solitude. Overnight accommodations are absent. For more information, visit https://wisconsinrivers.org/wp-content/uploads/2019/08/Southeastern-Rivers-FINAL.pdf.

Marquette County

MQ1 MUIR PARK, REFUGE AND OBSERVATORY HILL SNA: 43.690668, -89.396041. These combined properties encompass more than 1,400 acres. Primary features are the outstanding examples of sedge meadows, fen, oak savanna, and native and planted prairie. The Ice Age Trail traverses some of the three protected areas. Nature connections, such as Cognition Enrichment Areas and personal introspection, are abundant. The site can be an annual immersion site. For more information, visit https://www.fws.gov/refuge/fox_river/.

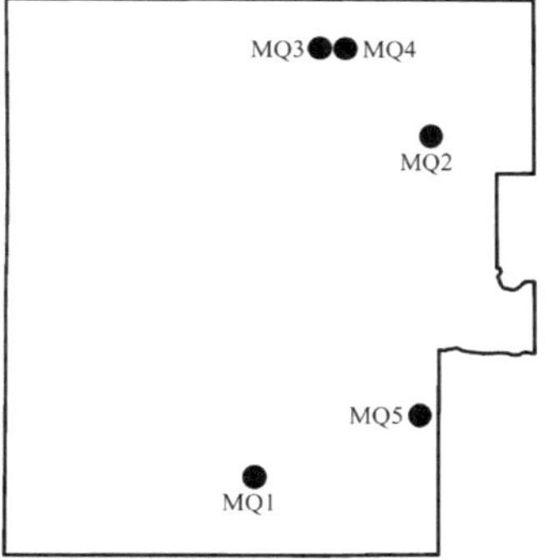

MQ2 GERMANIA MARSH WILDLIFE AREA: 43.899148, -89.252043. This wildlife area covers 2,400 acres. Primary cover types are wet meadows, marsh, swamp hardwoods, tamarack, native and planted prairie, and impoundments. The DNR manages the site using prescribed burning, invasive species treatments, and timber management. Amenities include opportunities for hiking, canoeing, and berry picking. Places of solitude, reflection, and wonder are possible, and the challenge provides more nature benefits. Overnight accommodations are absent. For more information, visit https://dnr.wisconsin.gov/topic/Lands/WildlifeAreas/germania.html.

MQ3 MECAN RIVER FISHERY AREA: 43.952196, -89.339373. The fishery area covers upland patches along 31 miles of high-quality trout water. The primary features are the outstanding examples of wet meadows, sand barrens, pine-oak forests, bottomland hardwoods, alder, and expansive wetlands. Volunteer fishing access trails are available for visitors. Nature connections, such as Cognition Enrichment Areas and personal introspection, are abundant. Overnight accommodations are absent. For more information, visit https://dnr.wisconsin.gov/topic/Lands/FisheriesAreas/1620mecanriver.html.

MQ4 MECAN RIVER PADDLE: 43.952204, -89.325696. The section described here is relatively flat water. The Marquette County water to the Germania dam has the best bank vegetation. Upstream sections have the most obstacles, with occasional deadfalls in the river, and experienced canoeists may be best suited for this adventure. Amenities include opportunities for wildlife observation and botanical forays. Nature connections are plentiful, especially goal setting and problem-solving. Overnight camping is not available. For more information, visit https://wisconsinrivers.org/wp-content/uploads/2017/12/East_Central_FINAL.pdf.

MQ5 GRAND RIVER PADDLE: 43.727855, -89.260990. From the Grand River Marsh dam downstream to the Fox River, then upstream for 3.4 miles can be an enjoyable paddle for novices and younger paddlers. This paddle has different amenities. Primary cover types along the river are cattails and marsh in the first portion, then floodplain trees along the Fox. Paddlers have opportunities for birdwatching, turtle-watching, and viewing floodplain forests. Stretches of river flow through incredible solitude. Overnight accommodations are absent. For more information, visit https://wisconsinrivers.org/wp-content/uploads/2017/12/East_Central_FINAL.pdf.

Rock County

RO1 AVON BOTTOMS WILDLIFE AREA: 42.517801, -89.306047. This wildlife area covers nearly 3,400 acres at the Illinois border. Primary cover types are wet sedge meadows, bottomland forests, shrubs, planted prairie, and oak woodland. The DNR manages the site using prescribed burning, invasive species treatments, and timber management. Amenities are few, which makes the site desirable for wilderness therapy. Overnight accommodations are absent. For more information, visit https://dnr.wisconsin.gov/topic/Lands/WildlifeAreas/avon.html.

RO2 LIMA MARSH WILDLIFE AREA: 42.805779, -88.842333. This wildlife area covers more than 2,500 acres in east central Rock County. Primary cover types are wet sedge meadows, oak woodland, shrubs, planted prairie, and a southern Wisconsin tamarack bog. The DNR manages the site using prescribed burning, invasive species treatments, and limited timber management. Amenities are few, which makes the site desirable for wilderness therapy. Overnight accommodations are absent. For more information, visit https://dnr.wisconsin.gov/topic/Lands/WildlifeAreas/lima.html.

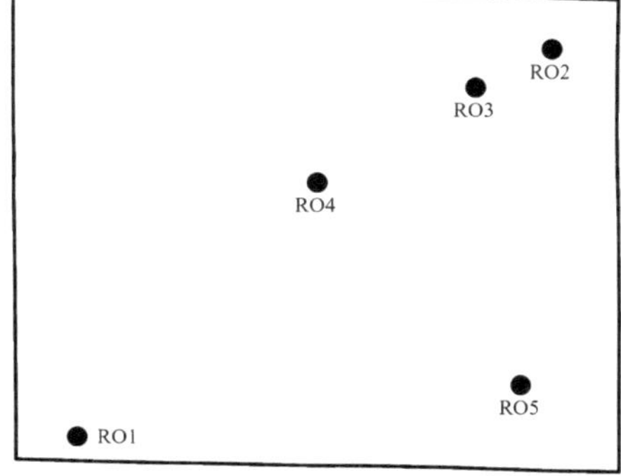

RO3 STORRS LAKE WILDLIFE AREA: 42.778389, -88.917518. This wildlife area covers approximately 750 acres east of Milton. Primary cover types are wet sedge meadows, oak woodland, shrubs, planted prairie, and a southern Wisconsin lake. The DNR manages the site using prescribed burning, invasive species treatments, and limited timber management. Amenities are many, which makes the site desirable for family visits. Overnight accommodations are absent. For more information, visit https://dnr.wisconsin.gov/topic/Lands/WildlifeAreas/storrs.html.

RO4 ROBERT O. COOK MEMORIAL ARBORETUM: 42.706892, -89.071933. The combined values of proximity to a dense population and nature immersion make this place special for the needs of younger nature enthusiasts. This Rock County gem features mature forest, prairie, marsh, and wetlands. Trails for hiking and snowshoeing crisscross the area, and there are many activities for kids. This Cognitive Enrichment Area is simple to access, but the interior can be maze-like for younger children. Overnight camping is not present. For more information, visit https://www.janesvillecvb.com/things_to_do/details/4364/216943/Robert_O_Cook_Memorial_Arboretum.

RO5 PELISHEK-TIFFANY NATURE TRAIL: 42.556804, -88.873187. In Rock County, the rail trail passes through many habitats. This flat trail passes through wetlands and native prairie and crosses streams and oak woodlands. The county manages the site with patchy prescribed burning and removing invasive species. Amenities include opportunities for biking and access to portions of the county formerly unavailable. Cognitive Enrichment Areas are easy to access, and immersion into nature provides many benefits. Overnight accommodations are absent. For more information, visit https://www.co.rock.wi.us/Home/Components/FacilityDirectory/FacilityDirectory/45/178.

Sauk County

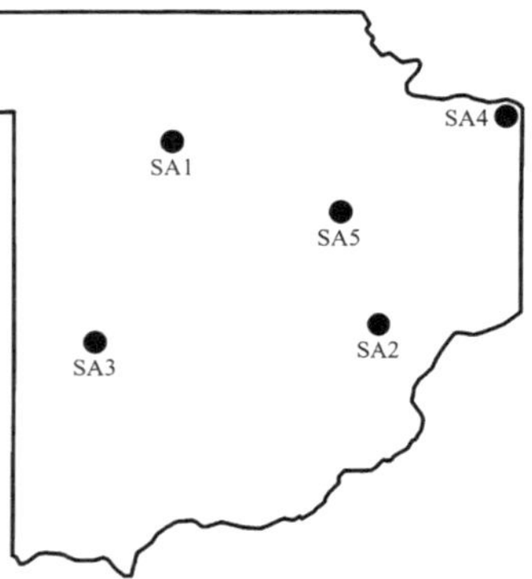

SA1 400 STATE TRAIL: $T. 43.529922, -90.007768. This 22-mile rail trail passes through several habitats in Sauk and Juneau Counties. This flat trail crosses wetlands, penetrates woodlots, crosses streams, and has views of many pine-clad sandstone bluffs. The DNR manages the site by keeping the lane open for use. The surrounding portions are passive. Amenities include opportunities for biking and hiking, as well as access to parts of the county that were formerly unavailable. Spiritual connections and personal introspection areas are easy to access. Overnight accommodations are absent. For more information, visit https://dnr.wisconsin.gov/topic/parks/400/info.

SA2 SAUK PRAIRIE RECREATION AREA AND MERRIMAC PRESERVE: 43.370063, -89.766431. These two recreation areas cover more than 5,000 acres. The significant feature is the wild aspect seen from the trails. Patches of hardwood forest cover portions, but the site is mostly wetlands and open grassland restorations. The DNR manages the site by using timber harvest and invasive species management. Amenities include opportunities for paved trail biking, hiking (11 miles), and snowshoeing. Nature connections are plentiful, especially personal cognition and solitude. Overnight accommodations are absent. For more information, visit https://dnr.wisconsin.gov/topic/parks/saukprairie, or https://riverlandconservancy.org/merrimac/.

SA3 WHITE MOUND COUNTY PARK: $E, C. 43.354677, -90.097743. The combined values of proximity to a dense population and nature immersion make this place special for the needs of younger nature enthusiasts. This 1,100-acre Sauk County gem features mature forest, prairie, marsh, lake, and wetlands. Trails for hiking and snowshoeing crisscross the area, and there are many activities for kids. This Cognitive Enrichment Area is simple to access, but the interior can be maze-like for younger children. Overnight camping is present. For more information, visit https://www.co.sauk.wi.us/parksandrecreation/white-mound-county-park.

SA4 WEST PINE ISLAND WILDLIFE AREA: 43.552681, -89.611421. This wildlife area covers 6,000 acres. Primary cover types are marsh, bottomland forest, oak savanna, and native prairie. The DNR manages the site by prescribing fire, invasive species control, and limited timber management techniques. Amenities include opportunities for wilderness immersion and berry picking. The solitude and personal challenges are at hand, and the challenge provides more nature benefits. Overnight accommodations are absent. For more information, visit https://dnr.wisconsin.gov/topic/lands/WildlifeAreas/pineisland.html.

SA5 BARABOO RIVER PADDLE (HATCHERY ROAD TO STATE HIGHWAY 113 BRIDGE): 43.468171, -89.810725. This seven-mile route is a leisurely family paddle with few obstructions and mild rapids. The mile downstream section from Highway 113 to the Wisconsin River is also possible, but takeout along the Wisconsin River is a challenge. Primary cover types along the river are wet meadows, narrow parallel lines of trees, and agricultural land. Amenities include opportunities for birdwatching and relaxation. Stretches of river flow through peaceful solitude. Overnight accommodations are present at the nearby state parks. For more information, visit https://wisconsinrivers.org/wp-content/uploads/2017/12/Southwestern_Wisconsin_Rivers-FINAL_1.pdf.

Crawford County

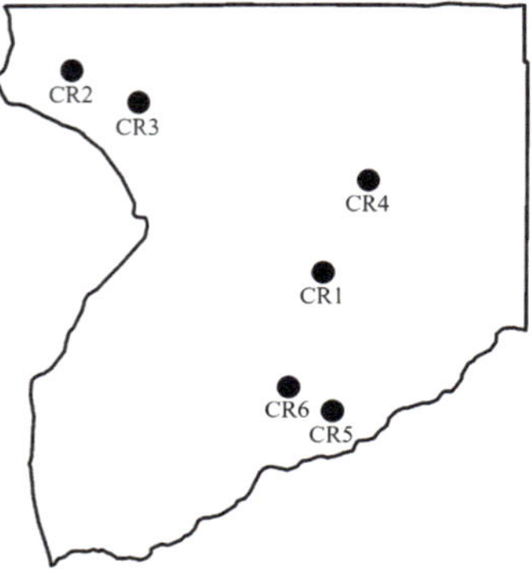

CR1 HOGBACK PRAIRIE STATE NATURAL AREA: 43.217608, -90.876783. This state natural area encompasses approximately 1,000 acres. Primary cover types are native prairie, restored prairie, and savanna restoration. The SNA Program manages the site to restore and increase the viability of the prairie ecosystem. It also protects rare species and provides research opportunities by using prescribed burning, goat grazing, and other techniques to manage the prairies and savanna communities. Amenities include immersion into a quality dry prairie ecosystem. Nature connections are plentiful, especially for those seeking solitude and improved cognition. Overnight accommodations are absent. For more information, visit https://dnr.wisconsin.gov/topic/statenaturalareas/HogbackPrairie.

CR2 RUSH CREEK STATE NATURAL AREA: 43.374059, -91.136761. This state natural area encompasses more than 3,000 acres. Primary cover types are native prairie, restored prairie, savanna restoration, oak woods, wetlands, and Rush Creek. The SNA Program manages the site to increase the viability of the prairie/savanna/oak forest ecotone. It also protects rare species and provides research opportunities by using prescribed burning and other techniques to manage the prairies and savanna communities. Amenities include immersion into various quality natural communities and a trail leading to an impressive view of the Mississippi River Palisades. Nature connections are plentiful, especially for those seeking solitude and improved cognition. Overnight accommodations are absent. For more information, visit https://dnr.wisconsin.gov/topic/statenaturalareas/RushCreek.

CR3 SUGAR CREEK BLUFF STATE NATURAL AREA: 43.350199, -91.067914. This Mississippi Valley Conservancy property encompasses approximately 430 acres. Primary cover types are native prairie, oak woods, and a section of Sugar Creek. The conservancy manages the site to maintain and increase the viability of the prairie ecosystem. It also protects rare species and provides research opportunities by using prescribed burning and other techniques to manage the prairies and savanna communities. Amenities include immersion into a quality dry prairie ecosystem and a trail system in the north unit. Nature connections are plentiful, especially for those seeking solitude and improved cognition. Overnight accommodations are absent. For more information, visit https://dnr.wisconsin.gov/topic/statenaturalareas/SugarCreekBluff.

CR4 BELL CENTER WILDLIFE AREA: 43.289096, -90.829782. This state wildlife area encompasses 1,550 acres. Primary cover types are native prairie, restored prairie, savanna restoration, oak woods, bottomland forest, and wetlands. The DNR manages the site to increase the viability of the prairie/savanna ecosystem by using prescribed burning and other techniques to manage the prairies and savanna communities. Amenities include immersion into several natural communities. Nature connections are plentiful, especially for those seeking solitude and improved cognition. Overnight accommodations are absent. For more information, visit https://dnr.wisconsin.gov/topic/Lands/WildlifeAreas/kickapoobcu.html.

CR5 WAUZEKA WILDLIFE AREA: 43.109396, -90.867052. This state wildlife area encompasses more than 1,900 acres of state-owned land. Restored prairie, oak woods, bottomland forests, and wetlands are the primary cover types. The DNR manages the site to maintain and increase the viability of the oak forest and bottomland hardwoods and is part of a UW–Madison forestry study area. A significant portion of the property is also a designated state natural area. Amenities include immersion into several natural communities. Nature connections are plentiful, especially for those seeking solitude and improved cognition. Overnight accommodations are absent. For more information, visit https://dnr.wisconsin.gov/topic/Lands/WildlifeAreas/kickapoowu.html.

CR6 LOWER KICKAPOO RIVER PADDLE: 43.127850, -90.9120005. The final 6.5 miles from Plum Creek landing to the Highway 60 bridge is scenic and seldom paddled. The first portion goes through grazed land, but the last section is scenic and wooded. This section travels through the wild country, and the final few miles flow through the Kickapoo Wildlife Area. The last section comprises many wetlands with abundant wildlife. More adventurous paddlers can plan longer routes upstream, putting in at Gays Mills. Amenities include opportunities for wildlife observation. Nature connections are plentiful, especially goal setting and problem-solving. Overnight camping is not available. For more information, visit https://wisconsinrivers.org/kark-paddle-guide/.

Grant County

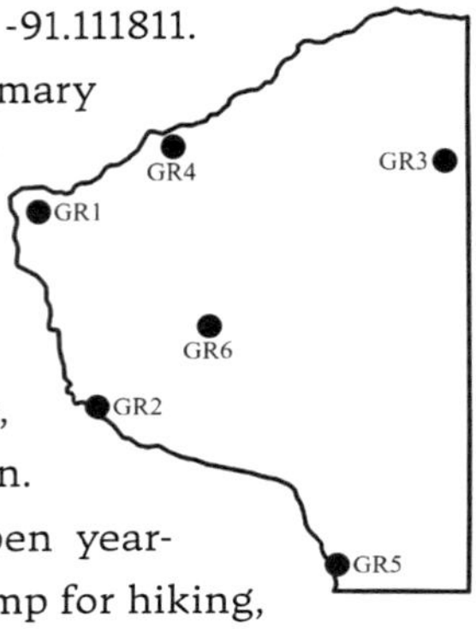

GR1 WYALUSING STATE PARK: $E, C. 42.971563, -91.111811. This state park encompasses 2,700 acres. The primary features are the outstanding views of the Wisconsin and Mississippi Rivers confluence, cliffs, floodplain forest, old-growth upland forest, and recovering old fields. The more than 14 miles of trails, including a nature trail and accessible trails, provide ample opportunities for nature immersion. Campgrounds with more than 100 sites are open year-round but limited in winter and provide a base camp for hiking, biking, fishing, and bird watching. Nature connections, such as spiritual connections and personal introspection, are abundant. The site can be an annual immersion site, especially for those with younger children. For more information, visit https://dnr.wisconsin.gov/topic/parks/wyalusing.

GR2 NELSON DEWEY STATE PARK: $E, C. 42.731942, -91.016121. This state park encompasses about 750 acres. The primary features are the outstanding views of the Mississippi River Palisades, effigy mounds, high-quality dry prairie, upland oak forest, and recovering old fields. The more than two miles of trails, including a nature trail, provide ample opportunities for nature immersion. Campgrounds with more than 45 sites are open seasonally and provide a base camp for hiking, nature observation, and historical understanding. Nature connections are abundant, such as spiritual connections and solitude. The site can be an annual immersion site, especially for those with younger children. For more information, visit https://dnr. wisconsin.gov/topic/parks/nelsondewey.

GR3 SNOW BOTTOM STATE NATURAL AREA: 43.031510, -90.465775. This state natural area encompasses 683 acres. It lies in the heart of a diverse and spectacular driftless area landscape. Significant pine relicts are the primary feature, and the site also has fen and springs, a southern dry-mesic forest, an oak woodland, riparian areas, and geological features. The SNA Program manages the site using prescribed burning and timber management. Amenities include opportunities for birdwatching, hiking, and berry picking. Nature connections are plentiful, especially in solitude. Overnight accommodations are absent. For more information, visit https://dnr.wisconsin.gov/topic/statenaturalareas/SnowBottom.

GR4 MILLVILLE OAK WOODLANDS STATE NATURAL AREA: 43.048636, -90.897573. This state natural area covers more than 1,200 acres. It lies south of the Wisconsin River valley in an outstanding driftless area landscape. The significant feature is the most extensive oak woodland in Wisconsin. Also featured are oak forests, maple forests, small prairie remnants, and geological features. The DNR manages the site using prescribed burning and invasive species management. Amenities include opportunities for birdwatching, hiking, and berry picking. Nature connections are plentiful, especially personal cognition and solitude. Overnight accommodations are absent. For more information, visit https://dnr.wisconsin.gov/topic/statenaturalareas/MillvilleOakWoodlands.

GR5 O'LEARY LAKE RECREATION AREA: 42.541562, -90.635382. O'Leary Lake is a seven-acre, 14-foot-deep lake within the Upper Mississippi River Refuge. The site encompasses several hundred acres, lies across the river from Dubuque, Iowa, and comprises lakes, backwater sloughs, marshes, and floodplain forests. The USF&WS manages the site by treating invasive species and maintaining the floodplain forest. Amenities include opportunities for exploring the river's backwater areas and a walking trail. Nature connections are best reached by canoe or small watercraft, especially spiritual connections and personal introspection. Overnight accommodations are absent. For more information, visit https://apps.dnr.wi.gov/lakes/lakepages/LakeDetail.aspx?wbic=721200.

GR6 GRANT RIVER PADDLE: 42.833764, -90.840576. This 11-mile paddle from Potter Bridge Road to County Highway U is filled with nature experiences. Primary cover types along the river are upland grassy fields, mixed hardwood upland forests, dripping cliffs, and wet meadows. Paddlers can extend the paddle another eight miles to Chaffee Hollow Road. Amenities include opportunities for birdwatching and viewing scenic cliffs topped with white pines. Stretches of river flow through incredible solitude. Overnight accommodations are absent. For more information, visit https://wisconsinrivers.org/wp-content/uploads/2017/12/Southwestern_Wisconsin_Rivers-FINAL_1.pdf.

Iowa County

IO1 GOVERNOR DODGE STATE PARK: $E, C. 43.016630, -90.141281. This state park encompasses about 5,000 acres. The primary features are the outstanding examples of driftless area topography and natural communities—cliffs, waterfalls, upland forest, impoundments, prairie plantings, and recovering old fields. The more than 40 miles of trails, including a nature trail, mountain bike trails, and accessible trails, provide ample opportunities for nature immersion. Campgrounds with more than 300 sites are open year-round but limited in winter and provide a base camp for hiking, biking, fishing, and swimming. Nature connections, such as spiritual connections and personal introspection, are abundant. The site can be an annual immersion site, especially for those with younger children. For more information, visit https://dnr.wisconsin.gov/topic/parks/govdodge.

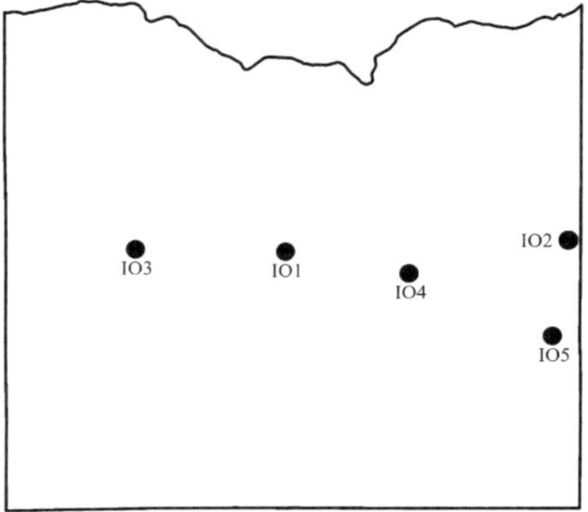

IO2 BLUE MOUND STATE PARK: $E, C. 43.023156, -89.834227. This state park encompasses almost 1,150 acres. The primary feature is Blue Mound and its associated natural communities. Talus fields, upland forests, prairie plantings, and recovering old fields provide at-hand nature. The more than 20 miles of trails, including interpretive trails and mountain bike trails, offer ample opportunities for nature immersion. Campgrounds with 77 sites, 12 walk-in sites, and an accessible cabin are open year-round but limited in winter and provide a base camp for hiking, biking, fishing, and swimming. Nature connections, such as spiritual connections and

personal introspection, are abundant. The site can be an annual immersion site, especially for those with younger children. For more information, visit https://dnr.wisconsin.gov/topic/parks/bluemound.

103 BLACKHAWK LAKE RECREATION AREA AND STATE WILDLIFE AREA: $E, C. 43.018834, -90.295047. This Iowa County recreation area covers approximately 200 acres, and the adjacent wildlife area occupies about 2,000 acres. The primary features are examples of driftless area topography and natural communities—oak savanna restorations, upland forest, impoundments, prairie plantings, and recovering old fields. The recreation area has nature trails and a swimming area. Campgrounds with more than 150 sites are open year-round but limited in winter and provide a base camp for hiking, fishing, and swimming. Nature connections, such as spiritual connections and personal introspection, are abundant. The site can be an annual immersion site, especially for those with younger children. For more information, visit https://dnr.wisconsin.gov/topic/Lands/WildlifeAreas/blackhawk.html.

104 RIDGEWAY PINE RELICT STATE NATURAL AREA: 42.999597, -90.014713. This state natural area encompasses 546 acres, and it lies at the eastern edge of the driftless area. Significant pine relicts are the primary feature, and the site also has meadows and springs, southern dry-mesic forest and oak woodland, and geological features. The SNA Program manages the site by using prescribed burning, invasive species removal, and limited timber management. Amenities include opportunities for birdwatching, off-trail hiking, and berry picking. Nature connections are plentiful, especially in solitude. Overnight accommodations are absent. For more information, visit https://dnr.wisconsin.gov/topic/statenaturalareas/RidgewayPineRelict.

105 MILITARY RIDGE PRAIRIE HERITAGE AREA: 42.949269, -89.867138. Several conservation organizations, especially The Nature Conservancy and The Prairie Enthusiasts, protect thousands of acres of grasslands south of Blue Mounds and Barneveld. These combined projects saved many small native prairie remnants and restored thousands of acres of prairie and savanna. The conservation organizations manage the sites by using prescribed burning, invasive species removal, and limited timber management. Amenities include opportunities for birdwatching, off-trail hiking, and berry picking. Nature connections are plentiful, especially in solitude. Overnight accommodations are present at nearby Blue Mound

State Park. For more information, visit https://www.nature.org/en-us/get-involved/how-to-help/places-we-protect/priority-area-military-ridge-prairie-heritage-area/.

La Crosse County

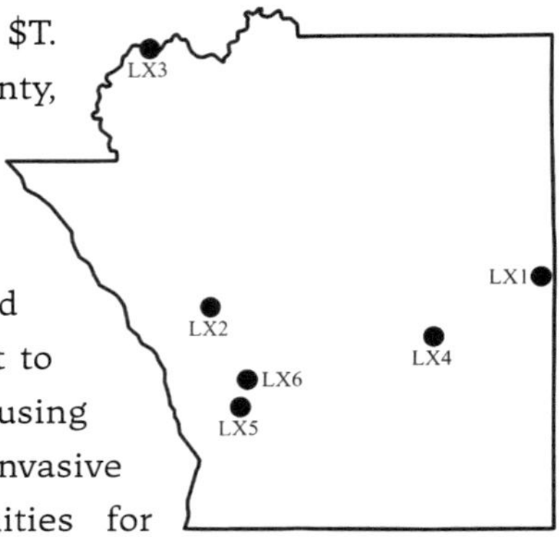

LX1 LA CROSSE RIVER STATE TRAIL: $T. 43.902863, -90.920182. In La Crosse County, the rail trail passes through many habitats. The 22-mile route passes through wetlands, woodlots, and agricultural land, crosses streams, and has patches of native sand prairie next to the trail. The DNR manages the site by using prescribed burning and removing invasive species. Amenities include opportunities for biking and access to portions of the La Crosse River Trail Prairie State Natural Area. Cognitive Enrichment Areas are simple to access, and immersion into nature provides many benefits. Overnight accommodations are absent. For more information, visit https://dnr.wisconsin.gov/topic/parks/lacrosseriver.

LX2 GREAT RIVER STATE TRAIL: $T. 43.881745, -91.234190. The 24-mile rail trail connects Onalaska with Trempealeau. The relatively flat trail passes through wetlands, woodlots, and agricultural land and crosses streams, with patches of native sand prairie next to the trail. DNR manages the site by using prescribed burning and removal of invasive species. Amenities include opportunities for biking and access to portions of the Van Loon Wildlife Area. Cognitive Enrichment Areas are easy to access, and immersion into nature provides many benefits. Overnight accommodations are absent. For more information, visit https://dnr.wisconsin.gov/topic/parks/greatriver.

LX3 VAN LOON WILDLIFE AREA: 44.061165, -91.291900. This wildlife area covers more than 3,700 acres. Primary cover types are floodplain forest, sand prairie, marsh, and oak savanna. The DNR manages the site by using prescribed burning, treating invasive species, and timber management. Amenities include opportunities for exploring the river's backwater areas in a wilderness setting. Nature connections are best secured by canoe or small watercraft, especially spiritual connections and personal introspection. Overnight accommodations are absent. For more information, visit https://dnr.wisconsin.gov/topic/Lands/WildlifeAreas/vanloon.html.

LX4 COULEE EXPERIMENTAL STATE FOREST: 43.860646, -91.023741. This state forest area covers about 3,000 acres. It lies east of La Crosse in typical driftless area topography. An expansive forest in a fragmented landscape is a significant feature. The site has an oak-hickory forest, maple forest, small prairie remnants, and geological features. DNR manages the site using experimental timber harvest, prescribed burning, and invasive species management. Amenities include opportunities for birdwatching, hiking, and berry picking. Nature connections are plentiful, especially personal cognition and solitude. Overnight accommodations are absent. For more information, visit https://dnr.wisconsin.gov/topic/StateForests/coulee.

LX5 HIXON FOREST AND GRANDAD BLUFF: 43.811658, -91.205407. This city of La Crosse property covers several hundred acres. It lies east of the city in typical driftless area topography. An expansive forest and outstanding views from the bluff overlook are significant features. The site has an oak-hickory forest, small prairie remnants, and geological features. The city of La Crosse manages the site for trail recreation and invasive species management. Amenities include opportunities for birdwatching, hiking, and skiing. Nature connections are plentiful, especially personal cognition and solitude. Overnight accommodations are absent. For more information, visit https://www.cityoflacrosse.org.

LX6 LA CROSSE BLUFFLANDS PRESERVE: 43.830360, -91.199166. The city of La Crosse and the Mississippi Valley Conservancy cooperate in protecting over 800 acres of bluff lands around La Crosse. Outstanding views from the bluffs are one of the significant features. The site has an oak-hickory forest, small prairie remnants, and geological features. Cooperative management for resource protection is the primary action. Amenities include opportunities for birdwatching, hiking, and skiing. Nature connections are plentiful, especially personal cognition and solitude. Overnight accommodations are absent. For more information, visit https://www.mississippivalleyconservancy.org/land-protection/la-crosse-blufflands.

Lafayette County

LF1 YELLOWSTONE LAKE STATE PARK AND WILDLIFE AREA: $E, C. 42.770080, -89.973696. This state park and adjacent wildlife area encompass 4,450 acres. The primary features are the impounded Yellowstone Lake, oak-hickory forest, oak savannas, small patches of native prairie, restored prairie, and shrublands. The more than 13 miles of trails, including mountain bike trails, provide abundant opportunities for nature immersion. Campgrounds with more than 128 sites are open year-round but limited in winter and provide a base camp. Nature connections are abundant, such as spiritual connections and solitude. The site can be an annual immersion site, especially for those with younger children. For more information, visit https://dnr.wisconsin.gov/topic/parks/yellowstone.

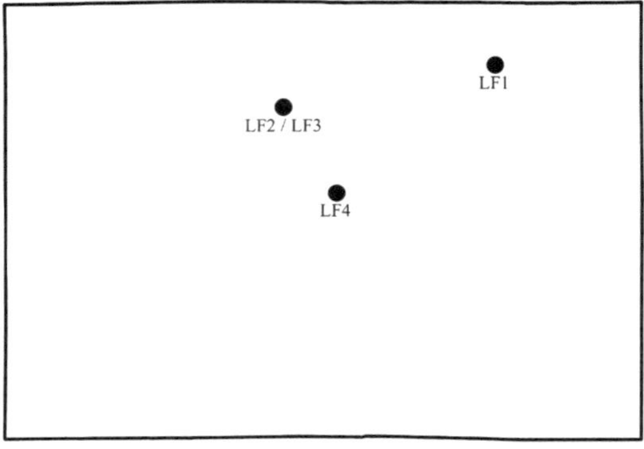

LF2 PECATONICA RIVER PADDLE: 42.741043, -90.168891. Nature experiences fill this eight-mile paddle from Calamine to Darlington. Primary cover types along the river are upland grassy fields, mixed hardwood upland forests, agricultural land, and wet meadows. Paddlers can extend the trip several more miles downstream, but this section is always deadfall free. Amenities include opportunities for birdwatching and relaxation. Stretches of river flow through incredible solitude. Overnight accommodations are absent. For more information, visit https://wisconsinrivers.org/wp-content/uploads/2017/12/Southwestern_Wisconsin_Rivers-FINAL_1.pdf.

LF3 PECATONICA RIVER TRAIL: $T. 42.740791, -90.170125. In Lafayette County, this 14-mile rail trail passes through many habitats, including wetlands, pastureland, and oak savannas, crosses streams, and has patches of native deep soil prairie next to the trail. DNR manages the site by using prescribed burning, removing invasive species, and turning it into the non-motorized Mound View Trail west of Belmont. Amenities include opportunities for biking and access to the Belmont Prairie State Natural Area. Cognitive Enrichment Areas are simple to access, and immersion into nature provides many benefits. Overnight accommodations are absent. For more information, visit https://dnr.wisconsin.gov/topic/parks/pecatonica.

LF4 CHEESE COUNTRY TRAIL: $T. 42.680988, -90.120268. This 40-mile rail trail passes through many habitats in Lafayette County. It passes through wetlands, pastureland, and oak savannas, crosses streams, and has patches of native deep soil prairie next to the trail. Motorized users are common. Therefore, hikers and bikers must know the traffic. Lafayette County manages the trail by using prescribed burning and removing invasive species. Amenities include opportunities for biking and hiking in a part of the state with sparse public land. Cognitive Enrichment Areas are simple to access, and immersion into nature provides many benefits. Overnight accommodations are present at Pecatonica River Trails Park. For more information, visit https://www.lafayettecountywi.org/trails.

Monroe County

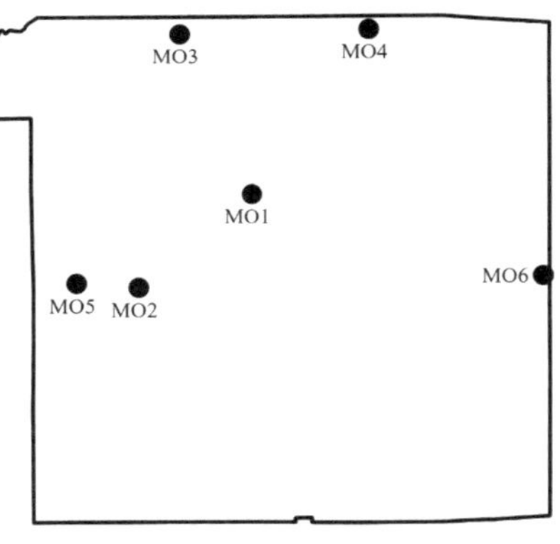

MO1 FORT MCCOY STATE NATURAL AREA: 44.007648, -90.657553. These two units of the state natural area encompass approximately 190 acres. The primary features are the outstanding examples of open barrens, red maple swamps, and sand-bottomed streams. A free Fort McCoy Access Pass is required for all activities, including hunting, fishing, and non-hunting/fishing activities. All recreational users need to update their accounts annually. Nature connections, such as spiritual connections and personal introspection, are abundant. Overnight accommodations are absent. For more information, visit https://dnr.wisconsin.gov/topic/StateNaturalAreas.

MO2 ELROY SPARTA STATE TRAIL: $T. 43.926652, -90.788241. This 32-mile rail trail passes through many habitats in Monroe County. The relatively flat trail passes through wetlands, woodlots, and agricultural land, crossing streams and three tunnels. DNR personnel manage the site by removing invasive species. Amenities include opportunities for biking and access to unforgettable ventures into the dark tunnels. Nature connections, such as spiritual connections and personal introspection, are abundant. Two walk-in campsites, one in Sparta and one in Elroy, offer limited overnight camping. For more information, visit https://dnr.wisconsin.gov/topic/parks/elroysparta.

MO3 MONROE COUNTY FOREST: 44.144653, -90.741254. In the northern part of Monroe County, the public forest covers more than 7,000 acres. An area of sandstone outcrops with remnant relict oak savanna is fascinating. Many additional acres of the county forest surrounding the savannas are available for exploration. The primary cover types are oak, pine, and aspen. These Wilderness Therapy and Cognitive Enrichment Areas are difficult to access, but immersion into nature provides many benefits. Overnight camping is absent. For more information, visit https://www.co.monroe.wi.us/departments/forestry-parks.

MO4 MCMULLEN COUNTY PARK: $C. 44.150265, -90.521624. This park and the surrounding county forest near Warrens cover more than 1,100 acres. Of particular interest are the 50-acre lake and its amenities. Primary cover types are oak, pine, and aspen. The park has a beach and hiking trails. These wilderness therapy and personal challenges off-trail provide many benefits. Overnight camping is available with 81 sites. For more information, visit https://www.co.monroe.wi.us/departments/forestry-parks/mcmullen-memorial-county-park.

MO5 LA CROSSE RIVER PADDLE: 43.929870, -90.860665. This 10-mile paddle from Hammer Road to Bangor is filled with nature experiences. Primary cover types along the river are upland grassy fields, mixed hardwood upland forests, agricultural land, and wet prairie meadows. Paddlers can extend the trip several more miles downstream to Neshonoc Lake at West Salem. Amenities include opportunities for birdwatching and relaxation. Stretches of river flow through incredible solitude. Overnight accommodations are absent. For more information, visit https://wisconsinrivers.org/wp-content/uploads/2017/12/Southwestern_Wisconsin_Rivers-FINAL_1.pdf.

MO6 OMAHA BIKE TRAIL: $T. 43.918425, -90.267152. This relatively flat 13-mile rail trail passes through many habitats in Juneau County, including wetlands, and the trail passes cliffs and crosses streams and agricultural land. The trail starts at Camp Douglas and ends in Elroy, connecting with other trails. Amenities include opportunities for biking and access to a 300-foot tunnel. Cognitive Enrichment Areas are easy to access, and immersion into nature provides many benefits. Overnight accommodations are absent. For more information, visit https://co.juneau.wi.gov/departments/land,_forestry,___parks/trails/omaha.php.

Richland County

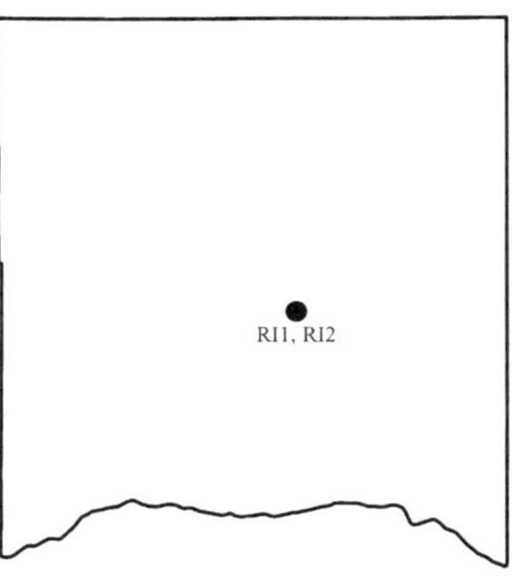

RI1 PINE RIVER PADDLE (RICHLAND CENTER TO SAWMILL ROAD): 43.346622, -90.388735. This is an easy family paddle with few obstructions. Enthusiasts can paddle the upstream section near Rockbridge, which has great sandstone cliffs for viewing, but deadfalls may be a concern. Primary cover types along the river are wet meadows, dense bottomland forest, and pine-studded cliffs in the upper portion. Amenities include opportunities for birdwatching and relaxation. Stretches of river flow through incredible solitude. Overnight accommodations are absent. For more information, visit https://wisconsinrivers.org/wp-content/uploads/2017/12/Southwestern_Wisconsin_Rivers-FINAL_1.pdf.

RI2 PINE RIVER TRAIL: 43.343154, -90.392038. This flat 14-mile rail trail passes through many habitats in Richland County, including wetlands, and the bottomland forest crosses streams and has views of cliffs. The DNR manages the site by removing invasive species. Amenities include opportunities for biking and access to portions of the county formerly unavailable. Cognitive Enrichment Areas are simple to access, and immersion into nature provides many benefits. Overnight accommodations are absent. For more information, visit https://parkscommission.co.richland.wi.us/points-of-interest/pine-river-trail/.

Vernon County

VE1 KICKAPOO VALLEY RESERVE: $C, T. 43.595890, -90.625419. This reserve covers more than 8,600 acres. The significant feature is the wild driftless area aspect. This site has hardwood forests, wetlands, open grasslands, and many cliffs and rock outcrops. The reserve manages the site using limited prescribed burns and invasive species management. Amenities include opportunities for mountain biking (May 1–November 15), hiking, fishing, and snowshoeing. Nature connections are plentiful, especially personal cognition and solitude. Twenty-five campsites provide potential overnight camping. For more information, visit http://kvr.state.wi.us/home.

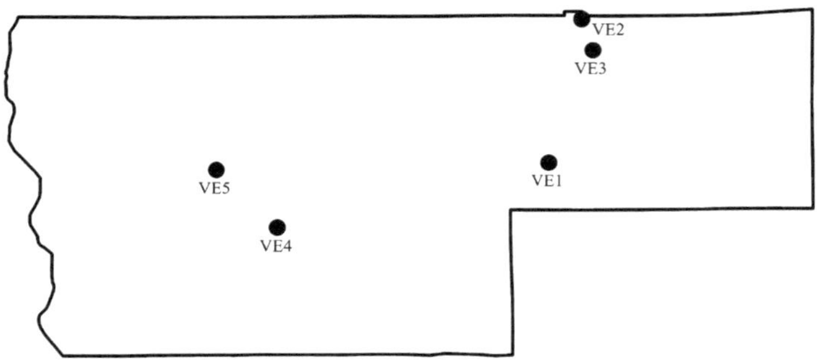

VE2 KICKAPOO RIVER PADDLE (ONTARIO TO LA FARGE): $ Rentals. 43.721447, -90.588153. This section is an easy family paddle with few obstructions and minimal rapids. Downstream paddles are also a possibility. Shorter paddles are available for more inexperienced paddlers. Primary cover types along the river are forests, wet meadows, and especially the dripping cliffs. Amenities include many liveries in Ontario, opportunities for viewing outstanding scenery, and relaxation. Paddlers and partyers can crowd stretches of river on summer weekends. Overnight accommodations are present at nearby Wildcat Mountain State Park. For more information, visit https://wisconsinrivers.org/wp-content/uploads/2017/12/Southwestern_Wisconsin_Rivers-FINAL_1.pdf.

VE3 WILDCAT MOUNTAIN STATE PARK: $E, C. 43.695513, -90.574495. This state park encompasses approximately 3,600 acres. The primary feature is an outstanding example of driftless area topography and vegetation. The 21 miles of trails include a nature trail and a 2.5-mile snowshoe trail. Fifty campsites are available, including several cart-in sites. Nature connections, such as spiritual connections and personal introspection, are abundant. The site can be an annual immersion site, especially for those with younger children. For more information, visit https://dnr. wisconsin.gov/topic/parks/wildcat.

VE4 SIDIE HOLLOW COUNTY PARK: $C. 43.538768, -90.948749. The combination of proximity to a dense population and nature immersion makes this place special for the needs of younger nature enthusiasts. This 520-acre Vernon County gem features mature forest, grassland, lake, and wetlands. Trails for hiking, mountain biking, and snowshoeing crisscross the area, and there are many activities for kids. This Cognitive Enrichment Area is simple to access, but the interior can be maze-like for younger children. Seventy-six sites are open for camping. For more information, visit https://www.vernoncounty.org/departments/land_and_water_conservation/parks_and_forests/sidie_hollow.php.

VE5 DUCK EGG COUNTY FOREST: 43.590466, -91.021909. The combination of proximity to a dense population and nature immersion opportunities makes this day-use area special for those seeking solitude. This 700-acre Vernon County Forest features a mature forest and 25 acres of prairie, stream, and wetlands. Ten miles of trails for hiking let the visitor enter the deep woods. This Wilderness Therapy Area is easy to access, but the interior can be maze-like for younger children. Overnight accommodations are absent. For more information, visit https://www. vernoncounty.org/departments/land_and_water_conservation/parks_and_forests/duck_egg.php.

West Central Wisconsin

Buffalo County

BU1 MERRICK STATE PARK: 44.161892, -91.758910. $E, C. This state park encompasses more than 300 acres. The primary feature is the Mississippi River, its backwaters, and its floodplain forest. Two miles of upland hiking trails and several miles of canoe trails provide ample opportunities for nature immersion. A campground with 65 sites is open year-round, providing a base camp for hiking, canoeing, fishing, and snowshoeing. Nature connections are abundant, especially in the maze of backwater sloughs. For more information, visit https://dnr.wisconsin.gov/topic/parks/merrick.

BU2 TREMPEALEAU NATIONAL WILDLIFE REFUGE (BUFFALO COUNTY PORTION): 44.068663, -91.597251. The federal government established this national wildlife refuge to protect migratory and breeding waterfowl and marshland species. It encompasses about 6,800 acres. Most of the facilities lie in Trempealeau County (see website for details). The Buffalo County portion is remote and offers visitors an immersion experience into the vast Mississippi River floodplain. Amenities include a six-mile trail into the forest and open wetlands. Nature connections are plentiful and significantly improve cognition and problem-solving. Overnight accommodations are available at nearby state parks. For more information, visit https://www.fws.gov/refuge/trempealeau/.

BU4
BU5
BU3
BU1
BU2

BU3 WHITMAN DAM WILDLIFE AREA: 44.175302, -91.797872. This state wildlife area encompasses 2,200 acres. Primary cover types are silver maple floodplain and marsh. The DNR manages the site for floodplain forest wildlife. Amenities include opportunities to experience the maze of bayou-like waterways along the Mississippi River for birdwatching, exploring, and berry picking. Nature connections are plentiful, especially for problem-solving and personal introspection. Overnight accommodations are present at Merrick State Park. For more information, visit https://dnr.wisconsin.gov/topic/Lands/WildlifeAreas/whitman.html.

BU4 BIG SWAMP WILDLIFE AREA: 44.578130, -91.798516. This state wildlife area encompasses almost 800 acres. Primary cover types are tamarack fen, shrub-carr, and upland hardwoods. The DNR manages the site as winter cover for pheasants. Amenities include opportunities to experience an unusual native plant community for birdwatching, exploring, and berry picking. Visitors should limit nature connections to experienced naturalists because of the access challenges and abundance of poison sumac on the property. Overnight accommodations are absent. For more information, visit https://dnr.wisconsin.gov/topic/Lands/WildlifeAreas/bigswamp.html. None.

BU5 BUFFALO RIVER PADDLE: 44.390927, -91.849902. Several sections of the Buffalo River from Mondovi to Rieck's Lake Park landing can be paddled. The most scenic is the section from Highway F to the park landing. The 24 miles from Mondovi to the landing is more of a challenge to finish in one day, with probable portages around logjams and fences. Paddlers should plan enough time to explore features along the river, especially the numerous wetland ponds south of Highway F. Amenities include opportunities for wildlife observation. Nature connections are plentiful, especially goal setting and problem-solving. If traffic noise does not bother you, overnight camping is available at Rieck's Lake Park. For more information, visit https://wisconsinrivers.org/kark-paddle-guide/.

Chippewa County

CH1 BRUNET ISLAND STATE PARK: $E, C. 45.179794, -91.162382. This state park encompasses more than 1,300 acres. The primary features are the multitude of islands and the mature hemlock-hardwood forest. More than eight miles of trails, including a nature trail, bike trail, and sand beach, provide ample opportunities for nature immersion. Campgrounds with 69 sites are open year-round but limited in winter and provide a base camp for hiking, canoeing, biking, fishing, snowshoeing, and swimming. Nature connections, such as spiritual connections and personal introspection, are abundant. For more information, visit https://dnr.wisconsin.gov/topic/parks/brunetisland.

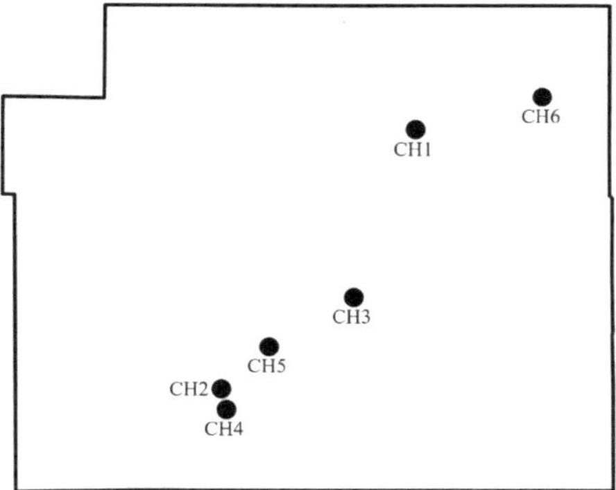

CH2 IRVINE PARK: 44.944514, -91.400085. This park encompasses approximately 320 acres. The primary features are the many typical urban park activities, plus a bear and cat zoo. Many historical buildings are present. In addition, the park offers solitude for those seeking it. The site is magnificent for younger nature enthusiasts. More than two miles of trails, including a nature trail, a cave, a stream, and forests, provide ample opportunities for nature immersion. Nature connections, such as spiritual connections and personal introspection, are abundant. For more information, visit https://www.chippewafalls-wi.gov.

CH3 TOM LAWIN WILDLIFE AREA: 45.028565, -91.237825. This state wildlife area encompasses 3,100 acres. Primary cover types are wetlands (including a high-quality sedge meadow), restored prairie, conifer swamp, and grasslands. The DNR manages the site for various wildlife by using prescribed burning and other techniques to manage the grasslands and timber harvest to manage the forest. Amenities include opportunities to experience an enormous expanse of different habitats for birdwatching, exploring, and berry picking. Nature connections are plentiful, especially for natural balance. Overnight accommodations are absent. For more information, visit https://dnr.wisconsin.gov/topic/Lands/WildlifeAreas/tomlawin.html.

CH4 CHIPPEWA RIVER UPPER DALLES PADDLE: 44.930396, -91.394124. This 12-mile section is semi-urban but features large sandstone cliffs and large pines. This section travels through developed cities but feels wild and scenic, especially downstream of Highway 53. The route concludes at the Dells Pond in Eau Claire, which has many formations around the shore. More adventurous paddlers can plan longer routes upstream. Amenities include opportunities for wildlife observation. Nature connections are plentiful, especially goal setting and problem-solving. Overnight camping is available at several nearby public campgrounds. For more information, visit https://wisconsin rivers.org/wp-content/uploads/2019/06/West-Central-FINAL.pdf.

CH5 OLD ABE TRAIL: $T. 44.984473, -91.341555. Old Abe State Trail is a paved 20-mile trail connecting Lake Wissota State Park to Brunet Island State Park. The trail is on an abandoned railroad grade and traverses agricultural and forest land. In many places, views of the Chippewa River are attained. Amenities include opportunities to view wildlife and natural beauty. Nature connections are plentiful, especially goal setting and problem-solving. Overnight camping is available at both state parks. For more information, visit https://dnr.wisconsin.gov/topic/parks/oldabe.

CH6 CHIPPEWA COUNTY FOREST (RUBY SECTION): 45.209061, -91.008010. This unit is in a seldom-visited portion of the county forest and features many acres of wetlands and managed forest land open for nature exploration. The need for more visitors offers the enthusiast opportunities for deep nature immersion. Hunter-walking trails or walking into remote

land can provide wilderness therapy. Primary cover types are aspen, hardwoods, and many types of wetlands. The county forest manages the resource, so care must be provided if timber operations occur or during hunting season. Remote camping is available. For more information, visit https://www.co.chippewa.wi.us.

Dunn County

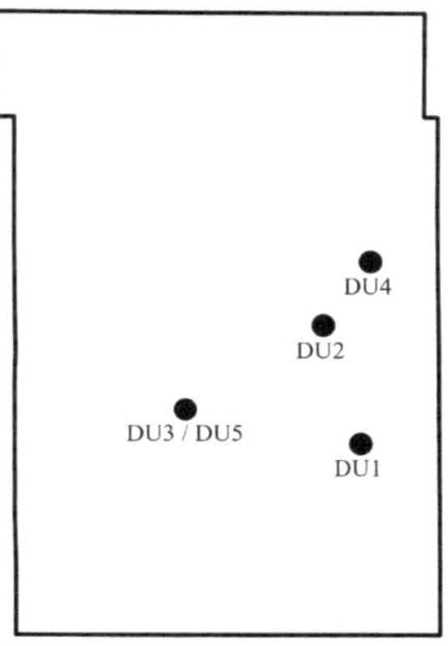

DU1 MUDDY CREEK WILDLIFE AREA: 44.845669, -91.740598. This state wildlife area covers more than 4,100 acres and is known locally as the Elk Mound Swamp. Primary cover types are upland grassy fields, mixed hardwood upland forest, sedge meadow, shrub-carr, and brushy areas. The DNR manages the site by using prescribed burning and timber management. Amenities include opportunities for birdwatching, hiking, and berry picking. Cognitive Enrichment Areas are tough to access, but the challenge provides more nature benefits. Overnight accommodations are absent. For more information, visit https://dnr.wisconsin.gov/topic/Lands/WildlifeAreas/muddycreek.html.

DU2 HOFFMAN HILLS STATE RECREATION AREA: $for skiing. 44.947149, -91.783345. This state recreation area features wooded aspen, maple, and oak hills. They have restored some places to prairie, and a few wetlands are mixed. The site covers over 700 acres, mostly hiking and cross-country skiing. An observation tower tops the highest point in Dunn County. Amenities include opportunities to experience nature and different habitats. Nature connections are plentiful, especially for creativity and wonder. Overnight accommodations are absent. The park is open year-round. For more information, visit https://dnr.wisconsin.gov/topic/parks/hoffmanhills/info.

DU3 RED CEDAR AND CHIPPEWA RIVER TRAILS: $T. 44.875567, -91.941123. These two connecting trails provide trail links between Menomonie and Eau Claire. The trails are partially paved and partly compact limestone, covering almost 45 miles. The trails are on abandoned railroad grades and traverse agricultural land, bottomland forests, prairies, and savannas.

Visitors garner great views of the Red Cedar and Chippewa Rivers in many places. Amenities include opportunities to view wildlife and natural beauty. Nature connections are plentiful, especially goal setting and problem-solving. Overnight accommodations are not available. For more information, visit https://dnr.wisconsin.gov/topic/parks/redcedar, or https://dnr.wisconsin.gov/topic/parks/chipriver.

DU4 MIDDLE RED CEDAR RIVER PADDLE: 45.001652, -91.729132. Enthusiasts can easily paddle several sections of the Red Cedar River in central Dunn County in one day. They should plan enough time to explore features along the river, especially the cliffs near Chetek. Another option is the short paddle from Chetek to the Russian Slough landing, where stops at Dobbs Landing and the Red Cedar River Savanna SNA can add memorable cognitive experiences. Amenities include opportunities for nature immersion. Nature connections are plentiful, especially goal setting and problem-solving. Overnight accommodations are absent along the river. For more information, visit https://wisconsinrivers.org/wp-content/uploads/2019/06/West-Central-FINAL.pdf.

DU5 LOWER RED CEDAR RIVER PADDLE: 44.872640, -91.940758. The lower section from Menomonie to Downsville or even the Chippewa River is a memorable paddle. Paddling several sections of the Red Cedar River and even the Yellow River from Barron downstream is accessible. Paddlers should plan enough time to explore features along the river, especially the cliffs near Menomonie, the floodplain forest, and the vast prairies at the Dunnville Wildlife Area. Amenities include opportunities for nature immersion. Nature connections are plentiful, especially goal setting and problem-solving. Overnight accommodations are absent along the river. For more information, visit https://wisconsinrivers.org/wp-content/uploads/2019/06/West-Central-FINAL.pdf.

Eau Claire County

EC1 AUGUSTA WILDLIFE AREA: 44.741799, -91.105342. This state wildlife area covers more than 2,500 acres and has three flowages. Primary cover types are upland grassy fields, restored barrens, mixed hardwood upland forest, sedge meadow, shrub-carr, and brushy areas. The DNR manages the site by using prescribed burning and timber management. Amenities include opportunities for birdwatching, hiking, and berry picking. Nature

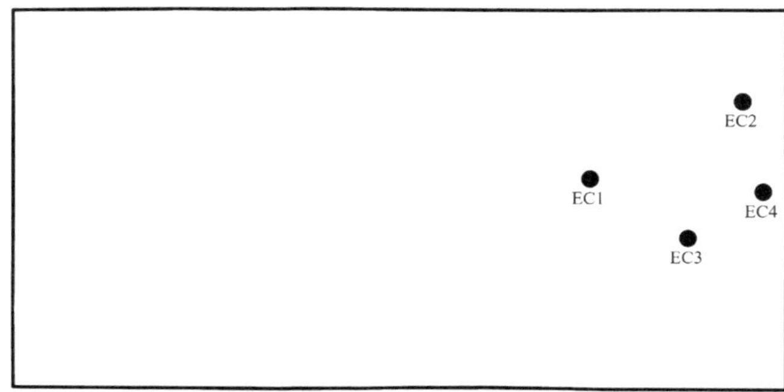

connection areas are difficult to access, but the challenge provides more nature benefits. Overnight accommodations are absent. For more information, visit https://dnr.wisconsin.gov/topic/Lands/WildlifeAreas/augusta.html.

EC2 NORTH FORK EAU CLAIRE RIVER PADDLE: 44.796630, -90.962655. For those naturalists who need a remote location, the paddle below Hamilton Falls at Wilson Park to the landing at Eisberner Park offers a near wilderness setting with many cliffs and towering pines. Canoe and kayak lovers could easily paddle this section in one day. They should plan enough time to explore features along the river, predominantly the dry prairie next to the landing, which can add memorable cognitive experiences. Amenities include opportunities for nature immersion. Nature connections are plentiful, especially goal setting and problem-solving. Overnight accommodations are absent along the river. For more information, visit https://wisconsinrivers.org/wp-content/uploads/2019/06/West-Central-FINAL.pdf.

EC3 EAU CLAIRE COUNTY FOREST (COON FORK PARK AND BARRENS): $E. 44.701569, -91.012985. Coon Fork Park occupies 383 acres of woods and lakeshore and harbors 108 campsites. Eau Claire County Forest land offers many nature immersion opportunities surrounding the park. Next to the park is the Coon Fork Barrens SNA, where visitors can experience high-quality pine barrens habitat. Walking paths lead into the vast forest areas that provide wilderness therapy and cognitive enrichment. The county forest manages the site, so care needs to be taken if timber operations occur or during hunting season. Camping is available. For more information, visit https://www.co.eau-claire.wi.us/.

EC4 EAU CLAIRE COUNTY FOREST (PRIMITIVE CAMPING): $C. 44.734381, -90.942995. The 52,000-acre county forest is open for exploration year-round. The county allows primitive camping for up to 14 days with a permit. The natural area features include extensive acid peatlands, pine forests, aspen and hardwood forests, many streams and rivers, and pine barrens. The Eau Claire County Forest offers remote wilderness therapy opportunities. The county forest manages the site, so care needs to be taken if timber operations occur or during hunting season. For more information, visit https://www.co.eau-claire.wi.us/.

Pepin County

PE1 CHIPPEWA RIVER PADDLE (COUNTY M TO ELLA): 44.678552, -91.901800. This paddle from the public launch at County Highway M to the boat ramp at Ella is about eight miles. Nature experiences abound in this vast and often shallow river. Primary cover types along the river are wet meadows, oak savanna, and dense bottomland forest. The paddle can be extended several more miles downstream, but these sections become a maze of channels. Amenities include opportunities for birdwatching and relaxation. Stretches of river flow through incredible solitude. Overnight camping on sandbars is possible. For more information, visit https://wisconsinrivers.org/wp-content/uploads/2019/06/West-Central-FINAL.pdf.

PE2 TIFFANY WILDLIFE AREA (FIVE-MILE BLUFF UNIT): 44.469940, -92.064736. The upland portion of the large Tiffany Wildlife Area covers bluff forests, savannas, and dry prairies. The DNR manages the site using limited timber management techniques to maintain savanna and dry prairie communities. Amenities include opportunities for wilderness immersion and berry picking. The solitude and personal challenges are at hand, and the challenge provides more nature benefits.

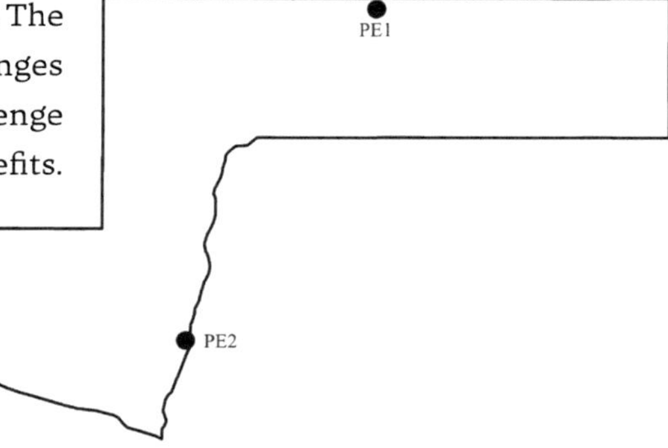

Overnight accommodations are absent. For more information, visit https://dnr.wisconsin.gov/topic/lands/WildlifeAreas/tiffany.html.

PE3 MAIDEN ROCK BLUFF STATE NATURAL AREA: 44.505064, -92.280579. This state natural area encompasses 263 acres. The primary features are the outstanding examples of dry prairie, oak savanna, open cliffs, hardwood forest, and driftless area topography. Sectioning the high-quality natural areas requires a long walk over the planted prairie. Nature connections, such as spiritual connections and personal introspection, are abundant. Overnight accommodations are absent. For more information, visit https://dnr.wisconsin.gov/topic/statenaturalareas/MaidenRockBluff.

Pierce County

PI1 PIERCE COUNTY ISLANDS WILDLIFE AREA: 44.579926, -92.455770. This wildlife area covers nearly 1,000 acres. Primary cover types are marsh, bottomland forest, bayous, and lakes. The DNR manages the site with limited timber management and invasive species removal. Access is by boat only. The solitude and personal challenges are at hand, and the challenge provides more nature benefits. Overnight accommodations are absent. For more information, visit https://dnr.wisconsin.gov/topic/Lands/WildlifeAreas/piercecountyislands.html.

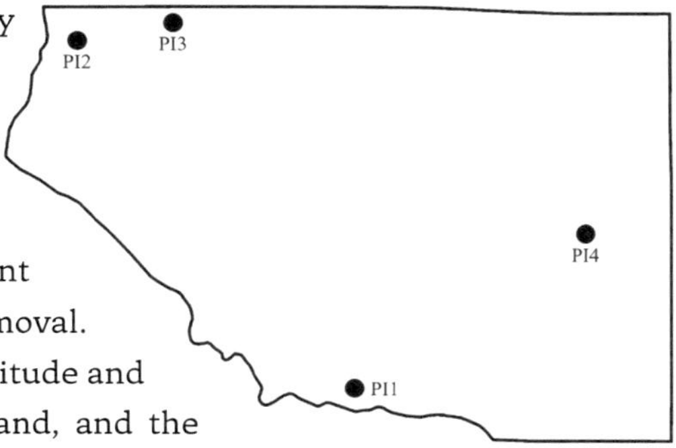

PI2 KINNICKINNIC STATE PARK AND NATURAL AREA: $E, C. 44.837266, -92.735380. This state park encompasses approximately 1,200 acres, of which a gorge is a designated state natural area. The primary feature is a fantastic gorge carved by the Kinnickinnic River. The 10 miles of trails include a nature trail, a mountain bike trail, and a swimming beach. In this day-use park, nature connections, such as spiritual connections and personal introspection, are abundant. The site can be an annual immersion site, especially for those with younger children. Camping is allowed in a boat mooring area only. For more information, visit https://dnr.wisconsin.gov/topic/parks/kinnickinnic.

PI3 KINNICKINNIC RIVER PADDLE: $P. 44.850761, -92.638900. This seven-mile paddle from the public launch at Glen Park to the County Highway F bridge is a beautiful experience. Parking at the takeout requires a state park sticker. The river flows through a gorge carved after the last glacier. Nature experiences abound in this narrow and often shallow river. Primary cover types along the river are cliffs, hardwood forests, and springs. Amenities include opportunities for solitude and relaxation in this urbanized part of the state. Overnight camping is absent. For more information, visit https://wisconsinrivers.org/wp-content/uploads/2019/06/West-Central-FINAL.pdf.

PI4 NUGGET LAKE COUNTY PARK: $E, C. 44.694112, -92.221516. Found in east-central Pierce County, this park has an impounded lake, forest, and examples of driftless area geology. Primary cover types in this 750-acre park are southern hardwood forest and an impoundment. Opportunities are present for fishing, hiking, and snowshoeing. Outstanding botanical areas are simple to access and provide excellent places for cognitive improvement. Overnight camping is available seasonally. For more information, visit https://www.co.pierce.wi.us/departments/nugget_lake/index.php.

St. Croix County

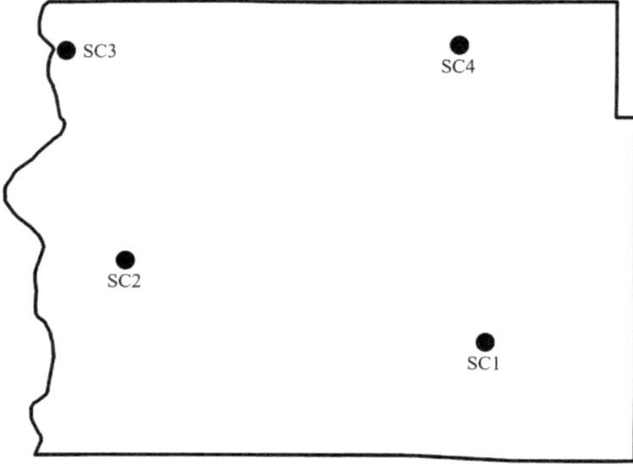

SC1 WILDWOOD TRAIL: 44.949754, -92.295213. In St. Croix County, the seven-mile rail trail passes through several habitats. The flat trail crosses wetlands, penetrates woodlots, crosses streams, and has views of pastoral lands. The county manages the site by removing debris and keeping the lane open. Vegetation next to the trail is left to develop on its own. Amenities include opportunities for biking, hiking, and access to portions of the county formerly unavailable. Spiritual connections and personal introspection areas are easy to access. Overnight accommodations are absent. For more information, visit https://www.sccwi.gov/350/Wildwood-Trail.

SC2 WILLOW RIVER STATE PARK: $E, C. 45.01716, -92.68777. This state park encompasses approximately 2,800 acres, including a superb waterfall. The primary feature is an amazing gorge carved by the Willow River. The 13 miles of trails include an accessible nature trail, a snowshoe trail, and a swimming beach. In this park, nature connections are abundant, such as spiritual connections and personal introspection. The site can be an annual immersion site, especially for those with younger children. Three campgrounds with over 170 sites are available. For more information, visit https://dnr.wisconsin.gov/topic/parks/willowriver.

SC3 ST. CROIX ISLANDS WILDLIFE AREA AND NATURAL AREA: 45.172142, -92.740832. This wildlife area covers more than 1,100 acres. Primary cover types are oaks, bottomland hardwoods, wet prairie, marsh, and the Apple River Canyon. The DNR manages the site by treating invasive species and timber management. Amenities include opportunities for exploring the natural communities in a wilderness setting. Nature connections are best sectioned by off-trail immersion, especially spiritual connections and personal introspection. Overnight accommodations are absent. For more information, visit https://dnr.wisconsin.gov/topic/Lands/WildlifeAreas/stcroixislands.html.

SC4 CYLON WILDLIFE AREA: 45.177163, -92.323698. This wildlife area covers more than 2,300 acres. Primary cover types are northern and southern hardwoods, sedge meadows, streams, and lowland brush. The DNR manages the site by treating invasive species, prescribed burning, and timber management. Amenities include opportunities for exploring the natural communities in a wilderness setting. Off-trail immersion is best for finding nature connections, especially spiritual connections and personal introspection. Overnight accommodations are absent. For more information, visit https://dnr.wisconsin.gov/topic/Lands/WildlifeAreas/cylon.html.

Trempealeau County

TR1 PERROT STATE PARK AND TREMPEALEAU NATIONAL WILDLIFE REFUGE: $E, C. 44.026647, -91.481227. This state park and adjacent national wildlife refuge encompass approximately 7,400 acres. The primary features include driftless area bluffs, native prairie, wetlands, and a large river delta. Twelve miles of trails, access to the 24-mile Great River Trail, and an educational auto tour highlight the properties. Over 100 campsites are available. Nature connections, such as spiritual connections and personal introspection, are abundant. The site can be an annual immersion site, especially for those with younger children. For more information, visit https://dnr.wisconsin.gov/topic/parks/perrot.

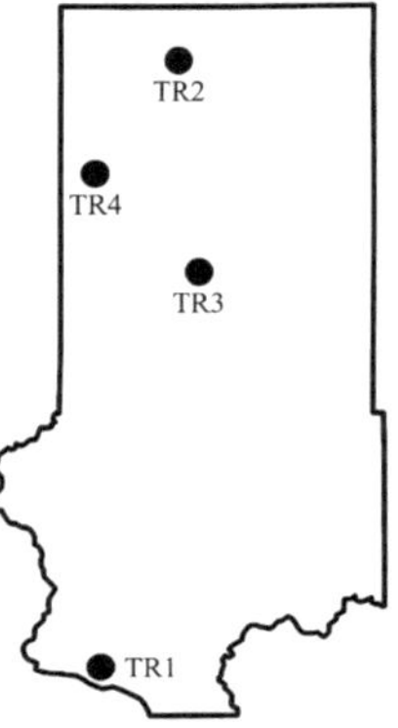

TR2 BUFFALO RIVER STATE TRAIL: $T. 44.551184, -91.392429. This flat 36-mile rail trail passes through several habitats in Trempealeau County, crosses wetlands, penetrates woodlots, crosses streams, and features several places where native prairie flourishes. The DNR manages the site by prescribed burning, removing invasive species, and keeping the lane open. Amenities include opportunities for biking, hiking, and access to portions of the county formerly unavailable. Spiritual connections and personal introspection areas are easy to access. Overnight accommodations are absent. For more information, visit https://dnr.wisconsin.gov/topic/parks/buffalo/info.

TR3 TREMPEALEAU RIVER PADDLE (WHITEHALL TO ARCADIA): 44.369129, -91.368493. This 16-mile paddle is an easy family paddle, with few obstructions and mild rapids. Downstream sections from Arcadia to Dodge are also possibilities. Primary cover types along the river are bottomland hardwoods, wet meadows, oak savannas, and agricultural land. Amenities include opportunities for wildlife observation and relaxation. Stretches of river flow through peaceful solitude. Overnight accommodations are absent. For more information, visit https://wisconsinrivers.org/wp-content/uploads/2019/06/West-Central-FINAL.pdf.

TR4 TAMARACK CREEK WILDLIFE AREA: 44.162741, -91.452523. This wildlife area covers more than 500 acres in west central Trempealeau County. Primary cover types are oak and other hardwoods, brushland, wetlands, and tamarack bog. The DNR manages the site by treating invasive species and timber management. Amenities include opportunities for a deep wilderness experience because of the difficult access. Off-trail immersion is best for finding nature connections, especially spiritual connections and personal introspection. Overnight accommodations are absent. For more information, visit https://dnr.wisconsin.gov/topic/Lands/WildlifeAreas/tamarack.html.

Central Wisconsin

Adams County

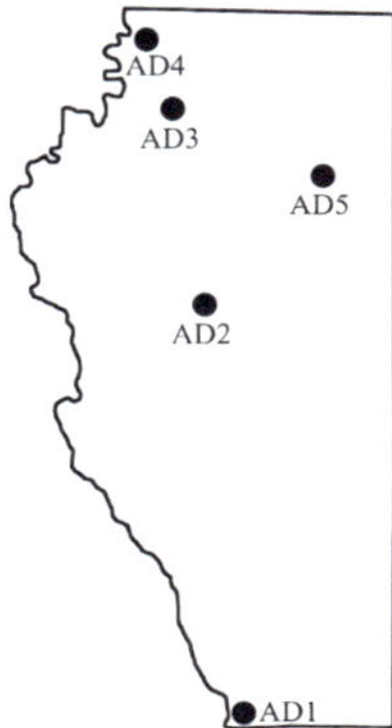

AD1 DELLS OF THE WISCONSIN RIVER SNA: $T. 43.648781, -89.775047. Trails direct visitors through old fields to pines and cliffs along the Wisconsin River. Biological diversity and scenic views abound. The focused nature connection opportunities point toward natural diversity patterns and color diversity but also provide areas for nature play and solitude. For additional information, visit https://dnr.wisconsin.gov/topic/statenaturalareas/DellsoftheWisconsinRiver.

AD2 ROCHE-A-CRI STATE PARK: $E, C. 44.001293, -89.812429. This state park features a forested mound and mixed conifer woods. Amenities are many, including on-site camping, several trails (including accessibility trails), restrooms, and areas of solitude. The park is open for automobile traffic from late spring to early fall. Walk-in access is available in winter. Nature connections opportunities include challenging hikes to the top of the mound, areas amenable for nature play, learning about the park's natural history, and serene areas for restorative contemplation. For additional information, visit https://dnr.wisconsin.gov/topic/parks/rocheacri.

AD3 SAND VALLEY TRAILS: 44.168056, -89.848131. This private recreation area has a series of trails open to the public. These trails travel through barrens, inland dunes, and prairie habitats. The Town of Rome worked with this private entity to provide opportunities to participate in nature immersion. The trails are not accessible compliant but offer the experience of viewing natural communities seldom seen by hikers elsewhere in the state. Visitors will find exceptional biological diversity, including many prairie species and several very rare species. For more information, visit https://www.visitromewi.com/hiking-biking.

AD4 VAN KUREN TRAILS: 44.224316, -89.877308. This private recreation area has 3.2 miles of trails open to the public. These trails travel through mature mixed conifer forest and wetland habitats. On-site facilities are not available. The owners limit nature connection opportunities to the trail, but the awe of traveling through the old forest helps ease anyone's anxiety. These woods are a wonderful place for spiritual reflection, personal introspection, and re-establishing your natural balance. For more information, visit https://www.visitromewi.com/hiking-biking.

AD5 COLBURN WILDLIFE AREA: 44.111994, -89.678737. Colburn Wildlife Area is a 4,965-acre property in north-central Adams County near the Waushara County border. The property comprises mainly lowland brush and sedge marsh with aspen and oak forest areas scattered throughout. Carter Creek passes through the middle of the property. Developed trails are not present, but hiking on wildlife maintenance lands or overland is available. Nature connections include therapeutic adventures, nature play, and finding wild edibles. For more information, visit https://dnr.wisconsin.gov/topic/Lands/WildlifeAreas/colburn.html.

Clark County

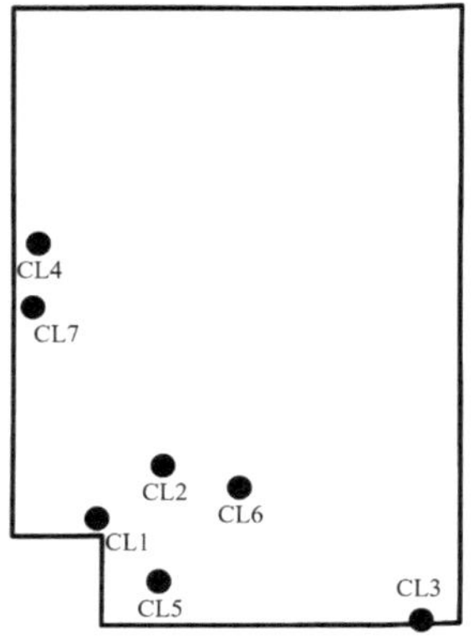

CL1 CLARK COUNTY FOREST (WILDCAT PARK): $C. 44.527597, -90.808727. This area is in a seldom-visited portion of the county forest. Wildcat Park is primitive and features scenic and extraordinary hiking. Near the trailhead, sandstone bluffs and cliffs abound, and close by are patches of old white pines, all of which are open for nature exploration. The need for more visitors offers the enthusiast opportunities for deep nature immersion. Simply walking into the remote land can provide wilderness therapy. Primary cover types are aspen, hardwoods, pines, and many wetlands. The county forest manages this resource, so care must be taken if timber operations occur or during hunting season. Remote camping is available.

For more information, visit https://www.clarkcountywi.gov/for-parks-wildcat.

CL2 CLARK COUNTY FOREST (SNYDER LAKE): $C. 44.580877, -90.717757. Snyder Lake Park has 45 campsites near the shores of Snyder Lake. The Clark County Forest surrounds the park, offering many nature immersion opportunities. Aspen, young hardwoods, and the wetlands provide most of the natural cover. Simply walking into the remote land can provide wilderness therapy. The lake is no-wake and provides a quiet water experience. The county forest manages the resource, so care must be taken if timber operations occur or during hunting season. Camping is available. For more information, visit https://www.clarkcountywi.gov/for-parks-snyder-park.

CL3 CLARK COUNTY FOREST (SHERWOOD PARK): $C. 44.427413, -90.368721. Sherwood Park has 31 campsites, including accessible sites near the shores of Sherwood Lake. The Clark County Forest surrounds the park, offering many nature immersion opportunities. Forests in the area are mostly covered with aspen and young hardwoods, and the wetlands can be extensive. Walking paths lead into the vast forest areas that provide wilderness therapy. The lake is no-wake and provides a quiet water experience. The county forest manages the resource, so care must be taken if timber operations occur or during hunting season. Camping is available. For more information, visit https://www.clarkcountywi.gov/for-parks-sherwood.

CL4 CLARK COUNTY FOREST (BLUE SWAMP PRIMITIVE AREA): 44.799445, -90.888807. The primitive area has the Blue Swamp State Natural Area at its core. This natural area features a large acid peatland comprising a central poor fen and a northern wet forest. Water from the swamp drains in two directions. The major plant communities are a tamarack-dominated conifer swamp and a brushy meadow dominated by sedges and bog birch. Blue Swamp is part of the Clark County Forest, offering remote wilderness therapy opportunities. The county forest manages the resource, so care must be provided if timber operations occur or during hunting season. Camping is not available. For more information, visit https://dnr.wisconsin.gov/topic/statenaturalareas/BlueSwamp.

CL5 CLARK COUNTY FOREST (LEVIS/TROW MOUND RECREATION AREA): $T, C. 44.466108, -90.723717. Levis/Trow Mound Recreational Area is located within the southwest corner of Clark County and provides more than 41 miles of trails that wind and loop through the forest. The area features sandstone bluffs and mounds—a distinctive feature of the trail system. Management seeks to maintain and protect the natural environment and wildlife habitat. Many nature immersion opportunities exist. Hiking the trails leads into the vast forest areas that provide wilderness therapy. The county forest manages the resource, so care must be taken if timber operations occur or during hunting season. Camping is available. For more information, visit https://www.clarkcountywi.gov/for-trails-levis-mound.

CL6 BLACK RIVER PADDLE (NEILLSVILLE TO LAKE ARBUTUS): 44.559796, -90.614630. This section has several rapids distinctively Class I in low water, but paddlers should consider either Class II or III in high water. The paddle features abundant rock features in the river, including the Neillsville Rapids and the Red Granite Rapids. This section travels through agricultural land but feels wild and scenic, especially downstream of Highway 95. The route concludes at Lake Arbutus in Jackson County. More adventurous paddlers can plan longer routes upstream. Amenities include opportunities for wildlife observation. Nature connections are plentiful, especially goal setting and problem-solving. Overnight camping is available at several nearby public campgrounds. For more information, visit https://wisconsinrivers.org/wp-content/uploads/2019/06/West-Central-FINAL.pdf.

CL7 SOUTH FORK EAU CLAIRE RIVER PADDLE: 44.737856, -90.895278. For those naturalists who need a remote location, the paddle from the Koehler's Ford landing to the County Road G bridge offers a near wilderness setting. The Class I rapids downstream from Highway H need at least medium water to run. Most users can easily paddle this section in one day. They should plan enough time to explore features along the river, especially the South Fork Barrens SNA, which can add memorable cognitive experiences. Amenities include opportunities for nature immersion. Nature connections are plentiful, especially goal setting and problem-solving. Overnight accommodations are absent along the river. For more information, visit https://wisconsinrivers.org/wp-content/uploads/2019/06/West-Central-FINAL.pdf.

Jackson County

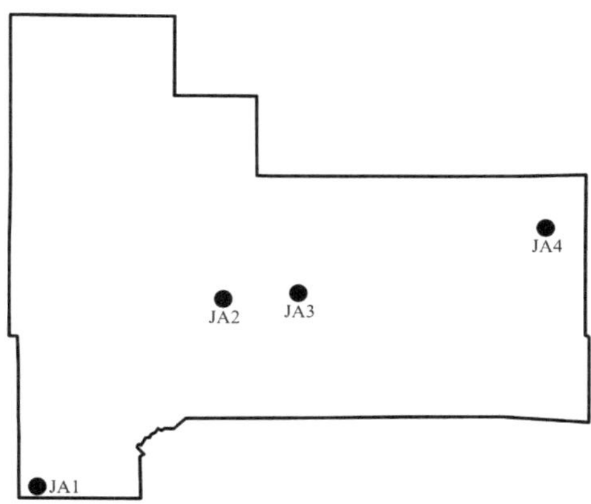

JA1 NORTH BEND BOTTOMS WILDLIFE AREA: 44.082517, -91.124874. This wildlife area covers more than 1,500 acres. Primary cover types are patches of floodplain prairie, oak savanna, marsh and oxbow lakes, floodplain forest, and grassy uplands. The DNR manages the site by using prescribed burning, treating invasive species, and timber management. Amenities include opportunities for canoeing, hiking, and berry picking. Places of solitude, reflection, and wonder are possible, and the challenge provides more nature benefits. Overnight accommodations are absent. For more information, visit https://dnr.wisconsin.gov/topic/Lands/WildlifeAreas/northbend.html.

JA2 BLACK RIVER PADDLE (BLACK RIVER FALLS TO HIGHWAY 53): 44.288641, -90.851281. This section is an outstanding family paddle. Slow, steady current, plenty of sandbars, and several drop-off and takeout locations make for a great family adventure. This section travels through state forests, wildlife areas, and natural bank vegetation. More adventurous paddlers can plan longer routes and camp on sandbars. Amenities include opportunities for wildlife observation. Nature connections are plentiful, especially goal setting and problem-solving. Overnight camping is available at several nearby public campgrounds and on sandbars. For more information, visit https://wisconsinrivers.org/wp-content/uploads/2019/06/West-Central-FINAL.pdf.

JA3 WAZEE LAKE RECREATION AREA: $E, C. 44.295338, -90.740922. This Jackson County Recreation Area covers approximately 1,300 acres, and the lake is 146 acres, clear and very deep. Crystal clear lake and pine barrens restoration are the main features. The recreation area has nine miles of hiking trails, three miles of paved bike trails, an accessible fishing pier, and a swimming area. The campground, with 12 sites, is open year-round, with reservations accepted from Memorial Day through Labor Day. Nature connections, such as spiritual connections and personal introspection, are abundant. The site can be an annual immersion site, especially for those with younger children. For more information, visit https://www.co.jackson.wi.us.

JA4 EAST FORK BLACK RIVER PADDLE: $C. 44.367205, -90.376469. The section described here has Class II rapids and requires only intermediate-skill whitewater or better paddlers. From the drop-off at the Knutes Road Bridge downstream to the East Fork Campground, the river flows through nearly human-free nature with rock outcrops and towering pines. More adventurous nature seekers can plan a two-day canoe camp overnight adventure. Amenities include opportunities for wildlife observation. Nature connections are plentiful, especially goal setting and problem-solving. Overnight camping is available along the route or at the State Forest Campground. For more information, visit https://wisconsinrivers.org/wp-content/uploads/2019/06/West-Central-FINAL.pdf.

Juneau County

JU1 BASS HOLLOW RECREATION AND STATE NATURAL AREA: 43.671771, -90.032072. This state natural area encompasses more than 500 acres. It lies in the heart of a diverse and spectacular driftless area landscape. Significant old oak-hickory forests and hemlock relicts are the primary features, and the site also has streams, springs, cliffs, and other geological features. The site is managed with trail maintenance and removal of invasive species. Amenities include opportunities for birdwatching, hiking, and berry picking. Nature connections are plentiful, especially in solitude. Overnight accommodations are absent. For more information, visit https://dnr.wisconsin.gov/topic/statenaturalareas/BassHollow.

JU2 MILL BLUFF STATE PARK AND NATURAL AREA: $E, C. 43.940339, -90.318671. This state park encompasses several hundred acres, of which 495 are a designated state natural area. The primary features are the outstanding examples of sandstone mesas, buttes, pinnacles, oak woodlands, pine forests, and red maple swamps. The two miles of trails include a nature trail and access to the top of Mill Bluff. Twenty-one sites are in the campground, close to the interstate highway. Nature connections, such as spiritual connections and personal introspection, are abundant. The site can be an annual immersion site, especially for those with younger children. For more information, visit https://dnr.wisconsin.gov/topic/parks/millbluff.

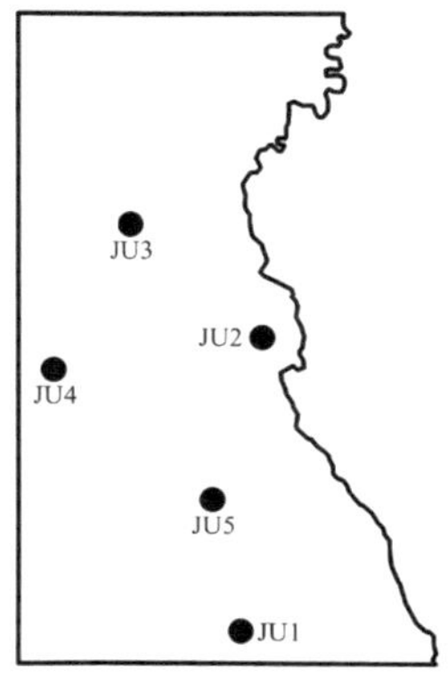

JU3 BUCKHORN STATE PARK AND WILDLIFE AREA: $E, C. 43.948110, -90.004290. The combined properties encompass more than 9,000 acres. The primary features are the outstanding examples of pine barrens, sand barrens, jack pine forests, bottomland hardwoods, and innumerable bayou sloughs. Nature and canoe trails are part of the 10 miles of trails. Buckthorn has 79 campsites, a swimming area, and access to the wild Yellow River bottoms. Nature connections, such as Cognition Enrichment Areas and personal introspection, are abundant. The site can be an annual immersion site. For more information, visit https://dnr.wisconsin.gov/topic/parks/buckhorn.

JU4 NECEDAH NATIONAL WILDLIFE REFUGE: 44.052853, -90.170517. The refuge encompasses more than 44,000 acres, but most are off-limits for non-hunters. The primary features are the outstanding examples of pine barrens, sand barrens, jack pine forests, bottomland hardwoods, flowages, and expansive wetlands. Six miles of trails are available for visitors. Nature connections, such as Cognition Enrichment Areas and personal introspection, are abundant. The site can be an annual immersion site. For more information, visit https://www.fws.gov/refuge/necedah.

JU5 LEMONWEIR RIVER PADDLE: 43.796193, -90.067853. The section described here is all flat water. The 16 miles from Mauston to Wisconsin Dells is a leisurely paddle. Upstream sections have many obstacles, especially deadfalls in the river, and may be best paddled by experienced canoeists. A short paddle from Kennedy Park to New Lisbon passes by sandstone cliffs called the "Little Dells." Amenities include opportunities for wildlife observation. Nature connections are plentiful, especially goal setting and problem-solving. Overnight camping is not available. For more information, visit https://wisconsinrivers.org/wp-content/uploads/2019/06/West-Central-FINAL.pdf.

Marathon County

MA1 MCMILLAN MARSH WILDLIFE AREA: 44.735748, -90.198455. This wildlife area covers 6,500 acres. Primary cover types are upland grassy fields, wet meadows, northern forests, marsh, and impoundments. The DNR manages this site using prescribed burning, invasive species treatments, and timber management. Amenities include opportunities for seasonal biking, hiking, and berry picking. Places of solitude, reflection, and wonder are possible, and the challenge provides more nature benefits. Overnight accommodations are absent. For more information, visit https://dnr.wisconsin.gov/topic/Lands/WildlifeAreas/mcmillan.html.

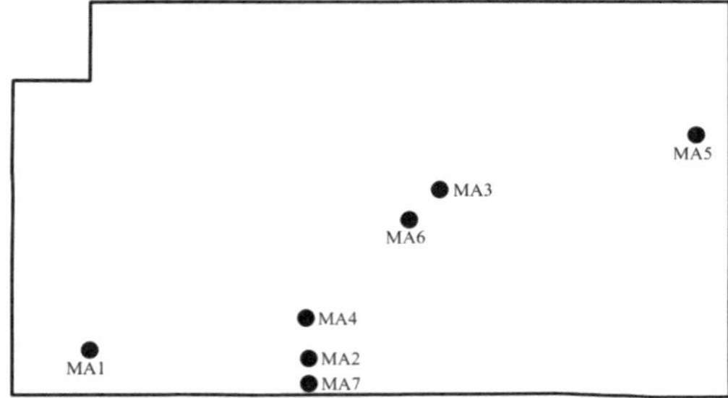

MA2 GEORGE W. MEAD WILDLIFE AREA: 44.725473, -89.865191. This wildlife area covers 33,000 acres in Marathon and Wood Counties. Primary cover types are upland grassy fields, hardwoods, aspen, marsh, impoundments, and bog. The DNR manages this site using prescribed burning, invasive species treatments, and timber management. Amenities include 70 miles of hiking trails, observation decks, and berry picking. Cognitive Enrichment Areas are difficult to access, but the challenge provides more nature benefits. Overnight accommodations are absent. For more information, visit https://dnr.wisconsin.gov/topic/Lands/WildlifeAreas/mead.html.

MA3 RIB MOUNTAIN STATE PARK AND NATURAL AREA: $E. 44.912151, -89.665389. This state park encompasses about 1,500 acres, of which 215 is talus forest and designated state natural area. The primary features are an outstanding example of a glacially scoured granite mountain, talus slopes, and dense woods. The 13 miles of trails include a nature trail and access to the top of Rib Mountain. In this day-use park, nature connections, such as spiritual connections and personal introspection, are abundant. The site can be an annual immersion site, especially for those with younger children. For more information, visit https://dnr.wisconsin.gov/topic/parks/ribmt.

MA4 BIG EAU PLEINE COUNTY PARK AND NATURAL AREA: $E, C. 44.770429, -89.869424. This Marathon County park has approximately 1,450 acres, including a 100-acre natural area of old-growth northern hardwoods. The primary features are a heavily wooded peninsula jutting into the Big Eau Pleine Reservoir. The park is much more amenable to younger children and those needing accessibility than other Marathon County sites. It has 12 miles of trails, water access, and over 100 campsites. Nature connections, such as spiritual connections and personal introspection, are abundant. The site can be an annual immersion site, especially for those with younger children. For more information, visit https://www.co.marathon.wi.us/.

MA5 PLOVER RIVER FISHERY AREA AND NATURAL AREA: 44.971917, -89.274446. This state fishery area covers several hundred acres, of which 250 is a designated state natural area. The primary feature is an outstanding example of a botanically rich landscape. The primary cover types are hardwood forest, white cedar, alder, the Plover River, and spring ponds. A short trail leads to the rich wildflower area. In this day-use area, nature connections are abundant, such as cognitive improvement, spiritual relationships, and personal introspection. Overnight accommodations are absent. For more information, visit https://dnr.wisconsin.gov/topic/Lands/FisheriesAreas/2000ploverriver.html.

MA6 MARATHON COUNTY FOREST (NINE MILE SWAMP UNIT): 44.878315, -89.711035. The Nine Mile Swamp Recreation Area is central to Marathon County. This 4,900-acre site has over 30 miles of trails, 10 miles of a mountain bike trail, and 6.7 miles of snowshoe trail. Primary cover types are aspen, hardwoods, and wetlands. The county forest manages this site for recreation opportunities and sustainable timber. Nature connections, such as spiritual connections and personal introspection, are abundant. Overnight camping is not permitted. For more information, visit https://www.co. marathon.wi.us/.

MA7 GEORGE W. MEAD WILDLIFE AREA (SOUTH): 44.697613, -89.865201. The wildlife area covers 33,000 acres in Marathon and Wood Counties. This portion of the wildlife area has many more amenities for casual nature enthusiasts. Parents with younger children or novice nature explores should visit this portion of the property. A visitor center, observation tower , and interpretive trails are close at hand. Overnight accommodations are absent. For more information, visit https://dnr.wisconsin.gov/topic/Lands/WildlifeAreas/mead.html.

Portage County

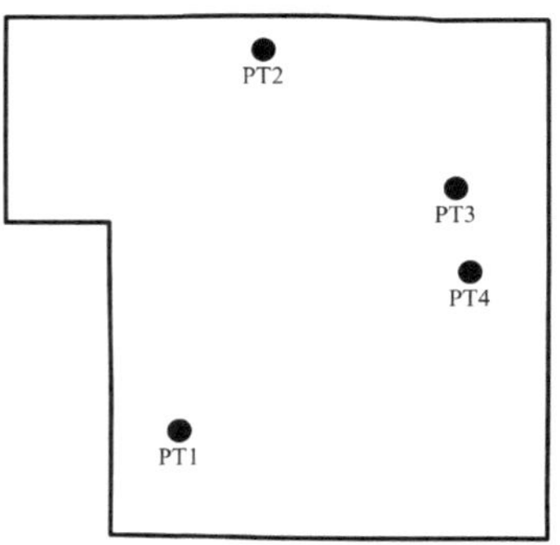

PT1 BUENA VISTA WILDLIFE AREA: 44.337274, -89.645876. This wildlife area covers nearly 12,700 acres. Primary cover types are open grasslands, wetlands, marsh, and patches of woody vegetation. The DNR manages the site to perpetuate Greater Prairie-Chickens by reducing wood vegetation, prescribed burning, and managed grazing to maintain the grasslands. Amenities include opportunities for wildlife observation (especially blinds to observe mating birds), off-trail hiking, and berry picking. The solitude and personal challenges are at hand, and the challenge provides more nature benefits. Overnight accommodations are not available. For more information, visit https://dnr.wisconsin.gov/topic/Lands/WildlifeAreas/buenavista.html.

PT2 DEWEY MARSH WILDLIFE AREA: 44.656874, -89.550355. This wildlife area covers more than 6,000 acres. Primary cover types are sedge meadows, northern forested wetlands, aspen patches, marsh, wet meadows, and streams. The DNR manages the site using prescribed burning, treating invasive species, and timber management. Amenities include opportunities for wildlife observation, hiking, and berry picking. Places of solitude, reflection, and wonder are possible, and the challenge provides more nature benefits. Overnight accommodations are absent. For more information, visit https://dnr.wisconsin.gov/topic/Lands/WildlifeAreas/dewey.html.

PT3 RICHARD HEMP FISHERY AREA: 44.540113, -89.329766. This large fishery area covers more than 1,300 acres. Primary cover types are patches of hemlock, white pine forest, oak-dominated hardwoods, trout streams, and alder. The DNR manages the site by treating invasive species and limited timber management. Amenities include opportunities for canoeing, fishing, hiking, and berry picking. Places of solitude, reflection, and wonder are possible, and the challenge provides more nature benefits.

Overnight accommodations are absent. For more information, visit https://dnr.wisconsin.gov/topic/Lands/FisheriesAreas/2122richardahemp.html.

PT4 TOMORROW RIVER STATE TRAIL: $T. 44.469067, -89.312965. In Portage County, this flat 29-mile rail trail passes through many habitats, including wetlands, pine forests, and hardwoods. It crosses streams and has views of glacial boulder fields. The DNR manages the site by removing invasive species. Amenities include opportunities for biking and access to portions of the county formerly unavailable. Cognitive Enrichment Areas are easy to access, and immersion into nature provides many benefits. Overnight accommodations are absent. For more information, visit https://dnr.wisconsin.gov/topic/parks/tomorrow.

Waushara County

WS1 MECAN RIVER PADDLE (MECAN SPRINGS TO COUNTY HIGHWAY JJ): 44.051189, -89.464111. This section can be a challenge because of the narrowness of the stream and deadfalls, but the exceptional nature immersion is beckoning. Downstream from Highway JJ to Marquette County is more amenable to family outings. Primary cover types along the river are patches of oak savanna, white pine, wet fen meadows, brushy bottomlands, and agricultural land. Amenities include opportunities for solitude and relaxation. Stretches of river flow through peaceful solitude. Overnight accommodations are absent. For more information, visit https://wisconsinrivers.org/wp-content/uploads/2017/12/East_Central_FINAL.pdf.

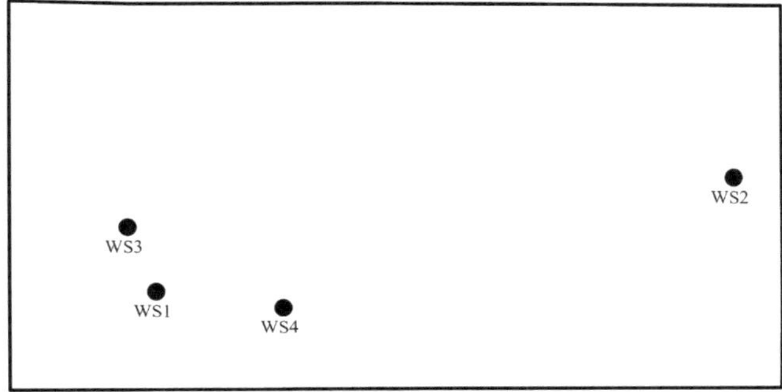

WS2 POYGAN MARSH WILDLIFE AREA: 44.126909, -88.930995. This wildlife area, which is more than 3,600 acres, has little visitation outside hunting season. Primary cover types are bottomland hardwoods, upland planted prairie, sedge meadow, cattail marsh, stream, and brushland. The DNR manages the site using prescribed burning and water management techniques to maintain productive wetlands. Amenities include opportunities for nature immersion. The solitude and personal challenges are at hand, and the challenge provides more nature benefits. Overnight accommodations are absent. For more information, visit https://dnr.wisconsin.gov/topic/Lands/WildlifeAreas/poygan.html.

WS3 GREENWOOD WILDLIFE AREA: 44.093731, -89.489131. This wildlife area covers more than 1,400 acres in west central Waushara County. Primary cover types are oak forest, oak savanna, native prairie, and planted prairie. The DNR manages the site by prescribed burning, treating invasive species, and timber management. Amenities include opportunities for a deep cognitive experience in an oak savanna-prairie landscape. Nature connections are best secured by off-trail immersion, especially spiritual connections and personal introspection. Overnight accommodations are absent. For more information, visit https://dnr.wisconsin.gov/topic/Lands/WildlifeAreas/greenwood.html.

WS4 LUNCH CREEK FISHERY AND STATE NATURAL AREA: 44.039945, -89.346287. These combined DNR properties cover more than 600 acres. The primary feature is one of the most diverse sedge meadows in the state. This site also contains an oak savanna, native prairie, fen, wetlands, and Lunch Creek. The state natural area provides access to advanced botanical and ornithological forays. State natural areas do not permit overnight camping. Nature connections, such as spiritual connections and personal introspection, are abundant. For more information, visit https://dnr.wisconsin.gov/topic/StateNaturalAreas.

Wood County

WO1 WOOD COUNTY WILDLIFE AREA: 44.306840, -90.253993. This nearly 21,000-acre wildlife area has minimal off-road visitation outside hunting season. Primary cover types are aspen islands in a sea of sedge meadow, tamarack-black spruce bog, impoundments, and brushland.

The DNR manages the site to perpetuate aspen, provide waterfowl habitat, maintain the swamps passively, and increase sedge meadow by prescribed burning. Amenities include opportunities for nature immersion. The solitude and personal challenges are at hand, and the challenge provides more nature benefits. Overnight camping is permitted during the spring and fall hunting seasons. For more information, visit https://dnr.wisconsin.gov/topic/Lands/WildlifeAreas/woodcounty.html.

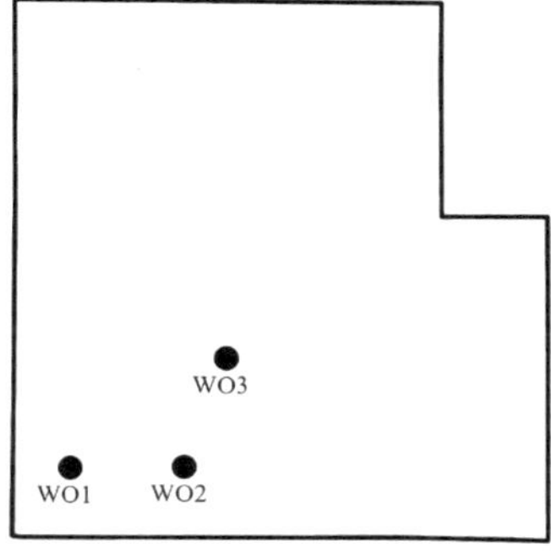

WO2 SANDHILL WILDLIFE AREA: 44.307239, -90.129780. This more than 9,100-acre wildlife area has a fenced enclosure for research purposes. Primary cover types are oak uplands, sedge meadows, tamarack-black spruce bog, impoundments, and native prairie/brushland. The DNR manages the site to perpetuate the cover types, provide waterfowl habitat, and increase barrens habitat with prescribed burning. Amenities include opportunities for accessible nature immersion from the auto tour. The solitude and personal challenges are at hand, and the challenge provides more nature benefits. Overnight camping is absent. For more information, visit https://dnr.wisconsin.gov/topic/Lands/WildlifeAreas/sandhill.

WO3 WOOD COUNTY FOREST (OWL CREEK FEN SAVANNA STATE NATURAL AREA): 44.394852, -90.082809. This more than 800-acre site features a large central Wisconsin fen. A classic wire-grass fen has islands of pine and spruce, but uniquely, a large portion of the site has scattered aspen with a savanna-like appearance. This wilderness immersion Cognitive Enrichment Area is difficult to access. This portion of the county forest provides wilderness therapy challenges. Wilderness enthusiasts can camp in a dispersed manner in the county forest with a permit. For more information, visit https://dnr.wisconsin.gov/topic/StateNaturalAreas.

East Central Wisconsin

Brown County

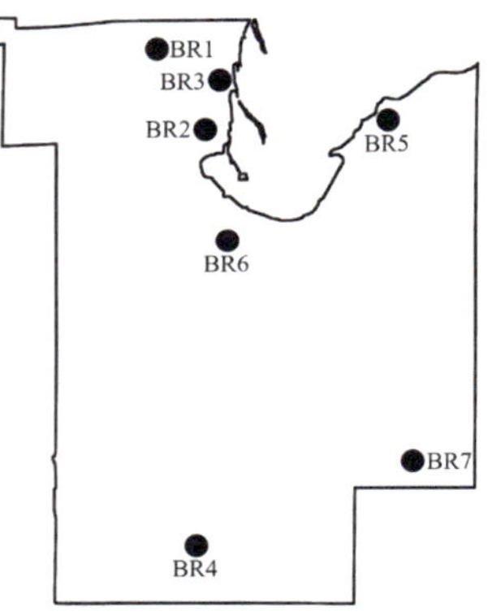

BR1 E.J. "OLLIE" SMITH REFORESTATION CAMP: 44.656813, -88.088372. The almost 1,500-acre reforestation camp harbors upland forests, ponds, and many wetlands. More than 6.5 miles of trails allow visitors to immerse in nature. Younger nature enthusiasts may also enjoy visiting the adjacent new zoo. Visitors can fish, hike, mountain bike, and snowshoe. They do not permit hiking in the winter; see park rules for activity restrictions. Nature connections are plentiful, especially personal introspection and wilderness therapy. For more information, visit https://www.browncountywi.gov/community/parks-department.

BR2 BARKHAUSEN WATERFOWL PRESERVE: 44.597240, -88.038719. The more than 900-acre site features upland forest, meadows, ponds, and many wetlands. More than nine miles of trails allow visitors to immerse in nature. The "Sensory Woods" provides access to many without other opportunities to experience nature. Visitors can fish, hike, mountain bike, and snowshoe. An interpretive center gives visitors a better understanding of the natural world. Nature connections are plentiful, especially personal introspection and wilderness therapy. For more information, visit https://www.browncountywi.gov/community/parks-department.

BR3 GREEN BAY WEST SHORES WILDLIFE AREA: 44.633325, -88.022309. This state wildlife area has four units in Brown County, encompassing 1,714 acres. Primary cover types are red maple swamps, marsh, and other wetlands. The DNR manages the site for waterfowl production by utilizing water control, invasive species reduction, and other techniques to maintain the wetlands. Amenities include opportunities for immersion into vast areas of coastal wetlands. Nature connections are plentiful, especially in wilderness therapy. Overnight accommodations are absent. For more information, visit https://dnr.wisconsin.gov/topic/Lands/WildlifeAreas/GBWS.html.

BR4 HOLLAND WILDLIFE AREA: 44.284993, -88.048324. This state wildlife area encompasses 536 acres. Primary cover types are red maple swamps, white cedar, and grasslands. The DNR manages the site for pheasant hunting using prescribed burning and other techniques to manage the grasslands. Amenities include opportunities to experience an old-growth red maple swamp for birdwatching, exploring, and berry picking. Nature connections are plentiful, especially for personal introspection. Overnight accommodations are absent. For more information, visit https://dnr.wisconsin.gov/topic/Lands/WildlifeAreas/holland.html. None

BR5 RED BANKS ALVAR STATE NATURAL AREA: 44.604130, -87.854054. This almost 344-acre unique site features the largest alvar in Wisconsin. An alvar is a natural community that forms on flat limestone bedrock with thin soils. A combination of boreal, savanna, and prairie species makes the site special. Visitors experience an intimate relationship with the unique botany of the site. The authors recommend that only experienced nature enthusiasts with a bent for botany visit the area because of its thin soils and fragile nature. Nature connections, such as spiritual connections and personal introspection, are abundant. For more information, visit https://dnr.wisconsin.gov/topic/statenaturalareas/RedBanksAlvar. None.

BR6 FOX RIVER STATE TRAIL: $T. 44.514471, -88.017323. The Fox River State Trail is a paved 25-mile trail connecting Green Bay to Hilbert. The trail is on an abandoned railroad grade and traverses urban and forest land, with especially great views of the Fox River. Amenities include opportunities to view wildlife and natural beauty. Nature connections are plentiful, especially goal setting and problem-solving. Overnight camping is not available. For more information, visit https://dnr.wisconsin.gov/topic/parks/foxriver/info.

BR7 DEVIL'S RIVER STATE TRAIL: $T. 44.348789, -87.829095. The Devil's River State Trail is a paved 14-mile trail connecting Denmark to Rockwood. The trail is on an abandoned railroad grade and traverses agricultural land, forests, streams, wetlands, and two high railroad trestles. Amenities include opportunities to view wildlife and natural beauty. Nature connections are plentiful, especially goal setting and problem-solving. Overnight camping is not available. For more information, visit https://dnr.wisconsin.gov/topic/parks/devilsriver/.

Calumet County

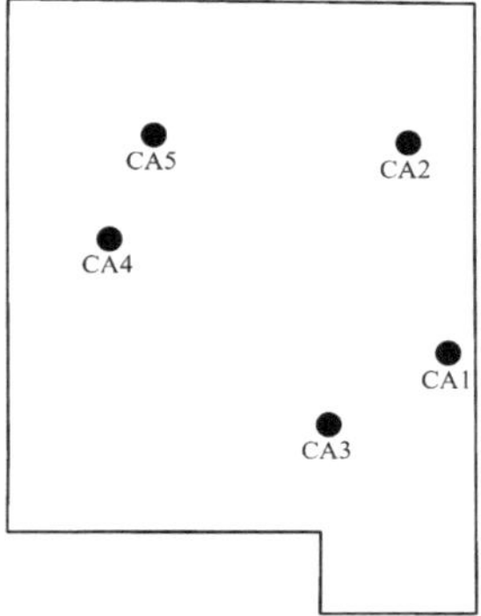

CA1 KILLSNAKE WILDLIFE AREA: 44.040977, -88.063333. This state wildlife area encompasses 7,000 acres. Primary cover types are wetlands, restored prairie, white cedar, and grasslands. The DNR manages the site for various wildlife by using prescribed burning and other techniques to manage the grasslands and timber harvest to manage the forest. Amenities include opportunities to experience an enormous expanse of different habitats for birdwatching, exploring, and berry picking. Nature connections are plentiful, especially for natural balance. Overnight accommodations are absent. For more information, visit https://dnr.wisconsin.gov/topic/Lands/WildlifeAreas/killsnake.html.

CA2 BRILLION WILDLIFE AREA AND BRILLION NATURE CENTER: 44.161075, -88.095042. This state wildlife area is a 4,800-acre property comprising bottomland hardwoods, prairie, marsh, wetlands, and upland hardwoods. The nature center is a nonprofit that was developed to provide educational opportunities for Brillion and surrounding communities. The DNR manages the site for various wildlife by using prescribed burning and other techniques to manage the grasslands and timber harvest to manage the forest. Amenities include opportunities for all abilities to experience nature and different habitats. Nature connections are plentiful, especially for creativity and wonder. Overnight accommodations are absent. For more information, visit https://dnr.wisconsin.gov/topic/Lands/WildlifeAreas/brillion.html.

CA3 LEDGE VIEW NATURE CENTER: 44.000335, -88.155877. Ledge View Nature Center is a 105-acre Calumet County park. The park is best identified as an environmental education center. Varied habitats include caves, hardwood forests, ledges, and prairie. The site has three miles of trails, a 60-foot observation tower, an arboretum, and gardens with native wildflowers. Visitors can also view displays and interactive exhibits inside the nature center building. Amenities include opportunities for all abilities to experience nature and different habitats. Nature connections are plentiful, especially for creativity and wonder. Overnight accommodations are absent. For more information, visit https://www.ledgeviewnaturecenter.org/.

CA4 CALUMET COUNTY PARK: $E, C. 44.107128, -88.325779. Calumet County Park is a 230-acre park with a campground, playgrounds, hiking and biking trails, and a modern boat launch facility. Winter activities at the park include snowshoeing, cross-country ski trails, and fat tire bike trails. The vegetation along the escarpment is hardwoods, with apparent areas of cliff species along the ledge. Amenities include opportunities to experience nature and different habitats. Nature connections are plentiful, especially for creativity and wonder. Overnight accommodations are present on-site. The park is open year-round. For more information, visit https://www.calumetcounty.org/650/Calumet-County-Park.

CA5 HIGH CLIFF STATE PARK: $E, C. 44.166648, -88.291447. This state park encompasses approximately 1,200 acres. The primary features are the open and shaded cliffs along the Niagara Escarpment. Forested tracts proceed from the ledge's crest to Lake Winnebago's shore. The more than seven miles of trails, including a nature trail, bike trail, and sand beach, provide ample opportunities for nature immersion. Campgrounds with 112 sites are open year-round but limited in winter and provide a base camp for hiking, biking, fishing, and swimming. Nature connections, such as spiritual connections and personal introspection, are abundant. The site can be an annual immersion site, especially for those with younger children. For more information, visit https://dnr.wisconsin.gov/topic/parks/highcliff.

Fond du Lac County

FD1 MULLET CREEK WILDLIFE AREA: 43.747858, -88.191224. This state wildlife area covers more than 2,200 acres. Primary cover types are upland grassy fields, mixed hardwoods, wetland forests, cattail marshes, sedge meadows, a white cedar swamp, shrub-carr, and brushy areas. The DNR manages the site using prescribed burning and timber management. Amenities include opportunities for birdwatching, hiking, and berry picking.

Cognitive Enrichment Areas are hard to access, but the challenge provides more nature benefits. Overnight accommodations are absent. For more information, visit https://dnr.wisconsin.gov/topic/Lands/WildlifeAreas/mullet.html.

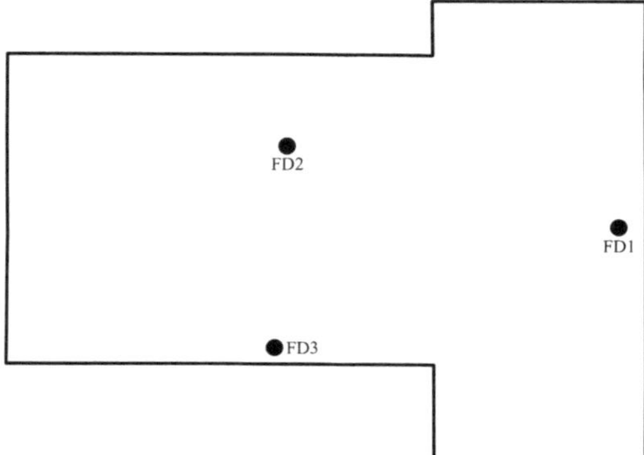

FD2 ELDORADO WILDLIFE AREA: 43.818345, -88.569045. This state wildlife area covers more than 6,300 acres. Primary cover types are several wetland types, upland grassy fields, restored savannas, flowages, shrub-carr, and brushy areas. The DNR manages the site by using prescribed burning and timber management. Amenities include opportunities for birdwatching, hiking, and berry picking. Wilderness Therapy Areas are tough to access, but the challenge provides more nature benefits. Overnight accommodations are absent. For more information, visit https://dnr.wisconsin.gov/topic/Lands/WildlifeAreas/eldorado.html.

FD3 OAKFIELD LEDGE STATE NATURAL AREA: 43.646684, -88.582177. While only covering slightly more than 200 acres, Oakfield Ledge can provide nature experiences hard to find elsewhere in the county. The site features an extensive portion of the Niagara Escarpment. Small cliffs and unusual rock formations are the features, but ledge-top savannas add complexity. The SNA Program manages the site by treating invasive species, tree thinning, and occasional burning. Amenities include opportunities for hiking and nature immersion. Cognitive Enrichment Areas are easy to locate, but the site suffers from those disrespecting nature by littering and graffiti. Overnight accommodations are absent. For more information, visit https://dnr.wisconsin.gov/topic/StateNaturalAreas.

Manitowoc County

MN1 KILLSNAKE WILDLIFE AREA: 44.058563, -88.037673. This wildlife area covers more than 7,000 acres (see Calumet County, page XXX). This section of the wildlife area is quite different from the western portion. Dense hardwood forest parallels the South Branch of the Manitowoc

River. Canoeing access is much easier here. Places of solitude, reflection, and wonder are possible, and the challenge provides more nature benefits. Overnight accommodations are absent. For more information, visit https://dnr. wisconsin. gov/topic/Lands/WildlifeAreas/killsnake. html.

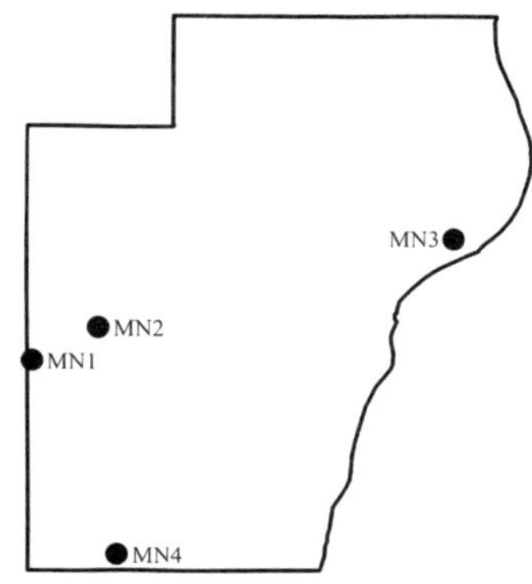

MN2 COLLINS MARSH WILDLIFE AREA: 44.083852, -87.967784. This wildlife area covers more than 4,200 acres. Primary cover types are patches of bottomland hardwoods, marsh, planted grasslands, and impoundments. The DNR manages this site using prescribed burning, treating invasive species, and timber management. Amenities include opportunities for canoeing, fishing, hiking, and berry picking. Places of solitude, reflection, and wonder are possible, and the challenge provides more nature benefits. Overnight accommodations are absent. For more information, visit https://dnr.wisconsin.gov/topic/Lands/WildlifeAreas/collins.html.

MN3 WOODLAND DUNES NATURE CENTER AND PRESERVE: $E. 44.153596, -87.589814. This private conservation organization protects over 1,500 acres of land. The primary features are hardwood and wetland forest types growing on ridge and swale topography. In addition, there are areas of wet shrubland, wetlands, marsh, and open water. The preserve has seven miles of hiking trails, a boardwalk, and observation decks overlooking the marsh. Nature connections, such as spiritual connections and personal introspection, are abundant. The site can be an annual immersion site, especially for those with younger children. For more information, visit https://www. woodlanddunes.org/.

MN4 WALLA HI COUNTY PARK: 43.905348, -87.948285. This forest occupies a rugged kettle moraine topography in the western part of Manitowoc County. Primary cover types in this 160-acre park are southern hardwood forest and small streams. Opportunities are present for fishing, hiking, and snowshoeing. These Cognitive Enrichment Areas are simple to access, and natural immersion provides many benefits. Overnight accommodations are absent. For more information, visit https://manitowoccountywi.gov/departments/parks/county-parks/walla-hi/.

Outagamie County

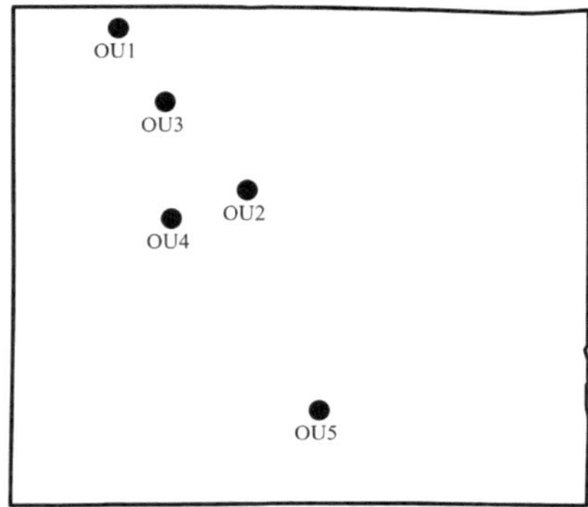

OU1 DEER CREEK WILDLIFE AREA: 44.576003, -88.636861. The wildlife area covers 1,500 acres. Primary cover types are upland grassy fields, northern forests, wetlands, and wet fields. The DNR manages the site using timber management techniques to maintain the aspen. Amenities include opportunities for wilderness immersion and berry picking. The solitude and personal challenges are at hand, and the challenge provides more nature benefits. Overnight accommodations are absent. For more information, visit https://dnr.wisconsin.gov/topic/Lands/WildlifeAreas/deercreek.html.

OU2 MACK WILDLIFE AREA: 44.463000, -88.514429. This wildlife area covers 1,350 acres. Primary cover types are upland grassy fields, swamp forests, wetlands, and brushland. The DNR manages the site using timber management techniques to maintain the aspen. Amenities include opportunities for wilderness immersion and berry picking. The solitude and personal challenges are at hand, and the challenge provides more nature benefits. Overnight accommodations are absent. For more information, visit https://dnr.wisconsin.gov/topic/Lands/WildlifeAreas/mack.html.

OU3 OUTAGAMIE WILDLIFE AREA AND HERB BEHNKE UNIT: 44.524975, -88.592522. This wildlife area covers 2,500 acres. Primary cover types are marsh, impoundment, bottomland forest, wetlands, and brushland. The DNR manages the site using timber management techniques to maintain the aspen. Amenities include opportunities for wilderness immersion and berry picking. The solitude and personal challenges are at hand, and the challenge provides more nature benefits. Overnight accommodations are absent. For more information, visit https://dnr.wisconsin.gov/topic/lands/WildlifeAreas/outagamie.html.

OU4 WOLF RIVER PADDLE (SHIOCTON TO NEW LONDON): 44.443662, -88.586857. Nature experiences fill this paddle from Shiocton to New London. Primary cover types along the river are wet meadows and dense bottomland forests. The paddle can be extended several more miles upstream, but these sections have deadfall concerns. Amenities include opportunities for birdwatching and relaxation. Stretches of river flow through incredible solitude. Overnight accommodations are absent. For more information, visit https://wipaddle.wordpress.com/2011/03/14/wolf-river-shiocton-to-new-london/.

OU5 GORDON BUBOLZ NATURE CENTER AND PRESERVE: $E. 44.310280, -88.446425. This private conservation organization protects over 775 acres of land. The primary features are hardwood and wetland forest types, marsh, and brushy wetlands. The preserve has miles of hiking trails, boardwalks, and observation decks overlooking a pond. Nature connections, such as spiritual connections and personal introspection, are abundant. The site can be an annual immersion site, especially for those with younger children. For more information, visit https://bubolzpreserve.org/about/trails-maps/.

Sheboygan County

SB1 BROUGHTON SHEBOYGAN MARSH PARK AND WILDLIFE AREA: $C. 43.848564, -88.042351. These combined county and state properties cover more than 13,000 acres. The primary features are wet forest, brushland, marsh, and impoundment. The park and wildlife area and preserve have access to a vast interior marsh and a very tall observation deck overlooking the impoundment. Fifty campsites provide overnight accommodations. Nature connections, such as spiritual connections and personal introspection, are abundant. For more information, visit https://www.sheboygancounty.com/.

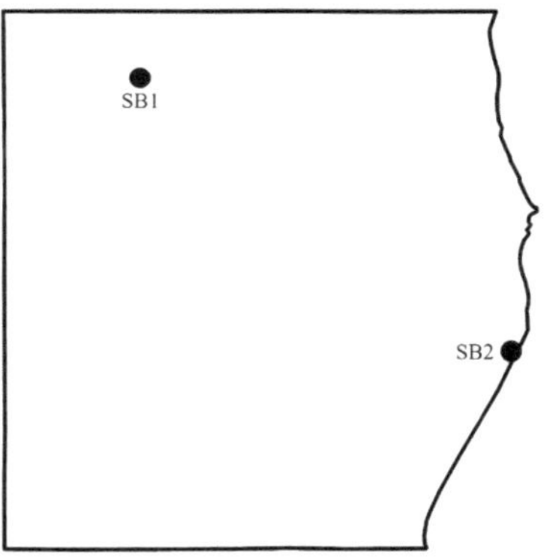

SB2 KOHLER-ANDRAE STATE PARK: $E, C. 43.672562, -87.717916. This state park encompasses approximately 1,000 acres, of which 20 is the beach. The primary features are an outstanding example of lakeside forests, wetlands, dunes, and beaches. The six miles of trails include a nature trail and an accessible cordwalk through the dunes. Over 130 campsites are available. Nature connections, such as spiritual connections and personal

introspection, are abundant. The site can be an annual immersion site, especially for those with younger children. For more information, visit https://dnr.wisconsin.gov/topic/parks/kohlerandrae.

Waupaca County

WP1 LITTLE WOLF RIVER PADDLE (MANAWA TO COUNTY HIGHWAY X): 44.464710, -88.923477. This 12-mile paddle is an easy family paddle, with few obstructions and mild rapids. Upstream sections to Big Falls are also possibilities. Primary cover types along the river are patches of hardwoods, wet meadows, marshland, brushy bottomlands, and agricultural land. Amenities include opportunities for solitude and relaxation. Overnight accommodations are absent. For more information, visit https://wisconsinrivers.org/wp-content/uploads/2017/12/East_Central_FINAL.pdf.

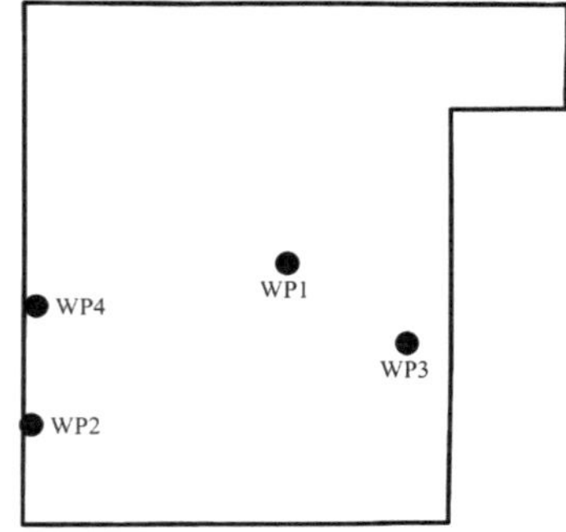

WP2 HARTMAN CREEK STATE PARK AND STATE NATURAL AREA: $E, C. 44.328863, -89.213864. This state park encompasses approximately 1,400 acres. The primary features are outstanding examples of the glacial moraine with pine-oak forests, streams, lakes, and wetlands. Twelve miles of off-road bike trails, 10 miles of hiking trails, and canoe routes highlight the park. Over 100 campsites are available. Nature connections, such as spiritual connections and personal introspection, are abundant. The site can be an annual immersion site, especially for those with younger children. For more information, visit https://dnr.wisconsin.gov/topic/parks/hartmancreek.

WP3 MUKWA WILDLIFE AREA: 44.398241, -88.786690. This wildlife area covers more than 1,400 acres in east central Waupaca County. Primary cover types are bottomland hardwoods, brushland, wetlands, and old oxbow lakes. The DNR manages the site by treating invasive species and timber management. Amenities include opportunities for a deep wilderness experience because of the difficult access. Nature connections are best secured off-trail immersion, especially spiritual connections and personal introspection. Overnight accommodations are absent. For more information, visit https://dnr.wisconsin.gov/topic/Lands/WildlifeAreas/mukwa.html.

WP4 SKUNK AND FOSTER LAKES STATE NATURAL AREA: 44.428306, -89.209120. This state natural area covers more than 250 acres, which includes portions of five small lakes. Pitted outwash topography, woods, wetlands, and lakes are the primary features. The trails permit access to wild lakes, which are very rare in this part of Wisconsin. State natural areas do not allow overnight camping. Nature connections, such as spiritual connections and personal introspection, are abundant. The site can be an annual immersion site, especially for those with younger children. For more information, visit https://dnr.wisconsin.gov/topic/statenaturalareas/SkunkandFosterLakes.

Winnebago County

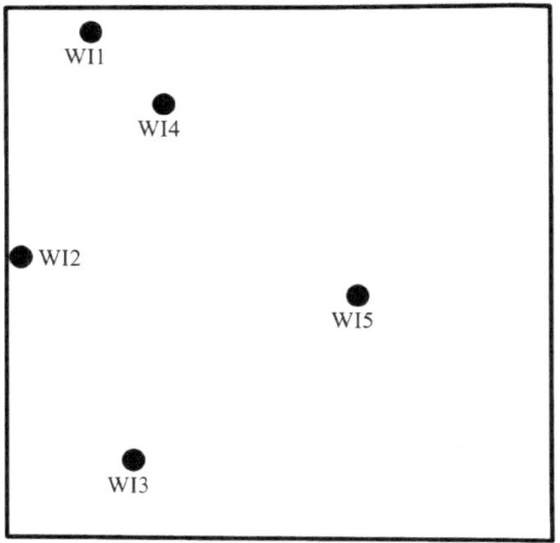

WI1 WOLF RIVER WILDLIFE AREA: 44.227438, -88.810835. This nearly 1,800-acre wildlife area has little visitation outside hunting season. Primary cover types are reed canary marsh and upland planted prairie, sedge meadow, cattail marsh, stream, and brushland. The DNR manages the site by reducing reed canary and increasing sedge meadow by herbicide treatment and prescribed burning. Amenities include opportunities for nature immersion. The solitude and personal challenges are at hand, and the challenge provides more nature benefits. Overnight accommodations are absent. For more information, visit https://dnr.wisconsin.gov/topic/Lands/WildlifeAreas/wolfriver.html.

WI2 DEPPE WILDLIFE AREA: 44.079879, -88.876566. This 430-acre wildlife area in western Winnebago County has minimal visitation outside hunting season. Primary cover types are marsh, upland planted prairie, cattail marsh, scattered trees, and brushland. The DNR manages the site by maintaining the grasslands through herbicide treatment and prescribed burning. Amenities include opportunities for nature immersion. The solitude and personal challenges are at hand, and the challenge provides more nature benefits. Overnight accommodations are absent. For more information, visit https://dnr.wisconsin.gov/topic/Lands/WildlifeAreas/deppe.html.

WI3 RUSH LAKE AND UIHLEIN WATERFOWL PRODUCTION AREA: 43.945978, -88.775001. This nearly 3,000-acre cooperative wildlife protection area lies in southwestern Winnebago County. Primary cover types are marsh, upland planted prairie, cattail marsh, scattered trees, and access to the largest prairie pothole in Wisconsin. The DNR manages the site by maintaining the grasslands through brush removal, herbicide treatment, and prescribed burning. Amenities include opportunities for nature immersion. The solitude and personal challenges are at hand, and the challenge provides more nature benefits. Overnight accommodations are absent. For more information, visit https://dnr.wisconsin.gov/topic/Lands/Other/ghra.html. and search around Rush Lake on the map.

WI4 WINCHESTER MEADOW STATE NATURAL AREA: 44.178668, -88.747076. This large state natural area covers more than 440 acres. The primary feature is one of the most diverse sedge meadows in the state. This site also contains wooded islands, native prairie and fen, and marsh. The state natural area provides access for advanced botanical and ornithological forays. State natural areas do not permit overnight camping; the access is a walk-in easement. Nature connections, such as spiritual connections and personal introspection, are abundant. For more information, visit https://dnr.wisconsin.gov/topic/statenaturalareas/WinchesterMeadow.

WI5 WIOUWASH STATE TRAIL (OSHKOSH TO HORTONVILLE): 44.053971, -88.574887. This 22-mile rail trail passes through several habitats in Winnebago County. This flat trail crosses wetlands, penetrates woodlots, crosses streams, and features several places where native prairie flourishes. The DNR manages the site by prescribed burning and removing invasive species. Amenities include opportunities for biking, hiking, and access to portions of the county formerly unavailable. Spiritual connections and personal introspection areas are easy to access. Overnight accommodations are absent. For more information, visit https://dnr.wisconsin.gov/topic/parks/wiouwash/info.

Northeast Wisconsin

Door County

DO1 PENINSULA STATE PARK: $E, C. 45.127263, -87.236481. This state park encompasses about 3,800 acres. The primary features are bedrock, rock beaches, white cedar swamp, old-growth forest, and bluffs. The more than 20 miles of trails, including a nature trail and accessible trails, provide ample opportunities for nature immersion. Campgrounds with more than 460 sites are open year-round but limited in winter and provide a base camp for hiking, biking, fishing, and swimming. Nature connections, such as spiritual connections and personal introspection, are abundant. The site can be an annual immersion site, especially for those with younger children. For more information, visit https://dnr.wisconsin.gov/topic/parks/peninsula.

DO2 WHITEFISH DUNES STATE PARK: $E. 44.929000, -87.182100. This state park and the adjacent county park encompass approximately 1,000 acres. The primary features are beaches, dunes, sphagnum bogs, old-growth forests, and bluffs. More than 14 miles of trails, including a nature trail and 1.2 miles of sand beach, provide ample opportunities for nature immersion. The park is open year-round but offers no camping. Overnight accommodations are plentiful in nearby locations. Nature connections, such as spiritual connections and personal introspection, are abundant. The site can be an annual immersion site, especially for those with younger children. For more information, visit https://dnr.wisconsin.gov/topic/parks/whitefish.

DO3 POTAWATOMI STATE PARK: $E, C. 44.851759, -87.427436. This state park encompasses about 1,200 acres. The primary features are bedrock beaches, hemlock cliffs, old-growth forests, and bluffs. The more than eight miles of trails, including a nature trail and accessible trails, provide ample opportunities for nature immersion. Campgrounds with more than 120 sites are open year-round but limited in winter and provide a base camp for hiking, biking, fishing, and swimming. Nature connections, such as spiritual connections and personal introspection, are abundant. The site can be an annual immersion site, especially for those with younger children. For more information, visit https://dnr.wisconsin.gov/topic/parks/potawatomi.

DO4 MUD LAKE (DOOR COUNTY) WILDLIFE AREA: 45.095788, -87.082082. The wildlife area covers more than 2,300 acres. Primary cover types are shallow lakes, sedge meadows, brushy swamps, boreal forests, and hardwoods. The DNR manages the site by treating invasive species and timber management. Amenities include opportunities for canoeing, hiking, and berry picking. Cognitive Enrichment Areas are tough to access, but the challenge provides more nature benefits. Overnight accommodations are absent. For more information, visit https://dnr.wisconsin.gov/topic/Lands/WildlifeAreas/mudlk.html.

DO5 GARDNER SWAMP WILDLIFE AREA: 44.800755, -87.599860. This wildlife area covers more than 2,300 acres. Primary cover types are sedge meadow, brushy swamp, white cedar swamp, and hardwoods. The DNR manages the site by prescribed burning, treating invasive species, and timber management. Amenities include opportunities for canoeing, hiking, and berry picking. The challenging aspect of access provides wilderness therapy opportunities, and the challenge provides more nature benefits. Overnight accommodations are absent. For more information, visit https://dnr.wisconsin.gov/topic/Lands/WildlifeAreas/gardner.html.

DO6 CAVE POINT TO CLAY BLUFFS STATE NATURAL AREA (SHIVERING SANDS UNIT): 44.879826, -87.207785. This unit of the state natural area covers more than 1,200 acres. Primary cover types are shallow lake, fen, brushy swamp, white cedar swamp, and hardwoods. The SNA Program manages the site, treating invasive species and limited timber management. Amenities include opportunities for hiking and deep nature immersion. Cognitive Enrichment Areas are hard to access, but the challenge provides more nature benefits. Overnight accommodations are absent. For more information, visit https://dnr.wisconsin.gov/topic/statenaturalareas/CavePointClayBanks.

Florence County

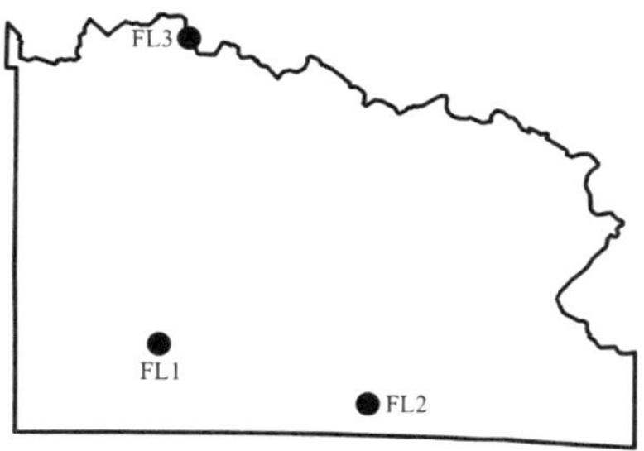

FL1 WHEELER LAKE STATE NATURAL AREA: 45.786742, -88.532074. This more than 750-acre state natural area is part of the Chequamegon-Nicolet National Forest. The site features a wetland complex with several scattered stands of older-growth hemlock and fire-origin red pine. Planning is required to find the site. The Forest Service manages the site by treating invasive species. Amenities include opportunities for hiking and deep nature immersion. Cognitive Enrichment Areas are hard to access, but the challenge provides more nature benefits. Overnight accommodations are present at nearby national forest campgrounds. For more information, visit https://dnr.wisconsin.gov/topic/statenaturalareas/WheelerLake.

FL2 FLORENCE COUNTY FOREST: 45.743811, -88.324670. This site is in an exceptionally diverse portion of the forest. The forest encompasses more than 36,000 acres, all of which are open for nature exploration. Visitors can use forest access roads for hiking and magnificent spots for nature immersion. Primary cover types are aspen, hardwoods, and many types of wetlands. The county forest manages the site, so care needs to be taken if timber operations occur or during hunting season. They permit primitive camping on county forest land. For more information, visit https://www.florencecountywi.com/departments/.

FL3 BRULE RIVER PADDLE: 46.001779, -88.500902. For those naturalists needing a remote location for a paddle, the 44 miles of the Brule, which forms the border with Michigan, is ideal. The river offers a wilderness setting with many cliffs, towering pines, and easy rapids. Several sections are available to the canoeist; therefore, trip planning is paramount. Users should plan enough time to explore features along the river, especially the botanically rich cliffs, which can add memorable cognitive experiences. Amenities include opportunities for nature immersion. Nature connections are plentiful, especially goal setting and problem-solving. Overnight accommodations are absent along the river. For more information, visit https://wisconsinrivers.org/wp-content/uploads/2019/08/Northeastern-Rivers-FINAL.pdf.

Forest County

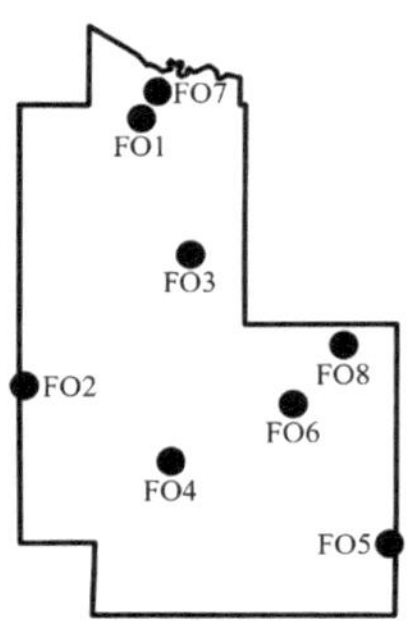

FO1 ALVIN CREEK HEADWATERS STATE NATURAL AREA: 45.967590, -88.846664. This state natural area covers more than 1,000 acres. Primary cover types are springs, ponds, bogs, white cedar swamps, and uplands of hardwoods and old-growth hemlocks. The Forest Service manages the site by treating invasive species and limiting access. Amenities include opportunities for hiking and deep nature immersion. Cognitive Enrichment Areas are difficult to access, but the challenge provides more nature benefits. Overnight accommodations are absent. For more information, visit https://dnr.wisconsin.gov/topic/statenaturalareas/AlvinCreekHeadwaters.

FO2 ATKINS LAKE AND HILES SWAMP STATE NATURAL AREA: 45.651258, -89.039971. This state natural area covers more than 2,500 acres. Primary cover types are a large shallow lake surrounded by a sedge meadow and a vast conifer swamp. The Forest Service manages the site by treating invasive species and limiting access. Amenities include opportunities for wilderness therapy and deep nature immersion. Goal-setting and high-performance areas are tough to access, but the challenge provides more nature benefits. Overnight accommodations are absent. For more information, visit https://dnr.wi.gov/topic/Lands/naturalareas/index.asp?SNA=238.

FO3 RAT LAKE SWAMP AND POPPLE RIVER HEADWATERS STATE NATURAL AREA: 45.806803, -88.764213. This State Natural Area covers more than 2,500 acres. Primary cover types are black spruce and tamaracks, white cedar, sedge meadows, and open bogs, which form the headwaters of the Popple River. The Forest Service manages the site by treating invasive species and limiting access. Amenities include opportunities for wilderness therapy and deep nature immersion. Goal-setting and high-performance areas are difficult to access, but the challenge provides more nature benefits. Overnight accommodations are absent. For more information, visit https://dnr.wisconsin.gov/topic/statenaturalareas/RatLakeSwampPoppleRiverHeadwaters.

FO4 WAUBIKON LAKE STATE NATURAL AREA: 45.561738, -88.798497. This state natural area covers more than 1,000 acres. Primary cover types are springs, large lakes, black spruce and tamaracks, white cedar, sedge meadows, and small patches of old-growth hemlock. The Forest Service manages the site by treating invasive species and limiting access. Amenities include opportunities for wilderness therapy and deep nature immersion. Goal-setting and high-performance areas are hard to access, but the challenge provides more nature benefits. Overnight accommodations are absent. For more information, visit https://dnr.wisconsin.gov/topic/statenaturalareas/WabikonLake.

FO5 DEER MOUNTAIN STATE NATURAL AREA: 45.463038, -88.437316. This state natural area covers more than 2,000 acres. Primary cover types are an upland forest of sugar maple, basswood, and occasional beech. The forest's rich habitat and leaf litter support a state-endangered fern found in the humus-rich soils of northern mesic forests. The Forest Service manages the site by treating invasive species and limiting access. Amenities include opportunities for wilderness therapy and deep nature immersion. Cognitive Enrichment Areas are difficult to access, but the challenge provides more nature benefits. Overnight accommodations are absent. For more information, visit https://dnr.wisconsin.gov/topic/statenaturalareas/DeerMountain.

FO6 CAMP THREE LAKE STATE NATURAL AREA: 45.628717, -88.595722. This state natural area covers more than 1,200 acres. Primary cover types are a deep, soft water lake, floodplain forest of silver maple, white cedar swamp, and upland forest of hardwoods and hemlock. Several northern warbler species nest within the state natural area. The Forest Service manages the site by treating invasive species and limiting access. Amenities include opportunities for wilderness therapy and deep nature immersion. Wilderness Therapy Areas are hard to access, but the challenge provides more nature benefits. Overnight accommodations are absent. For more information, visit https://dnr.wisconsin.gov/topic/statenaturalareas/CampThreeLake.

FO7 ALVIN/ALLEN CREEK OLD-GROWTH AREA: 45.998544, -88.819558. This federally designated area features a future old-growth forest and covers several hundred acres. Primary cover types are an upland forest of sugar maple, basswood, and hemlock. The rich habitat supports a diverse assembly of plants and many bird species. The Forest Service manages the site by treating invasive species and limiting access. Amenities include opportunities for wilderness therapy and deep nature immersion. Cognitive Enrichment Areas are difficult to access, but the challenge provides more nature benefits. Overnight accommodations are absent. For more information, visit https://www.fs.usda.gov/.

FO8 LAURA LAKE/GORDON LAKE RECREATION AREA: $C. 45.698989, -88.513266. For those Forest County nature enthusiasts with minor children or limited mobility, this area offers immersion into the county's natural wonders with more access options. This federally designated recreation area features two lakes, hardwoods, and hemlocks. The site has 41 campsites, a nature trail, a bike trail, and a swimming beach. Amenities include opportunities for wilderness therapy, personal introspection, and nature immersion. Places for creativity and wonder abound. Overnight accommodations are present at the Laura Lake Campground. For more information, visit https://www.fs.usda.gov/recarea/cnnf/recarea/?recid=27933.

Kewaunee County

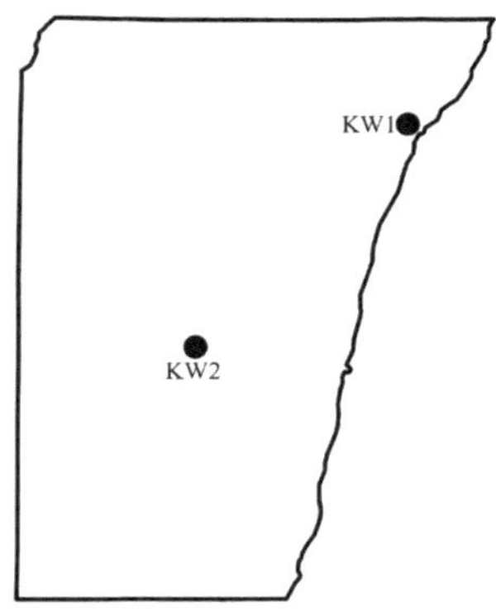

KW1 AHNAPEE STATE TRAIL: 44.612680, -87.445138. This 48-mile rail trail passes through many habitats in Kewaunee County. The relatively flat trail passes through agricultural areas, swamps, woodlots, streams, and millponds. This trail runs from Sturgeon Bay in Door County through much of Kewaunee County. Amenities include opportunities for biking and connections to access wet forests. Personal enrichment areas are simple to access, and immersion into nature provides many benefits. Overnight accommodations are absent. For more information, visit https://dnr.wisconsin.gov/topic/parks/ahnapee.

KW2 C.D. BESADNY FISH AND WILDLIFE AREA: 44.479788, -87.619655. The fish and wildlife area covers 2,600 acres in several units. Primary cover types are forest, wetlands, open marsh, upland grassy fields, prairie restorations, and rivers. The DNR manages the site using prescribed burning, invasive species treatments, and timber management. Amenities include opportunities for wildlife observation. Nature connections are plentiful, especially goal setting and problem-solving. Overnight accommodations are absent. For more information, visit https://dnr.wisconsin. gov/topic/Lands/WildlifeAreas/cdbesadny.html.

Marinette County

MR1 GREEN BAY WEST SHORES WILDLIFE AREA (PESHTIGO HARBOR UNIT) AND BLOCH OXBOW STATE NATURAL AREA: 44.994915, -87.694516. This wildlife area covers nearly 5,000 acres, and the adjacent state natural area protects 610 acres in Marinette County. Primary cover types are wet meadows, bottomland hardwoods, old-growth white pine forests, marsh, and rivers. DNR manages this site using prescribed burning, invasive species treatments, and timber management. Amenities include hiking trails, canoe trails, and berry picking. Cognitive Enrichment Areas are difficult to access, but the challenge provides more nature benefits. Overnight accommodations are absent. For more information, visit https://dnr.wisconsin.gov/topic/Lands/GBWS/peshtigoharbor.html.

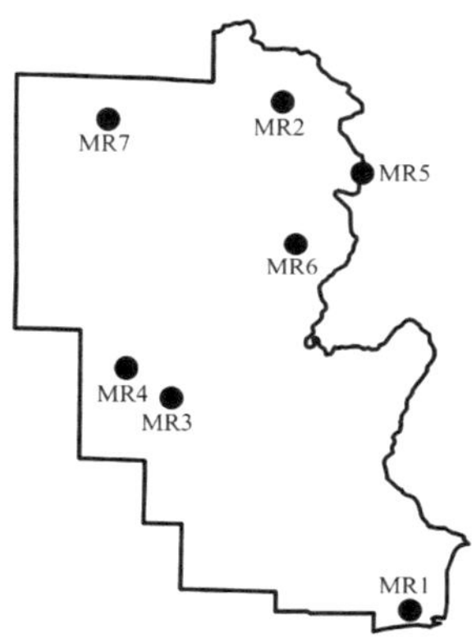

MR2 MARINETTE COUNTY FOREST: $C. 45.687089, -87.930009. Several bedrock-influenced areas are in the northeastern part of the vast Marinette County Forest—Long Slide Falls, Spikehorn Canyon, Twin Lakes Gorge, and north Branch Bedrock Glades. These four locations are prime for wilderness exploration. Many additional acres of the county forest surrounding the bedrock areas are available for exploration. Primary cover types are stunted glade communities, northern hardwood forests, and aspen. The county manages the area around the features for sustainable timber. These Wilderness Therapy and Cognitive Enrichment Areas are difficult to access, but immersion in nature provides many benefits. Overnight camping is allowed on county forest land with a permit. For more information, visit https://www.marinettecountywi.gov/departments/forestry-br/general-information/.

MR3 GOVERNOR EARL PESHTIGO RIVER STATE FOREST: $C. 45.284100, -88.138084. In central Marinette County, this forest covers 9,200 acres of land and over 3,000 acres of water. The linear forest follows the Peshtigo River and has all the native cover types for this part of the state. Eight miles of hiking trails, canoeing the Peshtigo, and fishing are primary activities. Nature connections, such as spiritual connections and personal introspection, are abundant. Overnight camping is available at Governor Thompson State Park or Twin Bridge Campground. For more information, visit https://dnr.wisconsin.gov/topic/StateForests/govearl.

MR4 GOVERNOR THOMPSON STATE PARK: $E, C. 45.323868, -88.222000. This state park covers over 3,000 acres of land and water in central Marinette County. The park has abundant water resources and has all the native cover types for this part of the state. Sixteen miles of hiking trails, swimming, water sports, and fishing are primary activities. Nature connections, such as spiritual connections and personal introspection, are abundant. Overnight camping is available at Governor Thompson State Park, with 170 sites. For more information, visit https://dnr. wisconsin.gov/topic/parks/govthompson.

MR5 MENOMINEE RIVER STATE RECREATION AREA: $C. 45.590020, -87.781283. In eastern Marinette County, along the border with Michigan, this state recreation area covers over 7,600 acres of land and water in Wisconsin and Michigan. The river is the focus of the recreation area, but it also includes many acres of uplands to explore. Visitors can find all the native cover types for this part of the state on the property. The primary activities include four miles of hiking trails, canoeing and kayaking, waterfall observation, and fishing. Nature connections, such as spiritual connections and personal introspection, are abundant. Overnight camping is available by reservation only at four canoe campsites. For more information, visit https://dnr.wisconsin.gov/topic/parks/menominee/recreation.

MR6 PIKE WILD RIVER: $C. 45.495566, -87.905587. In northeast Marinette County, this wild river land and water flows into the Menominee River north of Wausaukee. The Pike Wild River landscape has rock outcrops; most cover types are found in Marinette County. A no-cut buffer along the corridor provides for older-growth forest habitat. Canoeing and kayaking, waterfall observation, and fishing are the primary activities. Nature connections, such as spiritual connections and personal introspection, are abundant. Overnight camping is available by reservation on adjacent county forest land. For more information, visit https://dnr.wisconsin.gov/topic/lands/pikeriver.

MR7 DUNBAR BARRENS STATE NATURAL AREA: 45.662560, -88.255098. This state natural area encompasses around 1,400 acres. The primary features are outstanding examples of open barrens and pitted outwash glacial topography. Access via off-road trails gives visitors easy mobility to drive to a location and then make brief jaunts into the barrens habitat. Nature connections, such as spiritual connections and personal introspection, are abundant. The site can be an annual immersion site, especially for those with younger children. For more information, visit https://dnr.wisconsin.gov/topic/statenaturalareas/DunbarBarrens.

Menominee County

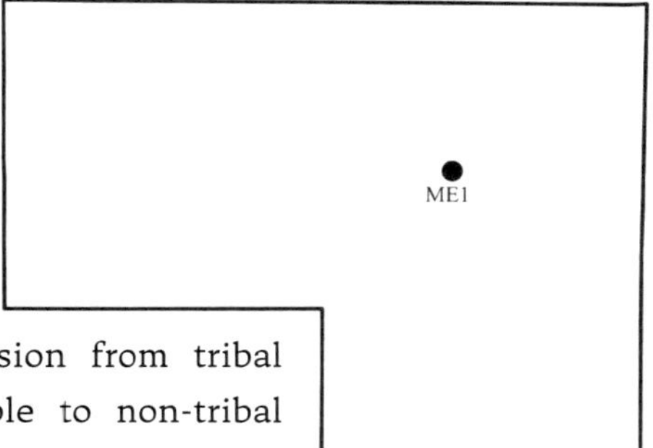

Most of Menominee County is a sovereign nation with private land limited to the Legend Lake Area. Outsiders consider most of the tribal land deep wilderness. Any access to wilderness therapy requires express permission from tribal officials. The one access available to non-tribal members is below:

ME1 WOLF RIVER PADDLE: 45.021188, -88.634882. The Wolf River is Wisconsin's most famous whitewater river. Menominee Nation opened some of the river for whitewater enthusiasts. The section that includes Sullivan Falls, the dells, and Big Smoky Falls is open for use. Primary cover types along the river are old-growth forests, northern hardwoods, hemlocks, stately white and red pines, gorge, and cliff communities. Stretches of the river require advanced whitewater skills. Overnight accommodations are present at private campgrounds. For more information, visit https://wisconsinrivers.org/wp-content/uploads/2019/08/Northeastern-Rivers-FINAL.pdf.

Oconto County

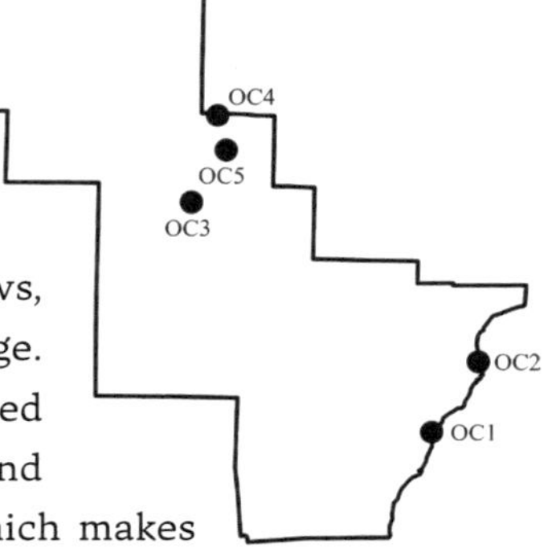

OC1 GREEN BAY WEST SHORES WILDLIFE AREA (PENSAUKEE UNIT): 44.808464, -87.917978. This unit of the wildlife area covers about 375 acres near Pensaukee. Primary cover types are wet sedge meadows, marsh, shrubs, and oak woodland on a ridge. The DNR manages the site using prescribed burning, invasive species treatments, and timber management. Amenities are few, which makes the site desirable for wilderness therapy. Overnight accommodations are absent. For more information, visit https://dnr.wisconsin.gov/topic/Lands/GBWS/pensaukee.html.

OC2 GREEN BAY WEST SHORES WILDLIFE AREA (OCONTO MARSH UNIT): 44.895838, -87.841468. This unit of the wildlife area covers nearly 1,000 acres north of Oconto. Primary cover types are wet sedge meadows, marsh, shrubs, a large impoundment, and aspen. The DNR manages the site using prescribed burning, invasive species treatments, and timber management. Amenities are few, which makes the site desirable for wilderness therapy. Overnight accommodations are absent. For more information, visit https://dnr.wisconsin.gov/topic/Lands/GBWS/ocontomarsh.html.

OC3 PESHTIGO BROOK WILDLIFE AREA: 45.093513, -88.326854. This wildlife area covers more than 2,300 acres. Primary cover types are sedge meadows, northern hardwoods, and aspen. The DNR manages the site by using prescribed burning, treating invasive species, and timber management. Amenities include opportunities for exploring the natural communities in a wilderness setting. Off-trail immersion is best for finding nature connections, especially spiritual connections and personal introspection. Overnight accommodations are absent. For more information, visit https://dnr.wisconsin.gov/topic/Lands/WildlifeAreas/peshtigobrook.html.

OC4 OCONTO COUNTY FOREST (BUTLER ROCK): 45.190015, -88.282448. The vast Oconto County Forest has an area of significant geological value. Butler Rock covers only 87 acres in size but harbors an outstanding bedrock glade scoured by the last glacier. Many additional acres of the county forest are available for exploration. Primary cover types are northern hardwood forest, oak, pine, and aspen. They manage areas around Butler Rock for sustainable timber. This Cognitive Enrichment Area is tough to access, but natural immersion provides many benefits. Overnight accommodations are absent. For more information, visit https://www.co.oconto.wi.us/.

OC5 OCONTO COUNTY FOREST (BRAZEAU SWAMP): 45.157099, -88.268216. Brazeau Swamp is a 2,200-acre area of 120-year-old white cedar in the Oconto County Forest. The swamp is dense, and past regeneration efforts have failed. They manage areas around the swamp for sustainable timber. This personal challenge area is easy to access, but the interior is maze-like and requires advanced orientation skills. Overnight accommodations are absent. For more information, visit https://www.co.oconto.wi.us/.

Shawano County

SH1 NAVARINO WILDLIFE AREA: 44.635263, -88.521376. This vast, nearly 15,000-acre wildlife area is popular with many in Shawano County. Primary cover types are upland planted prairie, ridges of oak and pine, aspen, sedge meadow, white cedar swamp, cattail marsh, impoundments, and brushland. The DNR manages the site using prescribed burning and timber management techniques to maintain cover types. Amenities include nature trails and a nature center. The solitude and personal challenges are at hand, and the challenge provides more nature benefits. Overnight accommodations are absent. For more information, visit https://dnr.wisconsin.gov/topic/Lands/WildlifeAreas/navarino.html.

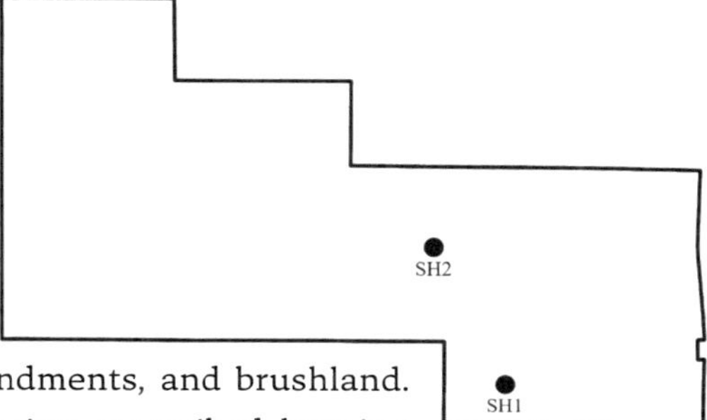

SH2 WOLF RIVER PADDLE (SHAWANO DAM TO HIGHWAY CCC BRIDGE): 44.773970, -88.619711. This six-mile paddle is an easy family paddle with few obstructions and mild rapids. Downstream sections from Highway CCC are also possibilities, but they may require more advanced skills to maneuver through the maze of bayous. Primary cover types along the river are wet meadows, bottomland hardwoods, and agricultural land. Amenities include opportunities for birdwatching and relaxation. Stretches of river

flow through peaceful solitude. Overnight accommodations are absent. For more information, visit https://wisconsinrivers.org/wp-content/uploads/2019/08/Northeastern-Rivers-FINAL.pdf.

North Central Wisconsin

Ashland County

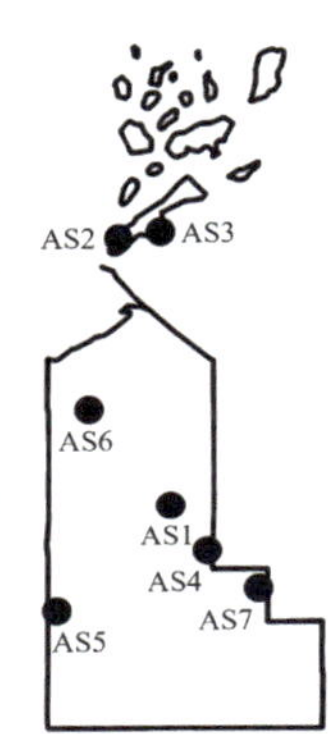

AS1 COPPER FALLS STATE PARK: $E, C. 46.351197, -90.642918. This state park encompasses more than 3,000 acres. The primary features are waterfalls, gorges, and an extensive forest of pine, hemlock, white cedar, aspen, and birch. The more than 17 miles of trails, including a 1.7-mile nature trail, provide ample opportunities for nature immersion. Two campgrounds with 55 sites are open year-round, providing a base camp for hiking, biking, fishing, and swimming. Nature connections are abundant, especially the awe of the Bad River Gorge. The site can be an annual immersion site, especially for those with younger children. For more information, visit https://dnr.wisconsin.gov/topic/parks/copperfalls.

AS2 MADELINE ISLAND WILDERNESS PRESERVE: 46.778378, -90.766740. These coordinates are for the southern unit trailhead of the Madeline Island Wilderness Preserve. This preserve encompasses 2,600 acres in the center of Madeline Island. The primary features of the preserve are two units of managed forest of aspen, birch, hemlock, fir, pine, and wetlands. The more than nine miles of trails are open to the public. No overnight options are available. Therefore, Big Bay State Park visitors can use these units for additional nature immersion opportunities. For more information, visit https://www.miwp.org.

AS3 BIG BAY STATE PARK: $E, C. 46.788502, -90.674005. This state park encompasses almost 2,350 acres. The primary features are dunes, sphagnum bogs, old-growth forests, and bluffs. The more than nine miles of trails, including a nature trail and 1.5 miles of sand beach, provide ample opportunities for nature immersion. Campgrounds with 60 sites are open year-round but limited in winter and provide a base camp for hiking, biking, fishing, and swimming. Nature connections, such as spiritual connections and personal introspection, are abundant. The site can be an annual immersion site, especially for those with younger children. For more information, visit https://dnr.wisconsin.gov/topic/parks/bigbay.

AS4 CAROLINE LAKE PRESERVE: 46.268400, -90.561658. The Nature Conservancy and the Wisconsin Department of Natural Resources own approximately 1,200 acres of this site. The primary feature is the clear, clean headwaters of the Bad River that feeds the incomparable Bad River Sloughs. They manage the forest to adapt to a changing climate and protect patches of old-growth white cedar. A rustic two-mile trail connects Caroline Lake with Twin Lakes. For more information, visit https://www.nature.org.

AS5 DAY LAKE CAMPGROUND: $C. 46.173981, -90.906031. This national forest campground features 52 sites in a towering pine forest. Amenities include opportunities for fishing and swimming, and it's a great place for elk viewing. The surrounding national forest offers many places for nature immersion. Nature connections, such as spiritual connections and personal introspection, are abundant. For more information, visit https://www.fs.usda.gov/recarea/cnnf/recarea/?recid=27725.

AS6 WHITE RIVER WILDLIFE AREA: 46.505463, -90.832690. This state wildlife area encompasses 1,120 acres. The site has much diversity. Flat uplands are mostly aspen, with scattered patches of pines. The steep clay banks harbor boreal forest species, and the floodplain has many southern Wisconsin plant species. Amenities include opportunities for nature immersion. Nature connections are plentiful, especially in improved cognition and problem-solving. Overnight accommodations are absent. For more information, visit https://dnr.wisconsin.gov/topic/Lands/WildlifeAreas/whiteriverwa.html.

AS7 ASHLAND COUNTY FOREST: 46.213044, -90.444134. This especially diverse portion of the forest encompasses more than 40,000 acres, all of which are open for nature exploration. Six designated hunter-walking trails covering 20 miles are magnificent spots for nature immersion. Primary cover types are aspen, hardwoods, and many types of wetlands.

The county manages the forest, so care must be taken if timber operations occur or during hunting season. Dispersed camping is permitted for up to 14 days. For more information, visit https://co.ashland.wi.us/forestry_recreation.

Iron County

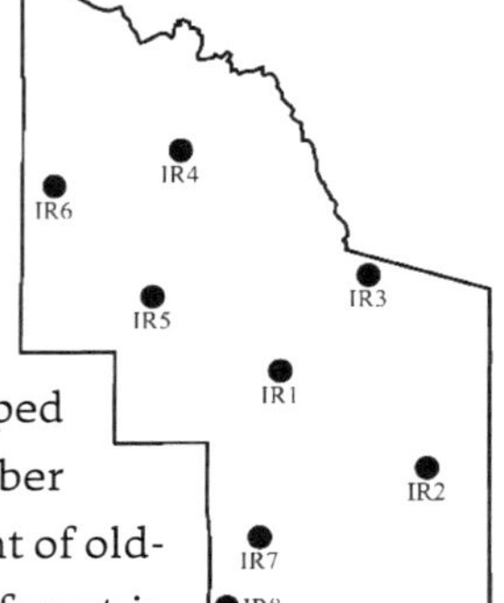

IR1 MOOSE LAKE STATE NATURAL AREA: 46.222487, -90.207180. This state natural area covers nearly 4,300 acres. It lies in the center of the south shore snowbelt. The most significant aspects are a sizeable interior forest with many acres of old-growth trees and a 270-acre undeveloped lake. The SNA Program manages the site using timber management techniques to hasten the development of old-growth characteristics. A vast area of old-growth forest is the most significant amenity. Only experienced wilderness enthusiasts should venture deep into this tract. Nature connections are plentiful, especially personal cognition and solitude. Overnight accommodations are absent. For more information, visit https://dnr.wisconsin.gov/topic/statenaturalareas/MooseLake.

IR2 MANITOWISH RIVER PADDLE: 46.130848, -90.012207. This river passes through the wilderness from the Highway 47 bridge in Manitowish downstream to Murray Landing on the Turtle-Flambeau Flowage. This section can be an enjoyable paddle for novices and younger paddlers. This paddle has different amenities. Primary cover types along the river are willow, alder, and marsh in the first portion, with patches of upland pine forest. Paddlers have opportunities for birdwatching, wilderness immersion, and viewing old-growth pine forests. Stretches of river flow through incredible solitude. Designated campsites are present. For more information, visit https://wisconsinrivers.org/wp-content/uploads/2018/02/North-Central-FINAL-1.pdf.

IR3 UNDERWOOD WILDLIFE AREA: 46.313970, -90.089951. This wildlife area covers more than 1,600 acres. Primary cover types are aspen, northern hardwoods, and grassy openings. The site was a former deer yard with cedar and hemlock, but most of those trees are gone, and the DNR now manages the site to maintain the aspen and uneven-age hardwoods.

Amenities include opportunities for immersion into the deep forest, hiking (off-trail), and berry picking. Places of solitude, reflection, and wonder are possible, and the challenge provides more nature benefits. Overnight accommodations are absent. For more information, visit https://dnr.wisconsin.gov/topic/Lands/WildlifeAreas/underwood.html.

IR4 IRON COUNTY FOREST (PENOKEE RANGE BIOLOGICAL RESERVE AREA): 46.431611, -90.339442. These coordinates are in the center of the reserve, and access can be from several directions. The site encompasses nearly 1,850 acres of passively managed county forest land. Older forests are developing in this area, and all are open for nature exploration. Visitors can explore anywhere in the reserve. Several open ridges give outstanding views of the forested range. The glacial features are ripe for overland exploration. Nature connections are plentiful, especially in wilderness therapy. This site is designated as an Important Bird Area. For more information, visit https://www.ironcounty.org.

IR5 IRON COUNTY FOREST (TYLER'S FORK MUSKEG): 46.294018, -90.376408. These coordinates are in the center of the muskeg, and access can be from several directions. The site encompasses a large acid muskeg passively managed on county forest land. The site is challenging to access, and penetration should be by experienced wilderness enthusiasts only. Visitors can explore anywhere in the muskeg. Nature connections are plentiful, especially in wilderness therapy. The site does not have any overnight accommodations. For more information, visit https://www.ironcounty.org.

IR6 IRON COUNTY FOREST (HIKE TO WATERFALLS): 46.397637, -90.507010. These coordinates are at Wren Falls. Many other hikes can lead to different waterfalls in the county. All the walks are publicly accessible on improved trails or via forest management access lanes. The sites pass through many habitats. Nature connections are plentiful, especially in wilderness therapy. The sites do not have any overnight accommodations. For more information, visit https://www.ironcounty.org.

IR7 HAY CREEK-HOFFMAN LAKE WILDLIFE AREA: 45.998522, -90.277537. This state wildlife area encompasses 13,800 acres. The site is primarily aspen, with scattered patches of hardwoods and wetlands. The DNR manages the site for white-tailed deer and ruffed grouse. Amenities include opportunities for fishing, hiking, and berry picking on the several miles of hunter-walking trails. Nature connections are plentiful, especially in wilderness therapy. Overnight accommodations are absent. For more information, visit https://dnr.wisconsin.gov/topic/Lands/WildlifeAreas/hayhoffman.html.

IR8 UPPER FLAMBEAU RIVER PADDLE: 46.065269, -90.233817. This 13.8-mile section of the North Fork of the Flambeau River is easy to paddle in one day. Paddlers should plan enough time to explore the Flambeau Wetlands SNA near the start of the journey or make a stop along the way. Amenities include opportunities for nature immersion. Nature connections are plentiful, especially goal setting and problem-solving. Overnight accommodations are absent. For more information, visit https://wisconsintrailguide.com/paddle/flambeau-river.html.

Langlade County

LA1 PETERS MARSH WILDLIFE AREA: 45.285074, -89.067952. This wildlife area covers 1,600 acres. Primary cover types are upland grassy fields, northern forests, wetlands, and fields. Maintenance of aspen is the primary timber management technique. Amenities include opportunities for camping, 10 miles of hiking on hunter-walking trails, and berry picking. The solitude and personal challenges are at hand, and the challenge provides more nature benefits. Overnight accommodations are possible. For more information, visit https://dnr.wisconsin.gov/topic/Lands/WildlifeAreas/petersmarsh.html.

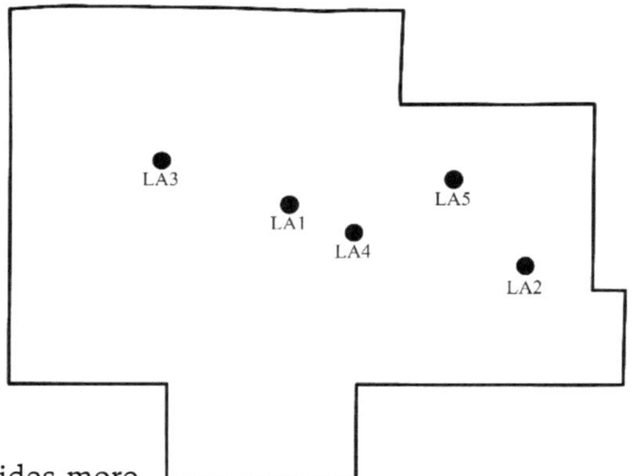

LA2 LANGLADE COUNTY FOREST (BEAR CAVES): 45.227705, -88.766456. The vast Langlade County Forest contains an area of unique geological value. The Bear Caves State Natural Area is only 50 acres in size but harbors enormous granite boulders left by the last glacier. Many additional acres of the county forest are available for exploration. Primary cover types are northern hardwood forests. The county forest manages areas

around the boulders for sustainable timber. This Cognitive Enrichment Area is hard to access, but natural immersion provides many benefits. Overnight accommodations are absent. For more information, visit https://dnr.wisconsin.gov/topic/statenaturalareas/BearCaves.

LA3 LANGLADE COUNTY FOREST (BOGUS SWAMP): 45.326002, -89.231084. The huge Langlade County Forest harbors an area of unique botanical value. The Bogus Swamp State Natural Area covers 870 acres and harbors large muskeg, with the northern portion developed into a patterned bog (only two are in the state). Many additional acres of the county forest are available for exploration. Primary cover types are black spruce swamp, muskeg, and patterned bog. The county forest manages areas for sustainable timber. This Cognitive Enrichment Area is easy to access, and natural immersion provides many benefits. Overnight accommodations are absent. For more information, visit https://dnr.wisconsin.gov/topic/statenaturalareas/BogusSwamp.

LA4 LANGLADE COUNTY FOREST (LAWRENCE LAKE): 45.258889, -88.985367. The Langlade County Forest has an undeveloped lake that is easily accessible for exploration. Lawrence Lake covers 50 acres, and the surrounding 276 acres are managed for mature trees. The steep hills have patches of hemlock mixed with maples and aspen. This Cognitive Enrichment Area is easy to access, and natural immersion provides many benefits. Overnight accommodations are absent. For more information, visit https://dnr.wisconsin.gov/topic/statenaturalareas/LawrenceLake.

LA5 WOLF RIVER PADDLE: 45.307714, -88.857989. The Wolf River is Wisconsin's most famous whitewater river. Abundant paddlers and tubers can make the river crowded. Nature enthusiasts seeking solitude must look at the options for paddling. Primary cover types along the river are marsh, alder, northern hardwoods, hemlocks, stately white and red pines, and dense white cedar swamps. Paddlers have opportunities to explore the streamside natural communities. Stretches of the river require at least intermediate whitewater skills. Overnight accommodations are present at private campgrounds. For more information, visit https://wisconsinrivers.org/wp-content/uploads/2019/08/Northeastern-Rivers-FINAL.pdf.

Lincoln County

LI1 NEW WOOD WILDLIFE AREA: 45.302365, -89.951380. This wildlife area covers 4,600 acres. Primary cover types are the nearly full range of northern forest types, wetlands, flowages, and streams. The DNR manages the site using timber management techniques to maintain the northern forest types and passively manage the white cedar swamp. Amenities include opportunities for camping during fall, off-trail hiking, canoeing, and berry picking. The solitude and personal challenges are at hand, and the challenge provides more nature benefits. Overnight accommodations are possible from September 1 to December 1. For more information, visit https://dnr.wisconsin.gov/topic/Lands/WildlifeAreas/newwood.html.

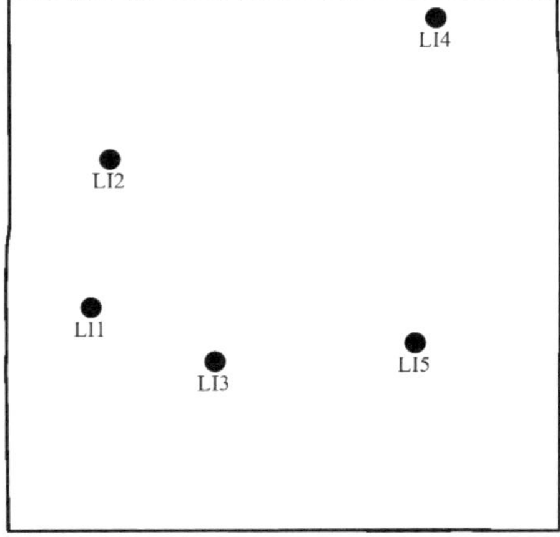

LI2 LINCOLN COUNTY FOREST (BOGS): 45.422994, -89.929830. In the western part of the vast Lincoln County Forest are three huge bog areas—Tomahawk Bog, Sparrow Bog, and Highway 8 Bog. These three locations are prime for wilderness exploration. Many additional acres of the county forest surrounding the bogs are available for exploration. Primary cover types are black spruce swamp, muskeg, northern hardwood forest, and aspen. The county forest manages the areas around the bog for sustainable timber. These Wilderness Therapy Areas are tough to access, but immersion into nature provides many benefits. Overnight camping is allowed on county forest land with a permit. For more information, visit https://co.lincoln.wi.us/forestry-land-and-parks.

LI3 BILL CROSS WILDLIFE AREA: 45.257628, -89.812340. This wildlife area covers 1,500 acres. Primary cover types are the nearly full range of northern forest types, wetlands, rock outcrops, and the Wisconsin River. The DNR manages the site using timber management techniques to maintain the northern forest types but passively manages the areas near the river.

Amenities include canoeing, fishing, off-trail hiking, and berry-picking opportunities. The solitude and personal challenges are at hand, and the challenge provides more nature benefits. Overnight accommodations are not available. For more information, visit https://dnr.wisconsin.gov/topic/Lands/WildlifeAreas/billcross.html.

LI4 MENARD ISLAND RESOURCE AREA: 45.536738, -89.564107. This resource area covers approximately 2,500 acres, including more than five miles of river frontage. The site is for day use only, providing fishing, canoeing, and hiking opportunities. Nature connections, such as spiritual connections and personal introspection, are abundant. Overnight accommodations are absent. For more information, visit https://dnr.wisconsin.gov/topic/lands.

LI5 HAYMEADOW COUNTY PARK: 45.264515, -89.552804. This park on the south shore of the Prairie River has northern forests, wetlands, and open meadows, and the adjacent Prairie River Dells has granite cliffs along the river. The county manages these sites by removing invasive species and timber management. Amenities include opportunities for hiking, mountain biking, and an accessible trail to the Dells. Nature connections are plentiful, especially in solitude. Overnight accommodations are absent. For more information, visit https://co.lincoln.wi.us/forestry-land-and-parks/page/haymeadow.

Oneida County

ON1 ONEIDA COUNTY FOREST (ENTERPRISE BLOCK): $C. 45.550230, -89.299915. Combining the Oneida County Forest with a state natural area forms the almost 1,500-acre Enterprise block. This area features old-growth hemlock and hardwood protected areas as well as a white cedar swamp surrounded by sustainably managed county forest land. Extensive, boggy wetlands are also part of the area. Ski and forest management trails cross the area and are open for hiking. This personal challenge area is easy to access, but the interior is maze-like and requires advanced orientation skills. Overnight camping is present, with 11 sites at the Enterprise Campground. For more information, visit https://www.oneidacountywi.gov/departments/fr/parks-campground/.

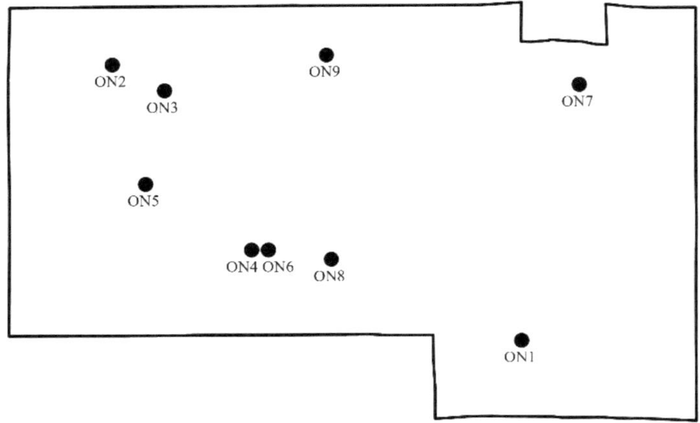

ON2 SQUIRREL RIVER PINES STATE NATURAL AREA AND SQUIRREL RIVER PADDLE: 45.836981, -89.894899. Squirrel River Pines SNA features over 1,300 acres of land harboring old-growth red pine. These natural-origin pines are a rarity in Wisconsin. Flowing through the site is the Squirrel River, which can be a leisurely paddle. Primary cover types along the river are sedge meadow, alder, red pines, and aspen. The flat water provides opportunities for exploring the streamside natural communities. Overnight accommodations are absent. For more information, visit https://dnr.wisconsin.gov/topic/statenaturalareas/SquirrelRiverPines.

ON3 TOMAHAWK RIVER PINES STATE NATURAL AREA AND TOMAHAWK RIVER PADDLE: 45.811105, -89.818359. Upper Tomahawk River Pines SNA features over 800 acres of land harboring old-growth red and white pine. These natural-origin pines are a rarity in Wisconsin. Flowing through the site is the Tomahawk River, which can be a leisurely paddle. Primary cover types along the river are sedge meadow, alder, and red and white pines. The flat water provides opportunities for exploring the streamside natural communities. Overnight accommodations are absent. For more information, visit https://dnr.wisconsin.gov/topic/statenaturalareas/UpperTomahawkRiverPines.

ON4 BEARSKIN STATE TRAIL: $T. 45.645147, -89.688025. This flat 21-mile rail trail in Oneida County passes through many habitats, including wetlands, pine forests, and hardwoods. It crosses streams and has views of many lakes. The DNR manages the site by removing invasive species. Amenities include opportunities for biking and access to portions of the county formerly unavailable. Cognitive Enrichment Areas are simple to access, and immersion into nature provides many benefits. Overnight accommodations are absent. For more information, visit https://dnr.wisconsin.gov/topic/parks/bearskin.

ON5 WILLOW FLOWAGE SCENIC WATERS AREA: $C. 45.713194, -89.845566. This scenic area covers more than 4,000 acres of water and 16,000 acres of land. The significant feature is the wild aspect seen from the water. This site has aspen and hardwood forest with patches of white pines. The DNR manages the site by using timber harvest and invasive species management. Amenities include opportunities for birdwatching, hiking, and berry picking. Nature connections are plentiful, especially personal cognition and solitude. Overnight accommodations are present, with 37 campsites. For more information, visit https://dnr.wisconsin.gov/topic/lands/willowflowage/.

ON6 WOODBORO LAKES WILDLIFE AREA: 45.644967, -89.670918. This wildlife area covers more than 3,000 acres. Primary cover types are northern hardwoods, aspen, birch, and six lakes. The DNR manages the site by treating invasive species and timber management. Amenities include opportunities for exploring the natural communities in a wilderness setting. Off-trail immersion is best for finding nature connections, especially spiritual connections and personal introspection. Overnight accommodations are absent, except for camping during the fall hunting season. For more information, visit https://dnr.wisconsin.gov/topic/Lands/WildlifeAreas/woodboro.html.

ON7 THUNDER LAKE WILDLIFE AREA: 45.815792, -89.216668. This wildlife area covers more than 3,000 acres. Primary cover types are northern peatlands, tamarack bog, sedge meadows, and lakes. The DNR manages the site by treating invasive species, prescribed burning, and timber management. Amenities include opportunities for exploring the natural communities in a wilderness setting. Off-trail immersion is best for finding nature connections, especially spiritual connections and personal introspection. Overnight accommodations are absent. For more information, visit https://dnr.wisconsin.gov/topic/Lands/WildlifeAreas/thunderlake.html.

ON8 WASHBURN LAKE SILENT SPORTS AREA (ONEIDA COUNTY FOREST): $T. 45.634705, -89.576016. This recreation area covers several thousands of acres of county forest land. The significant feature is the wild aspect seen from the trails. This site has aspen and hardwood forest with patches of red pines. The county manages the site by using timber harvest and invasive species management. Amenities include opportunities for mountain biking (11 miles), hiking (11 miles), and snowshoeing (5.5 miles). Nature connections are plentiful, especially personal cognition and solitude. Overnight accommodations are absent. For more information, visit https://www.co.oneida. wi.us/departments/fr/silent-sports-trails/.

ON9 NORTHERN HIGHLAND AMERICAN LEGION STATE FOREST: $C. 45.79944, -89.42986. A weekend camping in the Northern Highland American Legion State Forest and visiting the state natural areas provides opportunities for much of the public to benefit from nature. The nearby SNAs feature old-growth hemlock and pines, white cedar swamps, bogs, and extensive wetlands. These personal challenge areas are easy to access, but the interior of the vast wetlands requires advanced orientation skills. Overnight camping is available with hundreds of state forest campsites. For more information, visit https://dnr.wisconsin.gov/topic/StateForests/nhal.

Price County

PR1 FOULDS CREEK STATE NATURAL AREA AND ADJACENT BOGS: 45.848535, -90.073067. This state natural area covers 1,300 acres. Primary cover types are hemlock-hardwood forests, northern wet forests, and streams. In addition, within one mile to the east and west lie two huge bog areas (Riley Lake and Bootjack Bog). Passive management provides for wilderness experiences, although they need to be more amenable for novices. Places of solitude, reflection, and wonder are possible, and the challenge provides more nature benefits. Overnight accommodations are absent. For more information, visit https://dnr.wisconsin.gov/topic/statenaturalareas/FouldsCreek.

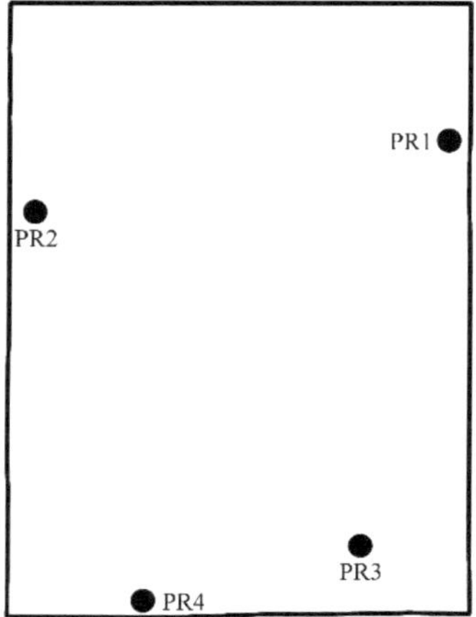

PR2 KIMBERLY CLARK WILDLIFE AREA: 45.776704, -90.643490. This wildlife area covers 8,700 acres. Wildlife managers keep 4,500 acres open for a remnant Sharp-tailed Grouse population.Primary cover types are upland grassy fields, aspen, cedar swamp, and bog. The DNR manages the site using prescribed burning, invasive species treatments, and timber management. Amenities include 17 miles of firebreaks for use as hiking trails and berry picking. Places of solitude, reflection, and wonder are possible. Overnight accommodations are absent. For more information, visit https://dnr.wisconsin.gov/topic/Lands/WildlifeAreas/kimberlyclark.html.

PR3 TIMM'S HILL COUNTY PARK: 45.450187, -90.192431. This Price County park is relatively small but contains many amenities. The primary features are the highest point in Wisconsin, plus two accessible lakes. The park is heavily wooded, dominated by hardwoods and hemlock. This park is much more amenable to younger children and those needing more accessibility than other Price County sites can offer. It has nature trails, a swimming beach, and an observation tower. Nature connections, such as spiritual connections and personal introspection, are abundant. The site can be an annual immersion site, especially for those with younger children. For more information, visit https://www.co.price.wi.us/Facilities/Facility/Details/Timms-Hill-County-Park.

PR4 JUMP RIVER PADDLE: 45.392813, -90.491438. This seven-mile paddle from County Highway I to Big Falls Park can be an exhilarating experience. Many rapids and abundant boulders are part of the scene. The river flows through Class II waters, and knowledge of water levels will be crucial for inexperienced paddlers. Nature experiences abound in this narrow and often flashy river. Primary cover types along the river are boulders, hardwood forests, and springs. Amenities include opportunities for solitude and physical challenges. Six campsites are available at Big Falls Park. For more information, visit https://wisconsinrivers.org/wp-content/uploads/2018/02/North-Central-FINAL-1.pdf.

Taylor County

TA1 PERSHING WILDLIFE AREA: 45.293769, -90.842491. This huge, nearly 7,900-acre wildlife area has two units. Primary cover types are upland brushlands, marsh, aspen, sedge meadow, and impoundments. The DNR

manages the site using prescribed burning and timber management techniques to maintain cover types. Amenities include hunter-walking trails and off-trail immersion. The solitude and personal challenges are at hand, and the challenge provides more nature benefits. Overnight accommodations are absent. For more information, visit https://dnr.wisconsin.gov/topic/Lands/WildlifeAreas/pershing.html.

TA2 JUMP RIVER PADDLE (JUMP RIVER TO SHELDON): 45.353739, -90.788868. This nine-mile paddle is a relatively easy family paddle, with few obstructions and mild rapids. Downstream sections from Sheldon are also possibilities. Primary cover types along the river are unique scoured bedrock glades with outstanding botanical values, wet meadows, bottomland hardwoods, and agricultural land. Amenities include opportunities for unique botany and relaxation. Stretches of river flow through peaceful solitude. Overnight accommodations are absent. For more information, visit https://wisconsinrivers.org/wp-content/uploads/2019/06/West-Central-FINAL.pdf.

TA3 TAYLOR COUNTY FOREST (GERTSBERGER PINES HCVF): 45.302221, -90.160169. While only 25 acres in size, this stand of old-growth pine is a destination for those seeking awe, creativity, and wonder. This area features old-growth pines and is part of the 17,500-acre managed county forest. This Cognitive Enrichment Area is easy to access with a complementary educational trail. Other portions of the county forest provide wilderness therapy challenges. Dispersed camping is allowed in the county forest without a permit. For more information, visit https://www.co.taylor.wi.us/departments/forestry-recreation-2/.

Vilas County

VI1 CATHERINE WOLTER WILDERNESS AREA: 46.230117, -89.673981. This 2,600-acre nature conservancy-owned property is open for day use. Wilderness lakes, wet forests, and northern hardwood forests are the primary features. Solitude abounds for hikers entering this immense Northwoods wilderness with 15 undeveloped lakes. Most of the fish populations in the lakes are unencumbered by fishing. Nature connections, such as spiritual connections and personal introspection, are abundant. For more information, visit https://www.nature.org/en-us/get-involved/how-to-help/places-we-protect/catherine-wolter-wilderness-area/.

VI2 VILAS COUNTY FOREST AND SPRUCE GROUSE SWAMP STATE NATURAL AREA: 46.080706, -89.197068. The 400-acre state natural area is surrounded by the Vilas County Forest, providing over 1,000 acres of wilderness. This area features upland jack pine mixed with abundant lowland pine spruce and tamarack. This Cognitive Enrichment Area is hard to access, which adds significant personal challenge values to the site. The combined properties provide cognitive improvement and wilderness therapy challenges. Wilderness enthusiasts can camp dispersedly in the county forest without a permit. For more information, visit https://dnr.wisconsin.gov/topic/StateNaturalAreas.

VI3 VAN VLIET HEMLOCKS STATE NATURAL AREA: 46.198682, -89.751348. While only 400 acres in size, this stand of old-growth hemlock, yellow, birch, and white pine is a destination for those seeking awe, creativity, and wonder. This site features an old-growth hemlock-hardwood forest and an immersion trail system. This Cognitive Enrichment Area is easy to access. Other nearby portions of the state forest provide wilderness therapy challenges. Overnight accommodations are absent. For more information, visit https://dnr.wisconsin.gov/topic/statenaturalareas/VanVlietHemlocks.

VI4 POWELL MARSH WILDLIFE AREA: 46.100776, -89.874925. This wildlife area covers 4,300 acres. Primary cover types are open peatland, marsh, wetland brush, and impoundments. The DNR manages the site by prescribed fire, invasive species control, and brush control techniques. Amenities include opportunities for hiking on the dike system and immersion into a vast open peatland. The solitude and personal challenges are at hand, and the challenge provides more nature benefits. Overnight accommodations are absent. For more information, visit https://dnr. wisconsin.gov/topic/lands/WildlifeAreas/powell.html.

VI5 NORTHERN HIGHLAND AMERICAN LEGION CANOE TRAIL: 46.018217, -89.473073. This state forest has five designated canoe routes, with some portaging through old-growth forests. Primary cover types along the lakes are wet meadows, aspen, hardwood, hemlock, and pine forest. Amenities include opportunities for birdwatching and relaxation. Stretches of the route glide through peaceful solitude. Over 100 canoe campsites are available along the route for one-night stays. For more information, visit https://silentsportsmagazine.com/2020/07/10/paddling-the-northern-highlands/.

Northwest Wisconsin

Barron County

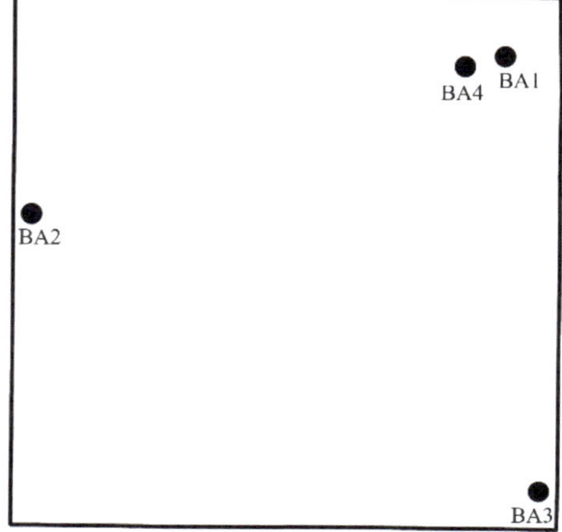

BA1 BARRON COUNTY FOREST (MIKANA UNIT TRAILS): 45.581296, -91.647153. This unit of the Barron County Forest has many trails. The topography permits mixed forest and wetland types and many wild lakes. Hiking, skiing, and multiple-use and primitive trails abound in this forest unit. Primitive camping is allowed. The county manages the trees, so care needs to be

taken if timber operations occur or during hunting season. Nature connections include wilderness therapy, problem-solving, and goal setting. For more information, visit https://www.barroncountywi.gov/county-forest.

BA2 LOON LAKE WILDLIFE AREA: 45.462967, -92.135075. This state wildlife area encompasses 3,100 acres. Primary cover types are oak, hardwoods, aspen, wetlands, and grasslands. The DNR manages the site using prescribed burning and timber management. Amenities include opportunities for fishing, hiking, and berry picking on the several miles of hunter-walking trails. Nature connections are plentiful, especially in wilderness therapy. Overnight accommodations are absent. For more information, visit https://dnr.wisconsin.gov/topic/Lands/WildlifeAreas/loonlake.html.

BA3 NEW AUBURN WILDLIFE AREA: 45.238280, -91.562334. This state wildlife area encompasses 1,100 acres. Primary cover types are mesic hardwoods, aspen, sedge meadows, and grasslands. The DNR manages the site using prescribed burning and timber management. Amenities include opportunities for birdwatching, hiking, and berry picking. Nature connections are plentiful, especially concentrations of Sandhill Cranes. Overnight accommodations are absent. For more information, visit https://dnr.wisconsin.gov/topic/Lands/WildlifeAreas/newauburn.html.

BA4 RED CEDAR RIVER PADDLE: 45.589150, -91.601741. Several sections of the Red Cedar River and even the Yellow from Barron downstream are a leisurely paddle in one day. Paddlers should plan enough time to explore features along the river, especially the cliffs near Chetek. Amenities include opportunities for nature immersion. Nature connections are plentiful, especially goal setting and problem-solving. Overnight accommodations are absent along the river. For more information, visit https://www.co.barron.wi.us/misc%20docs/maps/redcedarriver.pdf.

Bayfield County

BY1 WHITE RIVER PADDLE AND BIBON SWAMP STATE NATURAL AREA: 46.436145, -91.176324. Someone can easily paddle this section of the meandering White River in one day, with more experienced paddlers taking about five hours. Paddlers should plan enough time to make a stop or two within the vast, remote Bibon Swamp. Amenities include opportunities for deep nature immersion. Nature connections are plentiful, especially goal setting and problem-solving. Primitive camping is allowed in the Bayfield County portion of the property. For more information, visit https://dnr.wisconsin.gov/topic/StateNaturalAreas.

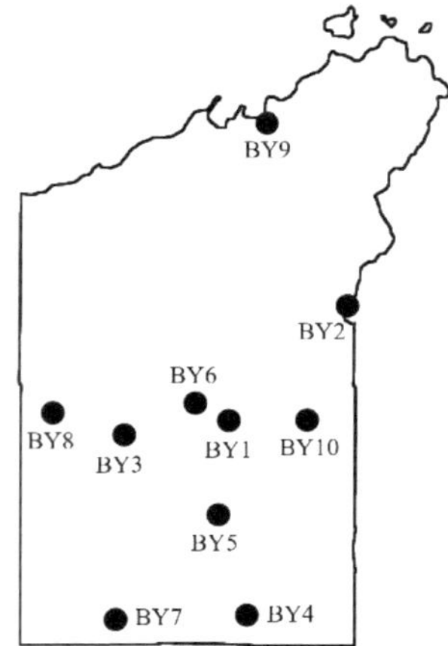

BY2 WHITTLESEY CREEK NATIONAL WILDLIFE REFUGE: 46.583970, -90.963775. This national wildlife refuge was established to protect the spawning habitat for the coaster brook trout. It encompasses about 400 acres and is an excellent location for younger children to explore nature. The associated Northern Great Lakes Visitor Center has interpretive displays and a mile-long trail and boardwalk into the wetlands. The site has much diversity. Amenities include opportunities for nature immersion. Nature connections are plentiful and significantly improve cognition and problem-solving. Overnight accommodations are nearby in Ashland. For more information, visit https://www.fws.gov/refuge/whittlesey_creek/.

BY3 CAMP NINE PINES STATE NATURAL AREA: 46.416917, -91.375741. This almost 3,000-acre research site features a natural origin: red and white pine forest with openings of frost pocket barrens. Visitors can experience a feel for the Northwoods pinery. Amenities include opportunities for hiking in a block of deep pine wood. The site abuts the Rainbow Lake Wilderness, which expands opportunities for deep nature immersion. Nature connections, such as spiritual connections and personal introspection, are abundant. Several national forest campgrounds are nearby. For more information, visit https://dnr.wisconsin.gov/topic/statenaturalareas/CampNinePines.

BY4 ROCK LAKE STATE NATURAL AREA: 46.172137, -91.143333. This almost 1,100-acre recreation site features an oak, maple, and natural origin red and white pine forest with scattered lakes. Visitors can experience immersion in an unfragmented forest. Amenities include hiking, skiing, and mountain biking opportunities in a block of deep pine wood. The site is close to other SNAs, which expands opportunities for deep nature immersion. Nature connections, such as spiritual connections and personal introspection, are abundant. Several national forest campgrounds are nearby. For more information, visit https://dnr.wisconsin.gov/topic/statenaturalareas/RockLake.

BY5 LAKE OWEN HARDWOODS AND NORTHEAST LAKE STATE NATURAL AREAS: 46.307813, -91.197084. These SNAs are close and can be explored together. The combined acreage is almost 2,400 acres. The sites feature old-growth and mature hemlock hardwoods, scattered old pines, and two large undeveloped lakes. Visitors can experience immersion into an unfragmented forest and peaceful solitude along the shores of pristine lakes. Nature connections, such as spiritual connections and personal introspection, are abundant. Several national forest campgrounds are nearby. For more information, visit https://dnr.wisconsin.gov/topic/statenaturalareas/LakeOwenHardwoods or https://dnr.wisconsin.gov/topic/statenaturalareas/NortheastLake.

BY6 UPPER WHITE RIVER FISHERY AREA AND PADDLE: 46.457139, -91.240305. Someone can easily paddle this section of the meandering White River from Pike River Road to Sutherland in one day. Numerous spring runs add diversity to the section. Visitors can spend a second weekend day at the Lake Two Pines SNA, which harbors old pines and several springs. Amenities include opportunities for nature immersion. Nature connections are plentiful, especially goal setting and problem-solving. Overnight accommodations are absent. For more information, visit https://dnr.wisconsin.gov/topic/statenaturalareas/LakeTwoPines.

BY7 TOTAGATIC LAKE WILDLIFE AREA: 46.162953, -91.391362. This state wildlife area encompasses 1,400 acres. The primary purpose of the wildlife area is wild rice production for waterfowl. Uplands have older trees near the shore and diverse age classes away from the water. The DNR manages the site for wild rice and may be closed for harvest in specific years. Amenities include opportunities for fishing, hiking, and berry picking. Nature connections are plentiful, especially in wilderness therapy. Overnight accommodations are absent. For more information, visit https://dnr.wisconsin.gov/topic/Lands/WildlifeAreas/totagaticlake.html.

BY8 BAYFIELD COUNTY FOREST (BARNES BARRENS): 46.446022, -91.510602. These coordinates are at the core of the Barnes Barrens management unit. The 11,500-acre management area focuses on maintaining open barrens, brushy areas, savanna-like barrens, and young jack pine forests, all available for nature exploration. Visitors can explore anywhere in the vast space. The county forest manages the site, so care needs to be taken if timber operations occur or during hunting season. Nature connections are plentiful, especially in wilderness therapy. For more information, visit https://www.bayfieldcounty.wi.gov/.

BY9 BAYFIELD COUNTY FOREST (GLACIAL KETTLES GEOLOGICAL AREA AND LOST CREEK FALLS SNA): 46.832791, -91.103487. These coordinates are at the trailhead for Lost Creek Falls. Visit the Bayfield County Forest site for access to the kettles area. The sites encompass almost 900 acres of passively managed county forest land. Older pine forests are developing in these areas, all of which are open for nature exploration. Visitors can explore anywhere on these two sites. An improved trail with boardwalks and bridges leads to Lost Creek Falls. The kettles area is ripe for overland exploration. Combining the two sites can make for a great weekend adventure. Nature connections are plentiful, especially in wilderness therapy. For more information, visit https://www.bayfieldcounty.wi.gov/.

BY10 WHITE RIVER FISHERY AREA AND PADDLE: 46.437742, -91.026624. This 14.9-mile section of the meandering White River is easy to paddle in one day. Paddlers should plan enough time to make a stop or two at the White River Breaks SNA, which harbors unique clay bank communities of plants. Amenities include opportunities for nature immersion. Nature connections are plentiful, especially goal setting and problem-solving. Overnight accommodations are absent. For more information, visit https://dnr.wisconsin.gov/topic/statenaturalareas/WhiteRiverBreaks.

Burnett County

BN1 CLAM RIVER PADDLE: 45.841323, -92.311762. Visitors can paddle several sections of the Clam River from Clam Dam Park to Highway F. An easy scenic section is from the park to Highway 35. This picturesque section has many bur oaks near its northern range limit. Farther downstream, the vegetation turns to pines and barrens species. More adventurous paddlers can plan longer routes. Amenities include opportunities for wildlife observation. Nature connections are plentiful, especially goal setting and problem-solving. Overnight camping is available at several nearby public campgrounds. For more information, visit https://wisconsinrivers.org/kark-paddle-guide/.

BN4
BN3
BN1
BN2

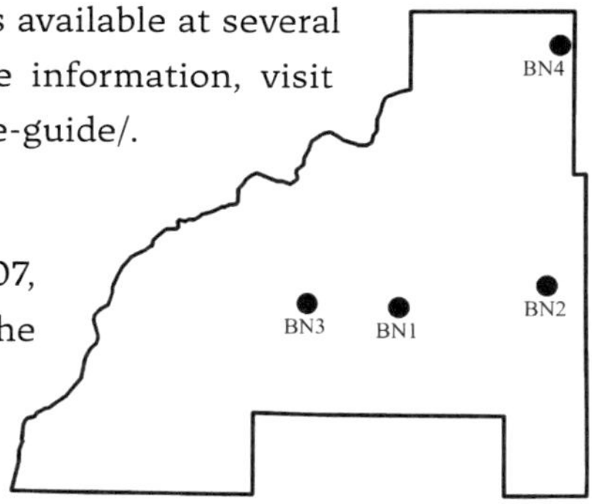

BN2 YELLOW RIVER PADDLE: 45.866207, -92.092009. Several sections of the Yellow River from Highway H to Highway 35 can be paddled. An easy scenic section is from Highway H to Emerson Road, about 20 miles. This panoramic section has many marshy wetlands, including patches of wild rice. Interspersed are upland with tall pines. Farther downstream, the vegetation turns to jack pines and barrens species. More adventurous paddlers can plan longer routes. Amenities include opportunities for wildlife observation. Nature connections are plentiful, especially goal setting and problem-solving. Overnight camping is available at several nearby public campgrounds. For more information, visit https://wisconsinrivers.org/kark-paddle-guide/.

BN3 AMSTERDAM SLOUGHS WILDLIFE AREA: 45.845053, -92.447001. This state wildlife area encompasses more than 6,000 acres. The primary purpose of the wildlife area is to re-establish the vegetation and wildlife found initially in the area. Uplands are managed for various forest age classes, and the wetlands were restored after past drainage attempts. The site has a one-mile out-and-back trail. Amenities include opportunities for fishing, hiking, and berry picking. Nature connections are plentiful, especially in wilderness therapy. Overnight accommodations are absent. For more information, visit https://dnr.wisconsin.gov/topic/Lands/WildlifeAreas/amsterdam.html.

BN4 NAMEKAGON BARRENS WILDLIFE AREA: 46.121503, -92.071313. This state wildlife area encompasses more than 6,400 acres. The primary purpose of the wildlife area is to re-establish the vegetation and wildlife initially found in the area. Uplands are managed for an open, barrens landscape. The site harbors remnant populations of sharp-tailed grouse and several other barrens species. There are two units on site separated by a few miles. Amenities include opportunities for hiking, berry picking, and observing Sharp-tailed Grouse mating. Nature connections are plentiful, especially in wilderness therapy. Overnight accommodations are absent. For more information, visit https://dnr.wisconsin.gov/topic/Lands/WildlifeAreas/namekagon.html.

Douglas County

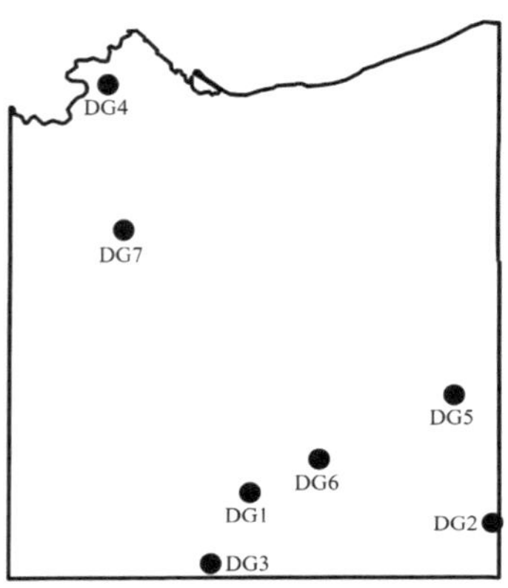

DG1 UPPER ST. CROIX RIVER PADDLE: $C. 46.253892, -91.929359. This 16.1-mile section of the St. Croix River is a leisurely one-day paddle. From the Gordon Dam to CCC Bridge Landing, the enthusiast is provided with class II rapids and a portage. Paddlers should plan enough time to stop and explore the shore locations along the way. Amenities include opportunities for nature immersion. Nature connections are plentiful, especially goal setting and problem-solving. Overnight accommodations are present but limited. For more information, visit https://www.nps.gov/sacn/planyourvisit/paddling.htm.

DG2 DOUGLAS COUNTY FOREST (OUNCE RIVER): 46.219458, -91.560362. This site is in an exciting portion of the county forest. Along the Ounce River and Coppermine Creek are ravines of talus and cliffs, contrasting the managed surrounding forest. The entire county forest area is open for nature exploration. Several timber management lanes permit easy access to interior locations, which are magnificent spots for nature immersion. Primary cover types are aspen, hardwoods, and many types of bedrock communities. Care must be taken if timber operations occur or during hunting season. Overnight accommodations are not available. For more information, visit https://www.douglascountywi.org/211/Forestry-Parks-Recreation.

DG3 DOUGLAS COUNTY FOREST (FIVE MILE BARRENS): 46.171973, -91.986051. These coordinates are in a significant part of the county forest. The barrens lie in the footprint of a massive forest fire that burned the area in 1977. This location provides insight into how pine barrens developed before the settlement. The entire county forest is open for nature exploration. Several timber management lanes permit easy access to interior locations, which are bright spots for nature immersion. The primary cover types are jack pine and northern pin oak. Care must be taken if timber operations occur or during hunting season. Overnight accommodations are absent. For more information, visit https://www.douglascountywi.org/211/Forestry-Parks-Recreation.

DG4 SUPERIOR MUNICIPAL FOREST (DWIGHT'S POINT STATE NATURAL AREA): 46.692006, -92.143663. These coordinates are centrally located within the forest, and several other access points are available. The Superior Municipal Forest comprises 4,400 acres of forest and wetlands. The best remaining example of a boreal forest (conifers and hardwood, including white and red pine, balsam, cedar, black spruce, white birch, and aspen) in Wisconsin is here. The entire municipal forest is open for nature exploration. Many miles of trails permit access into very remote peninsulas. Several recreational activities occur, so visitors need a plan to seek solitude. One remote campsite with access by water only is available on a first-come, first-served basis. Primary recreation is hiking, mountain biking, and cross-country skiing. For more information, visit https://www.ci.superior.wi.us/224/Superior-Municipal-Forest.

DG5 DOUGLAS COUNTY FOREST LEGACY AREA (DEER PRINT LAKE): 46.358216, -91.618738. This location is adjacent to Deer Print Lake in a significant part of the forest legacy land. Barrens and many shallow lakes permeate this portion of the forest legacy. This location provides opportunities for the visitor to immerse in the barrens habitat. The entire legacy area is open for nature exploration. Several timber management lanes permit easy access to interior locations, which are great spots for nature immersion. Primary cover types are red pine plantation, jack pine, and northern pin oak. Private timber companies manage the site, so care needs to be taken if timber operations occur or during hunting season. Overnight accommodations are absent. For more information, visit https://dnr.wisconsin.gov/topic/forestplanning/legacyareas.

DG6 DOUGLAS COUNTY WILDLIFE AREA: 46.288243, -91.823943. This state wildlife area encompasses more than 4,000 acres. The primary purpose of the wildlife area is to re-establish the vegetation and wildlife found initially in the area. The DNR manages an open, barrens landscape.

The site harbors remnant populations of Sharp-tailed Grouse and several other barrens species. Amenities include opportunities for hiking, berry picking, and observing Sharp-tailed Grouse mating. Nature connections are plentiful, especially in wilderness therapy. Overnight accommodations are absent. For more information, visit https://dnr.wisconsin.gov/topic/Lands/WildlifeAreas/douglas.html.

DG7 PATTISON STATE PARK: $E, C. 46.536934, -92.120043. This state park encompasses nearly 1,500 acres. The primary features are two outstanding waterfalls, gorges, old-growth forests, and wetlands. More than seven miles of trails, including a nature trail and accessible trails, provide ample opportunities for nature immersion. Campgrounds with more than 59 sites are open year-round but limited in winter and provide a base camp for hiking, biking, fishing, and swimming. Nature connections, such as spiritual connections and personal introspection, are abundant. The site can be an annual immersion site, especially for those with younger children. For more information, visit https://dnr.wisconsin.gov/topic/parks/pattison.

Polk County

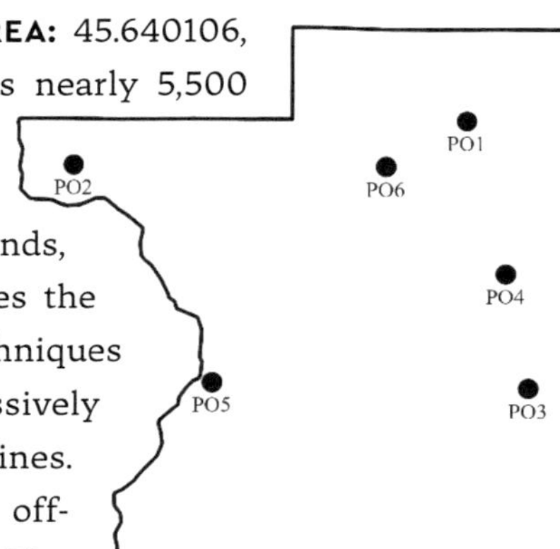

PO1 MCKENZIE CREEK WILDLIFE AREA: 45.640106, -92.300448. This wildlife area covers nearly 5,500 acres. Primary cover types are the almost full range of northern forest types (especially oak), bog, wetlands, lakes, and streams. The DNR manages the site using timber management techniques to maintain the forest types and passively manage bog and wild lake shorelines. Amenities include opportunities for off-trail hiking, fishing, and berry picking. The solitude and personal challenges are at hand, and the challenge provides more nature benefits. Overnight accommodations are absent. For more information, visit https://dnr.wisconsin.gov/topic/Lands/WildlifeAreas/mckenziecreek.html.

PO1
PO2
PO6
PO4
PO5
PO3

PO2 POLK COUNTY FOREST (STERLING UNIT): 45.600268, -92.816607. In the northwest part of Polk County, the forest lies on outwash sands deposited by the last glacier. These soils are poor, and even with advanced timber management, many patches of barrens persist. Primary cover types are red pine, jack pine, aspen, and northern pin oak. The county forest manages most areas for sustainable timber. Roads provide easy access to Wilderness Therapy Areas. Overnight camping is allowed on county forest land with a permit. For more information, visit https://co.polk.wi.us/.

PO3 JOEL MARSH WILDLIFE AREA: 45.388697, -92.219606. This wildlife area covers about 1,200 acres. Primary cover types are aspen, wetlands, marsh, and grassy uplands. The DNR manages the site using timber management techniques to maintain the aspen and prescribed burning to keep the grasslands. Amenities include wildlife observation, fishing, off-trail hiking, and berry-picking opportunities. The solitude and personal challenges are at hand, and the challenge provides more nature benefits. Overnight accommodations are not available. For more information, visit https://dnr.wisconsin.gov/topic/Lands/WildlifeAreas/joelmarsh.html.

PO4 RICE BEDS CREEK WILDLIFE AREA: 45.496450, -92.249038. This wildlife area covers over 3,100 acres. Primary cover types are oak, aspen, maple, wetlands, marsh, and streams. The DNR manages the site using timber management techniques to maintain the aspen and prescribed burning to keep the grasslands. Amenities include wildlife observation, fishing, off-trail hiking, and berry-picking opportunities. The solitude and personal challenges are at hand, and the challenge provides more nature benefits. Overnight accommodations are not available. For more information, visit https://dnr.wisconsin.gov/topic/Lands/WildlifeAreas/ricebeds.html.

PO5 INTERSTATE PARK AND NATURAL AREA: $E, C. 45.395319, -92.636679. This state park encompasses approximately 1,200 acres, of which many are designated bedrock glade SNAs. The primary feature is an impressive gorge carved by the St. Croix River. The nine miles of trails include access to outstanding views of the dalles. In this park, nature connections, such as spiritual connections and personal introspection, are abundant. The site can be an annual immersion site, especially for those with younger children. The campgrounds have over 80 sites. For more information, visit https://dnr.wisconsin.gov/topic/parks/interstate.

PO6 STRAIGHT LAKE PARK AND NATURAL AREA: $E, C. 45.597453, -92.406497. This state park, natural area, and wildlife area encompass almost 3,300 acres, of which glacial geology areas, tamarack fens, and old-growth oak woods are designated SNAs. The primary features are a tunnel channel and several lakes. The 8.5 miles of trails give access to the interior forest. There is a small swimming beach on Rainbow Lake. Nature connections, such as spiritual connections and personal introspection, are abundant in these adjacent public lands. The 10 campsites are hike-in only. For more information, visit https://dnr.wisconsin.gov/topic/parks/straightlake.

Rusk County

RU1 CHIPPEWA RIVER PADDLE (COUNTY HIGHWAY A TO BRUCE): 45.552198, -91.229995. This nine-mile paddle is an easy family paddle, with few obstructions and mild rapids. The 18-mile downstream section to the Lake Holcombe Flowage can also be a day trip. Primary cover types along the river are wet meadows, dense bottomland forests, and agricultural land. Amenities include opportunities for birdwatching and relaxation. Stretches of river flow through incredible solitude. Overnight accommodations are absent. For more information, visit https://wisconsinrivers.org/wp-content/uploads/2019/06/West-Central-FINAL.pdf.

RU2 SOUTHERN FLAMBEAU RIVER STATE FOREST AND SKINNER CREEK NATURAL AREA: 45.616412, -90.775178. Skinner Creek Hardwoods SNA features over 220 acres of land harboring old-growth northern hardwoods. These hardwoods have a vibrant ground layer, and the site provides a control for old-growth forest characteristics management on adjacent sections.

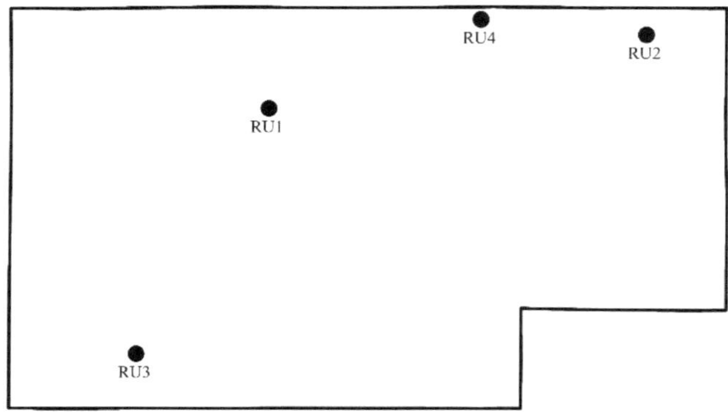

The Cognitive Enrichment Areas are close, with the road close to the site. Overnight accommodations are absent. For more information, visit https://dnr.wisconsin.gov/topic/statenaturalareas/SkinnerCreekHardwoods.

RU3 POTATO CREEK WILDLIFE AREA: 45.339827, -91.388406. This wildlife area covers more than 1,000 acres in southwestern Rusk County. Primary cover types are wetlands, wild rice marsh, cattails, northern hardwoods, aspen, and birch. The DNR manages the site by treating invasive species and timber management. Amenities include opportunities for exploring the natural communities in a wilderness setting. Off-trail immersion is best for finding nature connections, especially spiritual connections and personal introspection. Overnight accommodations are absent. For more information, visit https://dnr.wisconsin.gov/topic/Lands/WildlifeAreas/potato.html.

RU4 SILVERNAIL WILDLIFE AREA: 45.628943, -90.974772. This wildlife area covers more than 1,000 acres in north central Rusk County. Primary cover types are northern hardwoods, aspen, and hemlock. The DNR manages the site by treating invasive species and timber management. Amenities include opportunities for a deep wilderness experience because of the difficult access. Off-trail immersion is best for finding nature connections, especially spiritual connections and personal introspection. Overnight accommodations are absent. For more information, visit https://dnr.wisconsin.gov/topic/Lands/WildlifeAreas/silvernail.html.

Sawyer County

SW1 CHIPPEWA FLOWAGE STATE RECREATION AREA: 45.925203, -91.194563. The Chippewa Flowage encompasses approximately 15,000 acres, with over 230 miles of wild shoreline and 200 islands. The primary upland cover types are aspen, hardwoods, and pine. Access to most property requires a boat, but some places have road access. Eighteen primitive island campsites and two miles of hiking trails offer land access. The Wilderness Therapy Areas mostly require watercraft to experience. For more information, visit https://dnr.wisconsin.gov/topic/lands/chippewaflowage.

SW2 KISSICK SWAMP WILDLIFE AREA: 46.012171, -91.535855. This wildlife area covers nearly 1,000 acres. Primary cover types are upland grassy fields, northern forests, dense conifer swamps, and open bogs. The DNR manages the site using limited timber management techniques in the uplands and invasive species removal. Amenities include opportunities for wilderness immersion and berry picking. The solitude and cognitive improvement challenges are at hand, and the challenge provides more nature benefits. Overnight accommodations are absent. For more information, visit https://dnr.wisconsin.gov/topic/Lands/WildlifeAreas/kissick.html.

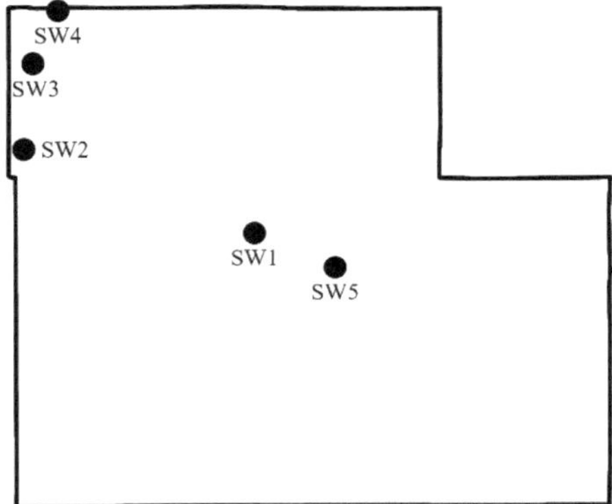

SW3 TOTOGATIC WILDLIFE AREA: 46.099847, -91.516629. This wildlife area covers 2,700 acres. Primary cover types are upland grassy fields, upland forest, cattail marsh, impoundment, and brushland. The DNR manages the site using timber management techniques to maintain the aspen. Amenities include opportunities for wilderness immersion and berry picking. The solitude and personal challenges are at hand, and the challenge provides more nature benefits. Overnight accommodations are absent. For more information, visit https://dnr.wisconsin.gov/topic/Lands/WildlifeAreas/totogatic.html.

SW4 SAWYER COUNTY FOREST (TOTOGATIC RIVER HEMLOCKS HCVF): 46.154752, -91.480529. While only 40 acres in size, this stand of old-growth hemlock and white cedar is a destination for those seeking awe, creativity, and wonder. This area features old-growth hemlock, and sustainably managed county forest land surrounds the old-growth and white cedar swamp. This personal challenge area is hard to access, but the benefits flow after locating the site. Overnight camping is not present. For more information, visit https://www.sawyercountygov.org.

SW5 CHIPPEWA RIVER PADDLE (WINTER DAM TO OJIBWA): 45.888182, -91.077200. This eight-mile paddle is an easy family paddle, with few obstructions and mild rapids. Downstream sections from Ojibwa are also possibilities but may require portages around dams. Primary cover types along the river are wet meadows, hardwoods, and pine forests. Amenities include opportunities for birdwatching and relaxation. Stretches of river flow through peaceful solitude. Overnight camping is not present. For more information, visit https://wisconsinrivers.org/wp-content/uploads/2019/06/West-Central-FINAL.pdf.

Washburn County

WB1 WASHBURN COUNTY FOREST AND TOTAGATIC HIGHLANDS HEMLOCKS STATE NATURAL AREA: 46.094279, -91.577250. While only 160 acres, this state natural area harbors old-growth hemlock, yellow birch, and white cedar. The difficult access draws those seeking awe, creativity, and solitude. This surrounding land is part of the Washburn County Forest, which is sustainably managed. This personal challenge area is tough to access, but the benefits flow after lcating the site. Overnight camping is absent within the state natural area. For more information, visit https://dnr.wisconsin.gov/topic/statenaturalareas/TotagaticHighlandsHemlocks.

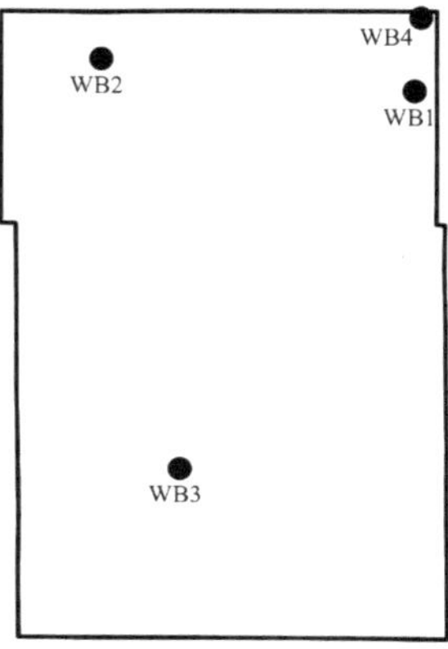

WB2 TOTOGATIC RIVER PADDLE (MINONG FLOWAGE TO THOMPSON BRIDGE ROAD) AND STATE NATURAL AREAS: 46.119264, -91.934951. This eight-mile paddle is an easy family paddle, with few obstructions and mild rapids. The takeout site needs advanced scouting, and the trip may need to go all the way to the Namekagon. Primary cover types along the river are sedge meadows, aspen, and pine forest. Amenities include opportunities for exploring old-growth red pines, pine barrens, and relaxation. Stretches of river flow through peaceful solitude. Overnight accommodations are absent. For more information, visit https://wisconsinrivers.org/wp-content/uploads/2019/08/Northwest-Rivers-FINAL.pdf.

WB3 BEAVER BROOK WILDLIFE AREA AND STATE NATURAL AREA: 45.780053, -91.846642. This 2,000-acre wildlife area lies south of Spooner. Primary cover types are upland forest, white pine, bur oak, marsh, aspen, sedge meadow, and trout stream. The DNR manages the site using timber management techniques to maintain cover types and a passively managed

300-acre state natural area. Amenities include hunter-walking trails and off-trail immersion. The solitude and personal challenges are at hand, and the challenge provides more nature benefits. Overnight accommodations are absent. For more information, visit https://dnr.wisconsin.gov/topic/Lands/WildlifeAreas/beaverbrook.html.

WB4 WASHBURN COUNTY FOREST (SILENT WOOD BENCHMARK AREA): $C. 46.153887, -91.569597. This site, bounded by the Totogatic River and the Douglas County line, has yet to see modern timber management. The county designated the site as a passive management zone. The area has old-growth aspen and a wild section of the river. The wilderness immersion area is hard to access. This portion of the county forest provides wilderness therapy challenges. Wilderness enthusiasts can camp dispersedly in the county forest with a permit. For more information, visit https://www.co.washburn.wi.us.

A Few Hours to Half-day Adventures

The Nature Pyramid states people should spend a few hours in nature every week to reap nature's benefits. Our conundrum was how to present the material in a cogent manner. If we listed every park and hiking trail in the state, our short book would be encyclopedic in content. Furthermore, many parks have neighborhood amenities, which are great for physical exercise, but many people need more natural settings other than mowed bluegrass.

In addition, Wisconsin's park and trail systems are vast. No matter how comprehensive our efforts would be, we would most assuredly miss outstanding sites that are many readers' favorites. We resolved to present hiking trails, accessible trails, lake swimming areas, dedicated snowshoe trails, and nature immersion areas with which we are familiar.

Many resources are available, especially for hiking, paddling, and parks, where the reader can obtain information. Our focus is on the benefits of the Nature Pyramid, foremost. Though many mental health benefits emanate from any walk in the woods, we focus our efforts on those sites we know.

Day adventures can catalyze curious youth imaginations. Adults can benefit by making connections or relieving stress. We present some of our favorite hiking trails for a few hours to a full day of adventure. Being trails, many have multiple access points. In this book, we listed our access points for GPS purposes. If additional resources are required, the reader may visit local or county websites.

Hiking Trails

ADAMS COUNTY: Castle Rock Flowage, Friendship. A trail along the flowage with views of the vast lake. 43.867016, -89.951895.

BARRON COUNTY: Hiawatha Park, Rice Lake. Wooded trails with heavily wooded footpaths. 45.520548, -91.724149.

BAYFIELD COUNTY: Frog Bay Tribal National Park, Bayfield. Outstanding botanical features and undeveloped Lake Superior shore. 46.907756, -90.788702.

BAYFIELD COUNTY: Big Rock Park, Bayfield. Footpaths through old red pines and along the scenic Sioux River. 46.709984, -90.925666.

BAYFIELD COUNTY: Houghton Falls State Natural Area, Bayfield. Trail with views of a sandstone gorge, waterfalls, and scenic views of the Lake Superior shoreline. 46.698622, -90.861776.

BROWN COUNTY: Neshota Park, Denmark. Trails through forest and along a river. 44.401153, -87.826431.

BROWN COUNTY: Baird Creek Parkway, Green Bay. Trails, boardwalks, and bluffs along Baird Creek. 44.504275, -87.940436.

BUFFALO COUNTY: Buena Vista Park, Alma. Outstanding views of the Mississippi River and a trail to 2nd Street in Alma. 44.323751, -91.910009.

BUFFALO COUNTY: Thrive! Park, Nelson. Steep trails along the bluff with great views of the Chippewa and Mississippi Rivers. 44.424031, -92.003479.

CALUMET COUNTY: Becker Lake, Brillion. Trails go through a prairie restoration to a lake view. 44.124735, -88.048727.

CALUMET COUNTY: Menasha Wetland Conservancy Area, Menasha. Featured are hiking trails through wetlands and pond views. 44.211897, -88.393455.

CHIPPEWA COUNTY: Chapman and Fandry Parks, Stanley. Several trails near the lake. 44.962287, -90.943571.

CHIPPEWA COUNTY: Joas Park Nature Preserve, Chippewa Falls. Trails lead visitors through prairies and lowland woods to a pond. 44.921366, -91.408454.

CLARK COUNTY: Listeman Arboretum, Neillsville. Primitive trails through a rich old forest with several views of the rocky Black River. 44.552676, -90.606119.

CLARK COUNTY: Conway Park, Thorp. Trails in a rich woodlot setting. 44.953341, -90.806140.

COLUMBIA COUNTY: Gibraltar Rock Ice Age Trail Unit, Lodi. Steep trails through dense woods and glades to an outstanding rock formation. 43.349614, -89.600576.

COLUMBIA COUNTY: Goose Pond, Arlington. Mowed trails through restored prairie with views of Goose Pond Sanctuary. 43.323045, -89.377840.

COLUMBIA COUNTY: Rowan Creek Fishery trails, Poynette. Trails along a trout stream that traverse oak savanna restoration and pines. 43.387254, -89.406454.

COLUMBIA COUNTY: Jamieson Park, Poynette. Trails lead through oak woodland to trout stream views. Rare plants. 43.385278, -89.430723.

COLUMBIA COUNTY: State Game Farm, Poynette. Featured are Wisconsin wildlife displays and different land management areas. 43.400633, -89.363410.

COLUMBIA COUNTY: Fox-Wisconsin Portage Canal, Portage. Trail along the historic canal connecting the Fox and Wisconsin Rivers. 43.549784, -89.441814.

COLUMBIA COUNTY: Otsego Marsh Preserve, Rio. This South Wisconsin Bird Alliance sanctuary has several trails through woods with great pond views. 43.402632, -89.224909.

CRAWFORD COUNTY: La Riviere Park, Prairie du Chien. Wooded trails with great views of the Wisconsin and Mississippi Rivers. 43.023622, -91.103099.

CRAWFORD COUNTY: Lawler Park, Prairie du Chien. Great for strolls along the Mississippi River. 43.054920, -91.160187.

DANE COUNTY: Stewart Park, Mount Horeb. Trails through deep woods around a pond. 43.018023, -89.744872.

DANE COUNTY: Madison School Forest, Olson Oak Woods. Old-growth oak forest with numerous trails. 42.945337, -89.588620.

DANE COUNTY: Brigham Park, Blue Mounds. Trails through rich woodland and adjacent planted prairie. 43.027082, -89.818314.

DANE COUNTY: Festge Park, Cross Plains. Savanna, prairie restoration, and rock outcrops. 43.122490, -89.685073.

DANE COUNTY: Cross Plains Ice Age Trail Unit, Cross Plains. Forest, prairie, and outstanding glacial features are highlighted here. 43.082125, -89.611346.

DANE COUNTY: Indian Lake County Park, Cross Plains. Wooded hills and trails circle the lake. 43.195583, -89.620503.

DANE COUNTY: Walking Iron County Park, Mazomanie. Native prairie and savanna restoration encompass most of the property. 43.187741, -89.823493.

DANE COUNTY: Cherokee Marsh, Madison. Trails through savanna and prairie restoration with boardwalks and marsh overlooks. 43.166256, -89.364063.

DANE COUNTY: Lussier Heritage Center and Lake Farm County Park, Madison. Interpretive Center with numerous trails through various habitats. 43.027120, -89.345170.

DANE COUNTY: Prairie Moraine County Park, Verona. Trails through diverse habitats. 42.961647, -89.513484.

DANE COUNTY: CamRock County Park, Cambridge. Wooded areas and marsh along a stream. 42.978038, -89.025059.

DANE COUNTY: Edna Taylor Conservation Park, Madison. Nature center and trails through various habitats. 43.051511, -89.316937.

DANE COUNTY: Door Creek Park, Madison. Wetlands, ponds, and open areas. 43.097111, -89.252897.

DANE COUNTY: Token Creek, Culver Wetlands Conservancy, DeForest. Trails through diverse habitats, including views of bubbling springs. 43.209311, -89.280953.

DODGE COUNTY: Astico Park, Columbus. Wooded trails with views of the Crawfish River. 43.325657, -88.956066.

DODGE COUNTY: Harnischfeger Park, Ixonia. Trails and boardwalk through wetlands to the Rock River. 43.211010, -88.544564.

DODGE COUNTY: Nitschke Park, Horicon. Effigy mounds and young forest. 43.473694, -88.695701.

DOOR COUNTY: Ellison Bay County Park, Ellison Bay. Trails through woods along the Niagara Escarpment with great lake views. 45.255215, -87.102701.

DOOR COUNTY: Door Bluff Headlands County Park, Ellison Bay. Escarpment edge trails with great lake views. 45.291573, -87.058762.

DOOR COUNTY: Little Lake Preserve, Washington Island. A 1.25-mile trail to the lakeshore. 45.413515, -86.931797.

DOOR COUNTY: Meridian County Park. Trails through the ridge and swale communities. 45.004579, -87.166319.

DOOR COUNTY: Three Springs Nature Preserve, Sister Bay. A 1.75-mile trail through the preserve. 45.178543, -87.081389.

DOOR COUNTY: White Cliff Fen Preserve, Fish Creek. A rich botanical site with trails. 45.076271, -87.274916.

DOOR COUNTY: Richter Community Forest Preserve, Washington Island. A 1.7-mile wooded trail. 45.344081, -86.942479.

DOOR COUNTY: Sturgeon Bay Ship Canal Nature Preserve, Sturgeon Bay. Trails through the ridge and swale dunes. 44.791891, -87.316894.

DOUGLAS COUNTY: Lucius Woods County Park, Solon Springs. Trails through old-growth red pines. 46.349217, -91.819043.

DOUGLAS COUNTY: Amnicon Falls State Park, Amnicon. Views of the falls and rock formations. 46.608556, -91.887579.

DOUGLAS COUNTY: Gordon MacQuarrie Wetlands, Superior. Trails, boardwalks, and observation decks in a vast wetland complex. 46.565904, -92.276070.

DUNN COUNTY: Lake Menomin Park, Menomonie. Wetlands, woods, and lake views along the trails. 44.895680, -91.890497.

DUNN COUNTY: Myran Park, Chetek. This small park has old pines growing along the Red Cedar River. 45.192017, -91.703000.

DUNN COUNTY: Bjornson Education Center, Menomonie School Forest, Lucas. Trails through rich woods and streams. 44.930531, -92.080744.

EAU CLAIRE COUNTY: Beaver Creek Reserve, Fall Creek. Diverse habitats along the Eau Claire River with wetland overlooks. Nature center. 44.814126, -91.270770.

EAU CLAIRE COUNTY: Putnam Park, Eau Claire. This urban park has many quiet trails featuring outstanding botany. 44.794509, -91.495174.

EAU CLAIRE COUNTY: L.L. Phillips Park, Eau Claire. Trails through woods and native prairie remnants. 44.820878, -91.377892.

EAU CLAIRE COUNTY: Lowes Creek County Park, Eau Claire. Oak woods and views of Lowes Creek. 44.756592, -91.472392.

EAU CLAIRE COUNTY: Carson Park, Eau Claire. This developed urban park has several trails through natural vegetation. 44.801749, -91.526508.

FOND DU LAC COUNTY: South Woods Nature Preserve, Ripon. Trails lead through some of the oldest trees in the county. 43.832383, -88.851331.

FOND DU LAC COUNTY: Waupun Maple Woods, Waupun. Many trails through rich maple woodland. 43.644092, -88.756059.

FOND DU LAC COUNTY: Gottfried Prairie and Arboretum, UW–Fond du Lac Campus, Fond du Lac. Trails through restored prairie and wetlands. 43.790095, -88.411363.

FOND DU LAC COUNTY: Hobbs Woods, Byron. Trails through woods and along Parsons Creek. 43.693573, -88.471870.

FOND DU LAC COUNTY: Riggs County Park, Ripon. Wetland restorations and an observation deck highlight the hikes. 43.838380, -88.820938.

FOND DU LAC COUNTY: Archer Thomas Olsen Trail, Fond du Lac. A trail through the Supple Marsh wetlands. 43.800911, -88.455310.

FOREST COUNTY: Stevens Lake Trails, Alvin. Mesic woods and old-growth hemlock are features. 45.925823, -88.719180.

FOREST COUNTY: Michigan Rapids Trail, Laona. Hike along the Peshtigo River to the rapids. 45.561972, -88.495248.

FOREST COUNTY: Ed's Lake National Recreation Trail, Crandon. The trail traverses many habitats. 45.469671, -88.791651.

GRANT COUNTY: Hallock Demonstration Forest, Millville. Hike the logging roads through the deciduous forest. 43.013939, -90.963715.

GRANT COUNTY: Memorial Park, Platteville. Trails along the Roundtree Branch. 42.730042, -90.500583.

GREEN COUNTY: Forest Prairie Park, Monroe. Recovering forests and native prairie are features. 42.617321, -89.584276.

GREEN LAKE COUNTY: Norwegian Bay Conservancy, Green Lake. Trail and boardwalk into wetlands and Green Lake. 43.811001, -89.041437.

GREEN LAKE COUNTY: Sunnyside Conservancy, Green Lake. Wetland restoration site. 43.839661, -88.925317.

IOWA COUNTY: Tower Hill State Park $, Spring Green. Trails to historic shot tower and along the Wisconsin River. 43.146518, -90.047510.

IOWA COUNTY: Dodgeville Arboretum, Dodgeville. A short trail through a woodlot. 42.962494, -90.143638.

IRON COUNTY: Potato River Falls, Gurney. Short trails to several outstanding waterfalls. 46.463432, -90.529339.

JACKSON COUNTY: Merlin Lambert County Park, Pittsville. Trails through pines and along the flowage. 44.304253, -90.502392.

JACKSON COUNTY:: Perry Creek Trail, Black River Falls. Old pines and sandstone cliffs are features along these trails. 44.266797, -90.860773.

JACKSON COUNTY: Lunda Community Park, Black River Falls. Trails go into the wooded area from the developed park. 44.294935, -90.870086.

JEFFERSON COUNTY: Holzhueter Farm State Park, Waterloo. The farmland is in the process of being converted to prairie and savanna. 43.175853, -88.909651.

JEFFERSON COUNTY: Aztalan State Park $, Jefferson. Unlike most trails in this book, the trails here focus on culture. 43.065228, -88.864681.

JEFFERSON COUNTY: Carlin Weld County Park, Palmyra. Trails through wetlands and prairie restoration. 42.906173, -88.542211.

JEFFERSON COUNTY: Korth Park, Lake Mills. Oak savanna and prairie restoration are features. 43.073799, -88.956044.

JEFFERSON COUNTY: Upper Rock Lake Park, Lake Mills. Nature trail through a woodlot. 43.098951, -88.929211.

JEFFERSON COUNTY: Rock River Park, Fort Atkinson. Trails through woods and wetlands. 42.928837, -88.860107.

JUNEAU COUNTY: Rocky Arbor State Park $, Wisconsin Dells. Trails through majestic pines and many rock formations. 43.643268, -89.804406.

JUNEAU COUNTY: Kennedy County Park, New Lisbon. The bottomland forest along the Lemonweir River is the main feature. 43.915933, -90.177491.

JUNEAU COUNTY: Juneau County Wilderness County Park, Necedah. Pine barrens and views of Petenwell Flowage are features. 44.154271, -89.985241.

KENOSHA COUNTY: Bristol Woods County Park, Bristol. More than four miles of wooded trails. 42.531479, -88.000796.

KENOSHA COUNTY: Salem Community Park, Salem. Wooded trails. 42.535377, -88.118510.

KENOSHA COUNTY: Seno K\RLT Conservancy, Burlington. A private land conservancy open for hiking. 42.604776, -88.302987.

KEWAUNEE COUNTY: Bruemmerville Park, Algoma. A trail along Silver Creek. 44.608021, -87.472164.

LA CROSSE COUNTY: Holland Sand Prairie State Natural Area, Holmen. Trails through the high-quality native sand prairie. 43.970051, -91.294673.

LA CROSSE COUNTY: Mindoro County Park, Mindoro. Maple forest is the highlight of this hike. 44.016100, -91.115158.

LA CROSSE COUNTY: Greens Coulee Savanna Oaks, Onalaska. More than one mile of trail through conservancy savanna restoration. 43.897614, -91.195357.

LAFAYETTE COUNTY: Belmont Mound State Park $, Platteville. Trails go through rich ground layers under maples. 42.766630, -90.351350.

LAFAYETTE COUNTY: Blackhawk Memorial Park, Woodford. Trails along the Pecatonica River with large cottonwoods. 42.661238, -89.876148.

LAFAYETTE COUNTY: Black Bridge Park, Darlington. A trail along the Pecatonica River. 42.685123, -90.120701.

LINCOLN COUNTY: Council Grounds State Park $, Merrill. Trails along the Wisconsin River and through old-growth pines. 45.184626, -89.734958.

LINCOLN COUNTY: Camp New Wood County Park, Merrill. Wooded trails along the Wisconsin River. 45.286336, -89.791451.

LINCOLN COUNTY: Hay Meadow County Park, Merrill. Also, visit the nearby Prairie River Dells Scenic Area. 45.265195, -89.550642.

LINCOLN COUNTY: Merrill Memorial Forest Wildlife Area, Merrill. More than 900 acres of forest and wetlands are open for hiking. 45.275279, -89.587437.

LINCOLN COUNTY: Bradley Park, Tomahawk. Miles of trail through old-growth pines. 45.469153, -89.739314.

MANITOWOC COUNTY: Cherney Maribel Caves County Park, Maribel. Cliffs, rich ground layers, plants, old-growth cedars, and cave tours. 44.283807, -87.777128.

MANITOWOC COUNTY: Manitou Park, Manitowoc. Riverside trails through woods and wetlands. 44.097406, -87.694409.

MANITOWOC COUNTY: Camp Vits Trails, Manitowoc. Predominately a mountain bike trail, open for hiking along the Manitowoc River. 44.088021, -87.719547.

MARATHON COUNTY: Cherokee Park, Colby. Trails along the Rib River through old-growth hemlocks. 44.902749, -90.217861.

MARATHON COUNTY: Dells of the Eau Claire County Park, Aniwa. Outstanding geology and botany along the trails. 45.003526, -89.339438.

MARATHON COUNTY: Rib Falls County Park, Edgar. Trails through woods to a cascade of the Big Rib River. 44.973827, -89.906457.

MARATHON COUNTY: Isle of Ferns Park, Wausau. Excellent views of the Wisconsin River. 44.953110, -89.628913.

MARATHON COUNTY: Paff Woods Nature Preserve, Wausau. Trails get close to old-growth hemlocks and white pines. 44.955795, -89.605082.

MARATHON COUNTY: Bitzke Bird Walk and Wildlife Refuge, Aniwa. Trails through wetlands to observation decks. 45.091716, -89.345838.

MARATHON COUNTY: McClintock County Park, Athelstane. Hike through mature forest to rapids on the Peshtigo River. 45.477341, -88.326641.

MARINETTE COUNTY: Twelve Foot Falls Park, Dunbar. The primary feature is the waterfalls, but trails go through mature woods. 45.580285, -88.140303.

MARINETTE COUNTY: Goodman County Park, Athelstane. Wooded trails and waterfalls. 45.523266, -88.333523.

MARINETTE COUNTY: Veterans Memorial Park, Crivitz. Old pines and Veterans waterfall. 45.268474, -88.212617.

MARINETTE COUNTY: Thunder Mountain Overlook Park, Crivitz. Trails with great views of the surrounding land. 45.305638, -88.297568.

MARINETTE COUNTY: Harmony Arboretum, Peshtigo. Trails through rich woods. 45.098758, -87.799321.

MARINETTE COUNTY: Menominee River County Park, Wausaukee. Wooded trails with views of the Menominee River. 45.279784, -87.702877.

MARINETTE COUNTY: Hemlock Curve Nature Trail, Peshtigo. More than two miles of trail near the Peshtigo River. 45.023551, -87.728487.

MARQUETTE COUNTY: Montello City Park, Montello. Hike next to the lake. 43.797791, -89.327985.

MILWAUKEE COUNTY: Cudahy Nature Preserve, Oak Creek. Trails through a rich ground layer of flowers. 42.929906, -87.904891.

MILWAUKEE COUNTY: Grant Park, Milwaukee. Great views of Lake Michigan from the trails. 42.918432, -87.844423.

MILWAUKEE COUNTY: Warnimont Park, Cudahy. Great views of Lake Michigan from the trails. 42.933602, -87.849787.

MILWAUKEE COUNTY: Greenfield Park, West Allis. Oak Leaf Trail around the wetland. Closed in 2024, open 2025. 43.009121, -88.064289.

MILWAUKEE COUNTY: Kohl Park, Milwaukee. Wooded trail off Fairy Chasm Drive. 43.185083, -88.021293.

MILWAUKEE COUNTY: Lincoln Park, Milwaukee. Trails along the Milwaukee River. 43.104546, -87.926774.

MILWAUKEE COUNTY: Underwood Creek Parkway, Deer Creek Trail, Milwaukee. Wooded trails along the stream. 43.023783, -88.067001.

MILWAUKEE COUNTY: Urban Ecology Center at Riverside Park, Milwaukee. Numerous trails along the river. 43.068712, -87.891493.

MILWAUKEE COUNTY: Schlitz Audubon Center, Bayside. Wooded trails, nature center, and lake views. 43.176471, -87.889674.

MONROE COUNTY: Amundson Park, Sparta. Wooded trails near the La Crosse River. 43.930601, -90.842325.

OCONTO COUNTY: Chute Pond County Park, Mountain. Trails through woods and bedrock glades with a view of the lake. 45.133162, -88.448042.

OCONTO COUNTY: North Bay Shore County Park, Oconto. Green Bay shoreland and wetlands are features. 44.965028, -87.783369.

OCONTO COUNTY: Oconto Breakwater Park, Oconto. The breakwater goes a significant distance into Green Bay. 44.895433, -87.830211.

ONEIDA COUNTY: Rhinelander Riverwalk, Rhinelander. Trail near the Pelican River. 45.628719, -89.417145.

ONEIDA COUNTY: Yawkey Forest Reserve, Hazelhurst. More than 400 acres on the shores of Katherine Lake are open for hiking. 45.813445, -89.694446.

OUTAGAMIE COUNTY: Mosquito Hill Nature Center, New London. Trails through bottomland forests, prairie restorations, and uplands with pond views. 44.386760, -88.707136.

OUTAGAMIE COUNTY: Plamann Park, Appleton. Children's farm and abundant trails. 44.324807, -88.388494.

OUTAGAMIE COUNTY: Appleton Memorial Park, Appleton. A trail along the pond with piers. 44.291479, -88.379535.

OZAUKEE COUNTY: Cedarburg Bog State Natural Area, Saukville. A trail through forested wetlands to a lake pier. 43.407132, -87.998028.

OZAUKEE COUNTY: Lion's Den Gorge Nature Preserve, Grafton. Cedar gorge and restored wetlands are features. 43.337874, -87.887907.

OZAUKEE COUNTY: Virmond Park, Mequon. Bluff top views of Lake Michigan. 43.210567, -87.903957.

OZAUKEE COUNTY: Waubedonia Park, Fredonia. Wooded trails along the river. 43.469549, -87.973816.

OZAUKEE COUNTY: Tendick Nature Park, Saukville. Old farm with trails. 43.419184, -87.955801.

OZAUKEE COUNTY: Riveredge Nature Center, Saukville. Nature center and trails through various habitats. 43.439972, -88.024272.

OZAUKEE COUNTY: Forest Beach Migratory Preserve, Port Washington. The site is managed to benefit migratory species. 43.458194, -87.815296.

OZAUKEE COUNTY: Huiras Lake State Natural Area, Fredonia. A trail through grassland restoration to a bog lake. 43.52195, -87.98335.

OZAUKEE COUNTY: Kurtz Woods State Natural Area, Grafton. Legal access is located at a gravel walkway between two homes. 43.363182, -87.951882.

PEPIN COUNTY: Arkansaw Stream Park, Arkansaw. A trail along a creek with numerous sandstone cliffs. 44.637589, -92.032496.

PIERCE COUNTY: Martell County Forest, Martell. Twenty-eight acres of managed forest with trails. 44.829714, -92.402308.

PIERCE COUNTY: Pierce County Educational Forest, Spring Valley. Selectively managed forest with trails. 44.830929, -92.338343.

PIERCE COUNTY: Kinnickinnic River Trail, River Falls. Trail along the river with savanna oaks. 44.851068, -92.636626.

PIERCE COUNTY: Halverson Park, River Falls. Trails through various habitats. 44.841168, -92.601261.

POLK COUNTY: Standing Cedars State Natural Area, Osceola. Restored prairie and riverside bluffs are features. 45.289164, -92.743161.

POLK COUNTY: Schillberg Park, Osceola. Various habitats and stream views. 45.329905, -92.684861.

POLK COUNTY: Wilke Glen and Cascade Falls, Osceola. A short trail to an outstanding waterfall. 45.319867, -92.706013.

POLK COUNTY: Osceola State Fish Hatchery, Chisago Loop Trail, Osceola. A trail through one of the best bedrock glades in the state. 45.348894, -92.682410.

POLK COUNTY: Ahlgren Wildlife Preserve and Recreation Area, Balsam Lake. Various habitats on 180 acres. 45.384991, -92.469219.

POLK COUNTY: Wert Family Nature Preserve, St. Croix Falls. Wooded trails lead to a vista overlooking the St. Croix River. 45.422572, -92.638423.

PORTAGE COUNTY: Standing Rocks County Park, Stevens Point. Trails through overgrown savanna with numerous large glacial rocks. 44.430952, -89.403319.

PORTAGE COUNTY: Schmeeckle Reserve, Stevens Point. Education center with many trails around the lake. 44.541218, -89.562868.

PORTAGE COUNTY: Steinhaugen Recreation Area, Custer. Trails through various habitats. 44.637222, -89.471919.

PRICE COUNTY: Big Falls County Park, Kennan. Outstanding rocky cascades on the Jump River. 45.406607, -90.637650.

PRICE COUNTY: Phillips School Forest, Phillips. More than three miles of trails through the woods. 45.708122, -90.350168.

RACINE COUNTY: Sander's Park and Campground, Mount Pleasant. Several trails through the wooded natural area with outstanding botany. 42.674528, -87.844215.

RACINE COUNTY: Bushnell County Park, Burlington. Trails through woods to the Fox River. 42.671132, -88.262811.

RACINE COUNTY: Cliffside Park, Racine. Wooded area along the shore of Lake Michigan. 42.818121, -87.825482.

RACINE COUNTY: Renak-Polak Maple-Beech Woods State Natural Area, Racine. Primitive trails in rich woods. 42.808553, -87.866799.

RACINE COUNTY: Nicholson Wildlife Refuge, Franksville. Trails and boardwalks through the wetlands. 42.799806, -87.904951.

RACINE COUNTY: W.R. Wadewitz Nature Camp, Burlington. Trails through various habitats. 42.750226, -88.230679.

RACINE COUNTY: Saller Woods, Rochester. Take the Seven Waters Bike Trail through woods, wetlands, and adjacent to bogs. 42.722620, -88.224059.

RACINE COUNTY: Pritchard Park, Racine. Trails through woods. 42.698839, -87.838507.

RACINE COUNTY: Wehmhoff Woodland Preserve, Burlington. Wooded trails over glacial features. 42.690592, -88.281915.

RICHLAND COUNTY: Ash Creek Community Forest, Richland Center. Four miles of primitive wooded trails. 43.291277, -90.419850.

RICHLAND COUNTY: Pier County Park, Rockbridge. Even though the park is small, it has outstanding scenic value. 43.445981, -90.363599.

RICHLAND COUNTY: Miner Hill Trail Park, Richland Center. Wooded trails over steep hills. 43.335745, -90.376755.

RICHLAND COUNTY: Krouskop Park, Richland Center. A trail on the levee. 43.345793, -90.389040.

ROCK COUNTY: Beckman Mill Park, Beloit. Short trails through oak opening restorations. 42.511862, -89.170106.

ROCK COUNTY: Carver-Roehl County Park, Clinton. Trails are adjacent to the stream with rock outcrops and wildflowers. 42.606137, -88.827384.

ROCK COUNTY: Gibbs Lake Park, Janesville. Trails through various habitats. 42.787618, -89.175299.

ROCK COUNTY: Happy Hollow Park, Janesville. This 200-acre park has numerous trails. 42.596643, -89.038968.

ROCK COUNTY: Lee Park, Janesville. Woodlot trails are the feature. 42.508057, -88.862564.

ROCK COUNTY: Magnolia Bluff Park, Evansville. Native prairie, rock outcrops, and oak woodland. 42.730432, -89.358365.

ROCK COUNTY: Riverside Park, Janesville. Devil's Staircase Trail overlooks the Rock River. 42.716761, -89.041371.

ROCK COUNTY: Peace Park, Janesville. Trails go through the woods and connect with Rockport Park. 42.671553, -89.065034.

ROCK COUNTY: Sheiffer Park, Janesville. Wooded trails are the feature. 42.720620, -88.966352.

ROCK COUNTY: Big Hill Park, Beloit. Steep wooded trails overlooking the Rock River. 42.556398, -89.051217.

RUSK COUNTY: Josie Creek County Park, Ladysmith. Wooded trails along Josie Creek. 45.520206, -90.965794.

RUSK COUNTY: Greenwood Park, Ladysmith. The only development in this 40-acre woods is the scenic trail. 45.469306, -91.083004.

RUSK COUNTY: O.J. Falge Park, Ladysmith. Featured is a boardwalk through the wetlands. 45.460471, -91.109874.

RUSK COUNTY: Ladysmith School Forest, Ladysmith. Trails through woods, including a boardwalk into a bog. 45.499104, -91.090139.

SAUK COUNTY: Natural Bridge State Park $, North Freedom. Trails through woodland to a natural rock bridge. 43.344109, -89.931167.

SAUK COUNTY: Parfrey's Glen State Natural Area $, Merrimac. Trail leads into a gorge with a stream. 43.409595, -89.636961.

SAUK COUNTY: Mirror Lake State Park $, Baraboo. Many trails into sandstone gorges, some with old-growth pines. 43.561579, -89.808107.

SAUK COUNTY: Hemlock County Park, LaValle. Hemlock trees festoon the cliffs. 43.594374, -90.137911.

SAUK COUNTY: Lake Redstone Park, LaValle. Trails go to a waterfall. 43.584046, -90.089696.

SAUK COUNTY: Smith Conservancy, Reedsburg. Trails through the woods along the Baraboo River. 43.529499, -90.012580.

SAUK COUNTY: Hartje Outdoor Learning Center, Reedsburg. Managed demonstration forest with hiking trails. 43.570784, -90.039096.

SAUK COUNTY: Moely Prairie, Prairie du Sac. A native sand prairie with numerous trails. 43.290905, -89.750365.

SAWYER COUNTY: Uhrenholdt Memorial Forest, Seeley. Trails through managed and unmanaged pine forests. 46.120707, -91.359214.

SAWYER COUNTY: Fish Hatchery County Park, Hayward. Trails through various habitats. 46.018929, -91.433823.

SHAWANO COUNTY: Hayman Falls County Park, Marion. Trails through woods to river cascades. 44.747544, -88.843392.

SHAWANO COUNTY: Gibson Island Trail, Clintonville. Nature trail with many lake vistas and giant pines. 44.692935, -88.660869.

SHAWANO COUNTY: Kuckuk Park, Shawano. A trail along the Wolf River. 44.767902, -88.617396.

SHEBOYGAN COUNTY: Sheboygan Indian Mound Park, Sheboygan. Trails to mounds in a wooded setting. 43.695429, -87.717067.

SHEBOYGAN COUNTY: Balzer Wilderness Park, Sheboygan. Wooded trails along a stream. 43.690755, -87.712424.

SHEBOYGAN COUNTY: Ellwood H. May Environmental (Maywood) Park. Trails and overlooks for many habitats. 43.782560, -87.756448.

SHEBOYGAN COUNTY: H.M. Meyer Nature Park, Plymouth. Trails with multiple views of the Mullet River. 43.743260, -87.984586.

ST. CROIX COUNTY: Mound Park Trails, River Falls. Wooded trails and prairie openings. 44.865784, -92.612583.

ST. CROIX COUNTY: Glover Park, Hudson. Trails through various habitats. 44.923406, -92.696611.

ST. CROIX COUNTY: Carpenter Nature Center, River Falls. A nature center and trails through various habitats. 44.909202, -92.744075.

ST. CROIX COUNTY: Glen Hills County Park, Glenwood City. Numerous trails through various habitats. 45.009378, -92.171005.

ST. CROIX COUNTY: Kinnickinnic County Forest, River Falls. Trails through 80 acres of pine plantation. 44.887690, -92.530533.

ST. CROIX COUNTY: Parnell Prairie Preserve, Somerset. Primitive trails through the native and restored prairie. 45.124868, -92.723116.

ST. CROIX COUNTY: Birkmose Park, Hudson. Short trails with river views. 44.967766, -92.754251.

ST. CROIX COUNTY: Eckert Blufflands Park, North Hudson. A new park with planned hiking trails. 45.022389, -92.750233.

TAYLOR COUNTY: Gilman Scout Park, Gilman. Wooded trails along the Yellow River. 45.162072, -90.808625.

TREMPEALEAU COUNTY: Pietrek Park, Arcadia. Bottomland forest trails along the Trempealeau River. 44.297534, -91.460788.

TREMPEALEAU COUNTY: Fireman's Park, Galesville. A trail along the river with a fishing pier. 44.100962, -91.351842.

VERNON COUNTY: Esofea County Park, Westby. Trails through wooded hills. 43.630869, -90.973350.

VERNON COUNTY: Tunnelville Cliffs State Natural Area, La Farge. More than two miles of wooded and wetland trails. 43.564072, -90.675088.

VERNON COUNTY: Kooyumjian Lost Creek Forest, Yuba. Trails through pine plantations and deciduous woods. 43.567211, -90.491340.

VERNON COUNTY: Davidson Park, Westby. Wooded trails in an urban setting. 43.656705, -90.861655.

VERNON COUNTY: Romance Woods, Genoa. Wooded trails on Mississippi Valley Conservancy land. 43.568015, -91.121899.

VILAS COUNTY: Lac Vieux Desert Park, Phelps. Short trails through old-growth pines to the headwaters of the Wisconsin River. 46.122704, -89.155354.

VILAS COUNTY: Marshall Wildlife Conservation Area, Lac du Flambeau. Wooded trails lead to a beaver pond observation deck. 45.908358, -89.982709.

WALWORTH COUNTY: Lulu Lake State Natural Area. Trails go through prairie restoration to bogs, fen, and Lulu Lake's shore. 42.822939, -88.443314.

WALWORTH COUNTY: Beulah Bog State Natural Area, East Troy. Trails go through the oak opening to a bog boardwalk. 42.818739, -88.414207.

WALWORTH COUNTY: Price Park Conservancy, Elkhorn. Trails through various habitats. 42.724934, -88.470190.

WALWORTH COUNTY: Natureland Park, Whitewater. Many habitat types along the trails. 42.742964, -88.715376.

WALWORTH COUNTY: White River County Park, Lake Geneva. Grassland restoration and streamside trails. 42.634209, -88.379392.

WALWORTH COUNTY: Kishwauketoe Nature Conservancy, Williams Bay. Prairie restoration and a boardwalk are highlights. 42.583104, -88.540314.

WALWORTH COUNTY: Wildwood Park, Darien. Wooded trails to several ponds. 42.599217, -88.700195.

WALWORTH COUNTY: Springs Park, Delavan. Wooded trails to streams and springs. 42.627857, -88.652007.

WALWORTH COUNTY: Petersen Island Woods Preserve, Elkhorn. Trails through the woodland preserve. 42.772609, -88.569825.

WASHBURN COUNTY: Hunt Hill Audubon Sanctuary, Sarona. Trails through an old-growth oak forest. 45.718008, -91.739134.

WASHBURN COUNTY: Totogatic Park, Minong. Lakeside trails and pine forest. 46.138543, -91.940823.

WASHBURN COUNTY: Stone Lake Community Wetland Park, Stone Lake. Trails into forested wetlands. 45.848754, -91.541388.

WASHINGTON COUNTY: Heritage Trails County Park, Slinger. Trails through various habitats. 43.295820, -88.266824.

WASHINGTON COUNTY: Lizard Mound County Park, West Bend. Wooded trails around numerous effigy mounds. 43.464655, -88.140696.

WASHINGTON COUNTY: Glacier Hills County Park, Hubertus. Trails cover outstanding glacial geology and rare plants. 43.247440, -88.286208.

WASHINGTON COUNTY: Kratzsch Conservancy, Newburg. Wildlife conservancy land with trails. 43.432404, -88.060617.

WASHINGTON COUNTY: Schoen Laufen Park, Germantown. Wooded trails are the primary feature. 43.213969, -88.139254.

WASHINGTON COUNTY: Fellenz Woods, West Bend. Grassland restoration and wooded trails with views of the Milwaukee River. 43.412710, -88.112988.

WASHINGTON COUNTY: Glacial Blue Hills Recreation Area, West Bend. An Ice Age Trail segment that goes through moraine topography. 43.444011, -88.213122.

WASHINGTON COUNTY: Polk Kames Ice Age Trail segment. Wooded trails with outstanding views of glacial kames. 43.353379, -88.271123.

WAUKESHA COUNTY: Fox River Park, Waukesha. Grassland and wooded trails with views of the Fox River. 42.961853, -88.275651.

WAUKESHA COUNTY: Muskego Park, Mukwonago. Wooded trails have abundant wildflowers adjacent to them. 42.894443, -88.164584.

WAUKESHA COUNTY: Mukwonago Park, Mukwonago. Hilly savanna restorations and patches of native prairie. 42.860868, -88.383431.

WAUKESHA COUNTY: Naga-Waukee Park, Delafield. Numerous trails for adventure seekers. 43.059448, -88.370878.

WAUKESHA COUNTY: Nashotah Park, Nashotah. Grassland, forest, and bog lakes. 43.110614, -88.404588.

WAUKESHA COUNTY: Ryan Park, Pewaukee. Hiking trails through old fields and grassland restorations. 43.101460, -88.269021.

WAUKESHA COUNTY: Moorewood Park, Waukesha. Wooded Trails in an urban setting. 42.997110, -88.191749.

WAUPACA COUNTY: Camp Vic-To-Rae, New London. Wooded trails along the Wolf River. 44.399388, -88.837430.

WAUPACA COUNTY: Pigeon River Park, Clintonville. Wooded trails along the Pigeon River. 44.652288, -88.828107.

WAUPACA COUNTY: Waupaca County Forest, Waupaca. Two hundred acres of pines and hardwoods with trails. 44.257295, -88.961613.

WAUPACA COUNTY: Waupaca Eco Park, Waupaca. Wooded trails lead to river views. 44.341182, -89.034459.

WAUPACA COUNTY: Seven Maples Nature Area, Clintonville. Wooded trails with lake views. 44.628778, -88.765662.

WAUPACA COUNTY: Jorgens Park Preserve, Scandinavia. Trails around Silver Lake. 44.467489, -89.137996.

WAUPACA COUNTY: Reeve Reserve, Big Falls. Trails cover many glacial features, including large boulder fields. 44.619107, -89.037233.

WAUSHARA COUNTY: Bohn Lake IAT Segment, Hancock. Follow the trail through the plantation, oak woods, and around Bohn Lake. 44.118440, -89.445827.

WAUSHARA COUNTY: Marl Lake County Park, Wautoma. Wooded trails that end at the lake. 44.109778, -89.384265.

WAUSHARA COUNTY: Mt. Morris County Park, Wild Rose. Trails through oak woods and overlooks. 44.118301, -89.198055.

WAUSHARA COUNTY: Whistler Mounds Park, Hancock. Trails to the mounds and lake. 44.127743, -89.501767.

WAUSHARA COUNTY: Bannerman Trail, Redgranite. A seven-mile snowmobile trail open for hiking. 44.041933, -89.099474.

WAUSHARA COUNTY: Kusel Lake, Wild Rose. Year-round wilderness hiking trail. 44.169302, -89.156257.

WAUSHARA COUNTY: Buehler Nature Area and Rattlesnake Springs Trail, Wautoma. Trails through woods to the springs. 44.109058, -89.178175.

WINNEBAGO COUNTY: Heckrodt Wetland Reserve, Menasha. Boardwalks into a forested wetland. 44.211629, -88.419897.

WINNEBAGO COUNTY: Lasley Point Archaeological Site, Winneconne. Wooded trails to archaeological features. 44.126960, -88.694011.

WINNEBAGO COUNTY: Terrell's Island Trails, Omro. Breakwater trails offer great lake and waterfowl viewing. 44.072669, -88.678883.

WINNEBAGO COUNTY: Sawyer Creek Nature Preserve, Oshkosh. Prairie restorations along the trails. 44.002040, -88.613113.

WOOD COUNTY: North Wood County Park, Arpin. A trail through the old forest to streamside locations. 44.520904, -90.139998.

WOOD COUNTY: Powers Bluff County Park, Arpin. Trails east of the ski slope have abundant wildflowers. 44.529024, -90.070896.

WOOD COUNTY: Wildwood Park, Marshfield. Trails through woods and grasslands, plus many zoo animals. 44.648765, -90.189299.

WOOD COUNTY: Weber's Nature Park, Marshfield. Wooded trails in an urban setting. 44.666730, -90.213611.

WOOD COUNTY: Hamus Nature Preserve, Marshfield. Wooded trails lead to ponds. 44.697494, -90.154731.

Accessible Trails

These paved or hard surface trails permit relatively easy access for those with mobility concerns. We do not include trails with amenities geared primarily for physical exercise. Included are accessible trails with opportunities to explore trailside features, such as native vegetation, views of scenic wonders, boardwalks and piers, and wildlife viewing.

BROWN COUNTY: Devil's River State Trail, Denmark. A 1.5-mile bike-hike trail starts in Denmark. 44.348686, -87.828970.

CALUMET COUNTY: Friendship State Trail, Hilbert. A non-motor crushed stone hiking trail between Brillion and Forest Junction. 44.178787, -88.071163.

COLUMBIA COUNTY: Schoenberg Marsh WPA, Leeds. A paved trail through the planted prairie to a marsh overlook. 43.339607, -89.307704.

DANE COUNTY: Pheasant Branch Park, Middleton. A four-mile trail that circles wetlands and springs. 43.122167, -89.491367.

DANE COUNTY: Western Green Area Park, DeForest. Several miles of paved and boardwalk trails through various habitats. 43.242266, -89.356420.

FLORENCE COUNTY: Nicolet State Trail, Tipler. A hard-packed ATV trail is open for others with accessibility concerns to the wild Pine River. 45.924576, -88.634308.

FOND DU LAC COUNTY: Mascoutin Valley State Trail, Rosendale. Hard-packed hiking trail east of Rosendale. 43.814409, -88.674348.

FOND DU LAC COUNTY: Eisenbahn State Trail, Eden. This former rail corridor provides access from Kewaskum to Eden. 43.692161, -88.362955.

FOND DU LAC COUNTY: Northwestern Trail, Ripon. This 2.5-mile-old rail line provides access from Ripon to the county line. 43.862893, -88.885287.

GRANT COUNTY: Mound View State Trail, Belmont. The hard-packed trail from Belmont part way to Platteville has native prairie alongside. 42.739556, -90.336856.

GREEN COUNTY: Montesian Gardens Trail, Monticello. The trail offers access to garden displays. 42.748656, -89.598315.

IOWA COUNTY: Military Ridge Trail. The trail runs through the communities of Barneveld, Ridgeway, and Dodgeville residents. 43.016824, -89.893766.

KEWAUNEE COUNTY: Blahnik Heritage Park, Algoma. Wooded trails, boardwalk, and access to Ahnapee State Trail. 44.645229, -87.470181.

KEWAUNEE COUNTY: Harold Reckelberg Park, Luxemburg. Access to Ahnapee State Trail from Luxemburg to Casco. 44.530492, -87.650180.

LA CROSSE COUNTY: Goose Island Interpretive Trail. A trail through the floodplain forest. 43.727613, -91.214293.

LAFAYETTE COUNTY: Pecatonica State Trail, Calamine. This accessible state trail had many wetlands and views of Bonner Branch. 42.740802, -90.170203.

LANGLADE COUNTY: Antigo Lake Park Trail, Antigo. Accessible trail and boardwalk through wetlands with lake views. 45.14270, -89.144452.

MARATHON COUNTY: Mountain-Bay State Trail $, Ringle. An accessible trail through woods that merges with the Ice Age Trail. 44.890874, -89.424451.

MILWAUKEE COUNTY: Menomonee River Parkway, Oak Leaf Trail, Wauwatosa. Riverside accessible trail through diverse habitats. 43.056626, -88.027338.

MILWAUKEE COUNTY: Kinnickinnic River Parkway, Jackson Park, Milwaukee. A wooded urban park with river access and a swimming lake. 42.997108, -87.963678.

MILWAUKEE COUNTY: Honey Creek Parkway, Milwaukee. Accessible trail with multiple access points to Honey Creek. 43.029580, -88.017077.

MILWAUKEE COUNTY: Oak Creek Parkway. An accessible trail through diverse habitats. 42.876373, -87.909058.

MONROE COUNTY: Tomah Recreation Trail, Tomah. Accessible trail with lake views and many habitats for viewing. 43.980368, -90.516257.

OUTAGAMIE COUNTY: Fox River Trail, Appleton. Paved trails along the north shore of the Fox River. 44.266626, -88.384126.

OUTAGAMIE COUNTY: Newberry Trail, Appleton. Paved trail adjacent to the Fox River. 44.254689, -88.394254.

OUTAGAMIE COUNTY: Newton-Blackmour State Trail, Black Creek. The trail to the east is more diverse and connects with Fallen Timbers Environmental Center. 44.475477, -88.450740.

POLK COUNTY: Cattail State Trail, Amery. The motorized trail is still suitable for accessible use from Amery to Beaver Brook. 45.311039, -92.356976.

PORTAGE COUNTY: Green Circle Trail, Stevens Point. A 27-mile accessible trail weaves through the city. 44.519537, -89.540890.

RACINE COUNTY: WE Energies Trail, Caledonia. An accessible trail through various habitats. 42.827843, -87.833975.

RACINE COUNTY: White River State Trail $, Burlington. An old rail trail that connects to Elkhorn. 42.659130, -88.308199.

RACINE COUNTY: Pike River Trail System, Mount Pleasant. Grassland, wetlands, and ponds are features along the trail. 42.737463, -87.872800.

ROCK COUNTY: Rock River Ice Age and Peace Trail, Janesville. The trail goes through many habitats along the Rock River. 42.664351, -89.055390.

SAUK COUNTY: Baraboo Riverwalk, Baraboo. A paved trail through the city along the Baraboo River. 43.468224, -89.754331.

SAUK COUNTY: Sauk City Riverfront Park, Sauk City. Accessible trails with views of and access to the Wisconsin River. 43.279133, -89.716437.

SAUK COUNTY: Great Sauk State Trail $, Prairie du Sac. Paved accessible trail within the former Badger Army Ammunition Plant. 43.343070, -89.742412.

SHAWANO COUNTY: Mountain-Bay State Trail $, Bonduel. Bike and horse trail with some accessible features near Bonduel. 44.749392, -88.459008.

SHEBOYGAN COUNTY: Interurban Trail, Cedar Grove. Accessible trail between Cedar Grove and Oostburg. 43.615650, -87.802341.

SHEBOYGAN COUNTY: Old Plank Road Trail, Plymouth. The section at Plymouth, where it crosses the Mullet River, has the best natural features. 43.760507, -87.980940.

SHEBOYGAN COUNTY: June Vollrath Park Trails, Elkhart Lake. The trail system skirts wooded areas. 43.841760, -88.013910.

WAUKESHA COUNTY: Waukesha River Walk, Waukesha. A trail along the Fox River in downtown Waukesha. 43.021979, -88.222460.

WAUPACA COUNTY: Wau-King Trail, Waupaca. An accessible trail through various habitats. 44.334043, -89.144764.

Lake Swimming Beaches

Lake swimming has many more amenities for nature lovers than splash pads or municipal pools. Opportunities exist for making sand castles, watching minnows, collecting shells, and exploring plant life. On the downside are algal blooms, turbid conditions, and, most importantly, limited use due to weather. Regardless, we love exploring available swimming in lakes. Here are some of our favorites for the reader to consider.

BARRON COUNTY: Cumberland Lakeside Beach Park, Cumberland. Sandy beach, accessible fishing pier.. 45.543409, -92.021445.

BAYFIELD COUNTY: Bayview Beach, Washburn. A long stretch of sandy beach along Chequamegon Bay with great botany inshore. 46.747336, -90.885933.

BAYFIELD COUNTY: Thompson's West End Park, Washburn. Beach and lakefront walking trail. 46.666437, -90.902482.

BAYFIELD COUNTY: Port Wing Boreal Forest State Natural Area, Port Wing. A one-half mile long section of sandy beach on Lake Superior. 46.792077, -91.402832.

BAYFIELD COUNTY: Twin Bear Campground, Iron River. Two beaches near wooded campsites. 46.506936, -91.359830.

BAYFIELD COUNTY: Atkins Lake County Park, Cable. Small beach on a clear, deep lake. 46.281152, -91.030145.

BURNETT COUNTY: Lake 26 Park, Danbury. Sandy beach in Swiss Township. 46.010875, -92.213903.

BURNETT COUNTY: Ralph Larrabee Park, Danbury. Sandy beach on the northeast shore of Round Lake. 45.987719, -92.368517.

CHIPPEWA COUNTY: Pine Point County Park, Holcombe. Beach on a peninsula into Lake Holcombe. 45.243882, -91.157130.

CLARK COUNTY: Mead Lake County Park, Greenwood. Small sandy beach at the campground. 44.791481, -90.759292.

DANE COUNTY: Marshall Park, Madison. This small beach is algae-free most of the time. 43.093600, -89.482105.

DODGE COUNTY: Crystal Lake Park, Beaver Dam. This lake is more developed than most in this section. 43.454900, -88.804343.

DOOR COUNTY: Baileys Harbor Ridges Park, Baileys Harbor. Excellent sand beach with outstanding beachside flora. 45.070245, -87.118323.

DOOR COUNTY: Frank E. Murphy Park, Egg Harbor. Several hundred feet of sandy beach. 45.013585, -87.334083.

DOOR COUNTY: Percy Johnson County Park, Washington Island. Sand to cobble beach to Eastside Park. 45.362962, -86.864700.

DOUGLAS COUNTY: Wisconsin Point, Superior. More than one mile of the sand spit. 46.686258, -91.974587.

EAU CLAIRE COUNTY: Lake Altoona Park, Altoona. Sandy beach on Lake Altoona. 44.811073, -91.423060.

EAU CLAIRE COUNTY: Big Falls County Park, Eau Claire. Sandbars on the Eau Claire River near Big Falls. 44.820874, -91.293161.

FLORENCE COUNTY: Lake Emily Park, Florence. Beach near the boat ramp. Also, the park has wooded trails. 45.873335, -88.275472.

FLORENCE COUNTY: American Legion Park and Beach at Keyes Lake, Florence. Public swimming beach. 45.894369, -88.302219.

FOREST COUNTY: Veterans Memorial Park, Crandon. A narrow beach on the south shore of Metonga Lake. 45.522012, -88.899777.

IRON COUNTY: Lake of the Falls County Park, Mercer. Wooded trails, waterfalls, and beaches are features. 46.149653, -90.160220.

IRON COUNTY: Weber Lake Park, Montreal. Deep in the heart of the Penokees, this lake has a beach. 46.409806, -90.392845.

JUNEAU COUNTY: Castle Rock Park, Mauston. Sandy beach on Castle Rock Lake. 43.889494, -89.972897.

KENOSHA COUNTY BEACH PARKS: Old Settlers Park – 42.569563, -88.098172. Silver Lake Park – 42.556754, -88.144617. Simmons Island Beach – 42.591403, -87.813976. Alford Park – 42.612607, -87.820091.

KEWAUNEE COUNTY: Bay Shore Park, New Franken. Beach along Green Bay and wooded trails. 44.637696, -87.801275.

LINCOLN COUNTY: Otter Lake Recreation Area, Gleason. Primitive campground with wooded trails and a small beach. 45.437898, -89.544495.

LINCOLN COUNTY: SARA Park, Tomahawk. City Park with a beach. 45.474696, -89.742091.

MANITOWOC COUNTY: Point Creek Natural Area, Manitowoc. Wooded trails and a section of Lake Michigan beach. 43.971378, -87.701767.

MANITOWOC COUNTY: Neshotah Beach, Two Rivers. Wide sandy beach on the north side of Two Rivers. 44.151409, -87.553954.

MARATHON COUNTY: Mission Lake County Park, Hatley. Sandy beach with natural vegetation nearby. 44.778085, -89.356120.

MARINETTE COUNTY: Lake Noquebay Park, Crivitz. Sandy beach on the lake's south shore. 45.246075, -87.905017.

MARINETTE COUNTY: Morgan County Park, Niagra. Trails, bedrock glades, and a sandy beach are features. 45.670594, -87.893744.

MILWAUKEE COUNTY: Bradford Beach. Large beach along Lake Michigan. 43.061289, -87.874241.

OCONTO COUNTY: North Bay Shore County Park, Oconto. Large beach on the north shore of Green Bay. 44.961329, -87.781909.

OCONTO COUNTY: Oconto City Park, Oconto. Sandy beach on the west shore of Green Bay. 44.858818, -87.855095.

ONEIDA COUNTY: Perch Lake Park, Rhinelander. A small beach on the east shore of Perch Lake. 45.632352, -89.573963.

OZAUKEE COUNTY: Port Washington South Beach Park, Port Washington. Extensive beach along Lake Michigan. 43.382407, -87.870567.

PEPIN COUNTY: Stockholm Village Park, Stockholm. Beach near rock jetty extending well into Lake Pepin. 44.479519, -92.263199.

PIERCE COUNTY: Prescott Beach, Prescott. Large sandy beach along the shore of the St. Croix River. 44.756254, -92.804233.

PORTAGE COUNTY BEACH PARKS: Jordan County Park – 44.578644, -89.498643. Lake Emily County Park – 44.470266, -89.332243. Lake Helen County Park – 44.620303, -89.239016. DuBay County Park – 44.675591, -89.690078. Collins County Park – 44.601204, -89.343105.

PRICE COUNTY: Solberg Lake County Park, Phillips. Park on the north shore of Solberg Lake. 45.761674, -90.366762.

PRICE COUNTY: Smith Lake County Park, Park Falls. A small beach on the lake. 45.903195, -90.498502.

RACINE COUNTY: Fischer Park, Burlington. Sandy beach on the south shore of Browns Lake. 42.681360, -88.237321.

RUSK COUNTY: Memorial Park, Ladysmith. Beach on a flowage of the Flambeau River. 45.468866, -91.101732.

SHAWANO COUNTY: Shawano Lake County Park, Shawano. Extensive beach on the north shore of Shawano Lake. 44.825484, -88.532937.

SHEBOYGAN COUNTY: North Side Municipal Beach, Sheboygan. Expansive beach and play area. 43.756213, -87.703383.

SHEBOYGAN COUNTY: South Side Municipal Beach, Sheboygan. Extensive beach and dunes system. 43.744069, -87.706902.

ST. CROIX COUNTY: Homestead Parklands County Park, Hudson. Sandy beach on Perch Lake. 45.056590, -92.698155.

ST. CROIX COUNTY: Troy Beach, Hudson. Steep road to a beach on the St. Croix River. 44.934700, -92.739252.

WALWORTH COUNTY: Williams Bay Beach $, Lake Geneva. Across East Geneva Street is a nature conservancy. 42.578530, -88.534857.

WALWORTH COUNTY: Fontana Beach $, Lake Geneva. Urban beach is adjacent to the harbor. 42.547214, -88.571190.

WALWORTH COUNTY: Big Foot Beach State Park $, Lake Geneva. This small state park has an outstanding beach. 42.566331, -88.433546.

WASHBURN COUNTY: Mayne Beach, Shell Lake. Large sandy beach and play area. 45.742914, -91.921645.

WASHINGTON COUNTY: Leonard J. Yahr County Park, West Bend. Sandy beach on Erler Lake. 43.478974, -88.095076.

WAUKESHA COUNTY: Fox Brook Park, Brookfield. Expansive beach and play area on Fox Brook Lake. 43.073932, -88.169856.

WAUKESHA COUNTY: Menomonee Park, Menomonee Falls. Sandy beach on Trout Lake. 43.157218, -88.173492.

WAUKESHA COUNTY: Minooka Park, Waukesha. Small beach on a pond in the park. 42.986459, -88.197049.

WAUSHARA COUNTY: Lake Alpine County Park, Wautoma. Sandy beach with adjacent woods ready for exploration. 44.059307, -89.190388.

WOOD COUNTY: Dexter Park, Dexterville. Sand beach on Lake Dexter with nearby woods ripe for exploring. 44.385840, -90.122279.

WOOD COUNTY: Nepco Lake Park, Port Edwards. A popular park just south of Wisconsin Rapids. 44.343796, -89.815365.

WOOD COUNTY: South Wood County Park, Wisconsin Rapids. Beach with a grassy area. 44.366732, -89.756571.

Designated Snowshoe Trails

Snowshoeing has a significant advantage over many other outdoor sports, except hiking, in that a person can do it almost anywhere there's access. The creation of the snowshoe purposefully allows the user to go nearly anywhere in winter. Most outdoor enthusiasts, however, prefer to do their snowshoeing on trails specifically designed for such activity. We present a few of our favorite snowshoe-specific tracks outside those mentioned in earlier sections.

BAYFIELD COUNTY: Diamond Lake Snowshoe Hike, Grandview. Fall hunter-walking trails are designated snowshoe trails in winter. 46.264013, -91.155019.

LANGLADE COUNTY: Gartzke Flowage Trails, Polar. This recreation area has designated snowshoe trails. 45.132467, -88.964542.

LINCOLN COUNTY: Underdown Recreation Area, Gleason. This recreation area has designated snowshoe trails. 45.276600, -89.585323.

POLK COUNTY: Somers Lake Recreation Area Trails, Frederic. This winter recreation area has wooded trails. 45.659833, -92.364918.

SAWYER COUNTY: Hatchery Creek Trails, Hayward. Several miles of snowshoe trails are found in the county park. 46.021177, -91.432094.

SHAWANO COUNTY: Maple Hills Recreation Area, Shawano. Designated snowshoe trails go through the wooded hills. 44.741642, -88.636939.

VILAS COUNTY: The Tamaracks OHM Snowshoe Trails $, Conover. Trails through wetlands and pine forests are features. 46.090976, -89.312118.

Nature Immersion Sites

These sites are places with few or no amenities. The visitor is responsible for their personal safety needs. Knowledge of natural systems and orienteering are a must. We present here some of our favorite immersion sites. The focus is primarily on botanical richness, but sometimes, animal concentrations are featured. Areas with extreme sensitivity to human disturbance, such as fens, floating bogs, and rookeries, are purposefully left off our list for obvious reasons.

ADAMS COUNTY: Sohlberg Silver Lake State Natural Area, Friendship. Undeveloped lake with rare shoreline plants. 43.892441, -89.917735.

ADAMS COUNTY: Burt Morris Land, Adams. Over 1,000 acres of wetland swales in deciduous uplands. Foot traffic only. 44.171034, -89.762854.

ADAMS COUNTY: New Chester Waterfowl Production Area. More than 300 acres of grassland, woods, and wetlands for exploring. 43.854239, -89.627884.

ASHLAND COUNTY: Dry Lake State Natural Area, Glidden. Pristine wetlands and old-growth forests around Dry Lake. 46.227980, -90.584317.

ASHLAND COUNTY: Caroline Lake State Natural Area, Ballou. Bad River headwaters with managed old forest surrounding it. 46.268285, -90.561635.

BARRON COUNTY: Prairie Farm Cliffs, Prairie Farm. Just south of Pioneer Park is a series of public-owned wooded cliffs with many prairie elements. 45.240334, -91.985997.

BAYFIELD COUNTY: Nourse Sugarbush State Natural Area, Bayfield. Old sugarbush maples, some with Native American workings. 46.780519, -90.902116.

BAYFIELD COUNTY: Inch Lake State Natural Area, Iron River. Undeveloped lake with patches of old red pines. 46.495657, -91.349401.

BUFFALO COUNTY: Trempealeau River Meadow State Natural Area, Fountain City. Wet prairie restoration dominates the site. 44.189574, -91.621280.

BURNETT COUNTY: Clam Lake State, Wildlife Area, Siren. Grasslands, woods, and abundant wetlands are features. 45.770144, -92.311113.

BURNETT COUNTY: Fish Lake Pines State Natural Area, Grantsburg. This primitive trail leads to old-growth red pines. 45.708137, -92.720268.

CALUMET COUNTY: Kiel Marsh State Wildlife Area, Kiel. Extensive wetlands are ripe for exploration. 43.901678, -88.058417.

CALUMET COUNTY: Stockbridge Ledge Woods State Natural Area, Stockbridge. Outstanding botany occurs over thin ledge-top soils. 44.046101, -88.281448.

CHIPPEWA COUNTY: Plagge Woods State Natural Area, Holcombe. Old forest with abundant wildflowers. 45.278027, -91.199983.

CHIPPEWA COUNTY: Kemper Woods, Lake Hallie. An 80-acre forest with 50 years of bird study. 44.914938, -91.358650.

CLARK COUNTY: Bald Peak Marsh, High Conservation Value Resource, Foster. Extensive sedge meadow west of Bald Peak. 44.629977, -90.802081.

CLARK COUNTY: Horse Creek Marsh, Fairchild. Extensive sedge meadow in a forest matrix. 44.667214, -90.895293.

COLUMBIA COUNTY: Gibraltar Rock State Natural Area, Lodi. The Ice Age Trail provides access, but immersion is possible. 43.349731, -89.600558.

COLUMBIA COUNTY: Becker Waterfowl Production Area, Pardeeville. More than 350 acres are open for exploration of wetlands and restored prairie. 43.561595, -89.306116.

DANE COUNTY: Badfish Creek State Wildlife Area, Madison. Spring seeps and sedge meadows mix with non-native grasses. 42.880036, -89.276361.

DANE COUNTY: Waubesa Wetlands State Natural Area, Oregon. Deep springs and wet meadows are featured along with upland woods. 42.993128, -89.361705.

DANE COUNTY: Hook Lake Wildlife Area, Oregon. Featured is a bog lake with a restored prairie in the uplands. 42.933307, -89.321946.

DANE COUNTY: Lake Barney Waterfowl Production Area, Fitchburg. Fall hotspot for LeConte's and Nelson sparrows. 42.950333, -89.417347.

DANE COUNTY: Erbe Grassland, The Prairie Enthusiasts, Blue Mounds. Restored tall grass prairie. 42.999494, -89.787261.

DOOR COUNTY: Big and Little Marsh State Natural Area, Washington. These wetlands contain fen elements and have great wildflower displays. 45.370094, -86.878631.

DOOR COUNTY: Jackson Harbor Ridges State Natural Area, Washington Island. Dunes, forested ridges, and swale have outstanding botany. 45.398932, -86.855843.

DOOR COUNTY: Bayshore Blufflands State Natural Area, Sturgeon Bay. The Niagara Escarpment and woods are primary features. 44.935155, -87.390418.

DOOR COUNTY: Kangaroo Lake, Peninsula Center. Dense woodland and wetlands are features. 45.054864, -87.172816.

DOUGLAS COUNTY: Upper Nemadji River SNA, Superior. The floodplain along the Nemadji River contains many southern Wisconsin wildflowers. 46.550987, -92.246616.

DUNN COUNTY: Otter Creek Oak Barrens State Natural Area, Wheeler. A significant oak barrens restoration is featured. 45.096273, -91.839500.

DUNN COUNTY: Big Beaver Wildlife Area, Baxter. Sedge meadow wetlands with patches of wet prairie and tamaracks are highlights. 45.121115, -91.996699.

DUNN COUNTY: Russian Slough County Park, Colfax. Floodplain forests and shrub-carr are challenges for the nature immersion enthusiast. 44.991101, -91.807721.

DUNN COUNTY: Rock Falls Wildlife Area, Rock Falls. Restored prairie and prairie potholes draw visitors. 44.711467, -91.690884.

FOND DU LAC COUNTY: Calvary Marsh, Mount Calvary. Paddle upstream on the Sheboygan River to the marsh-sedge meadow. 43.815946, -88.212494.

FOND DU LAC COUNTY: Guskey-Miller Prairie Conservancy, Ripon. Thirty-eight acres of native and restored prairies are prime for exploration. 43.85851, -88.85694.

FOREST COUNTY: Little Rice Lake Wildlife Area, Crandon. Access makes this immersion site a challenge. 45.619657, -88.978843.

GRANT COUNTY: Devil's Backbone State Natural Area, Glen Haven. Steep bluffs and tufa formations capture the nature enthusiast's imagination. 42.846747, -91.071814.

GRANT COUNTY: Cassville Bluffs State Natural Area, Cassville. Steep bluffs with native goat prairies are features. 42.700206, -90.939356.

GRANT COUNTY: Borah Creek Prairie State Natural Area, Lancaster. Native and restored prairie offers visitors a view of the presettlement of Grant County. 42.939624, -90.691970.

GRANT COUNTY: Bagley Bottoms, Bagley. Federal Refuge land featuring floodplain forest and backwater sloughs. 42.909822, -91.122625.

GRANT COUNTY: Grant River Paddle from Hwy 35/81 bridge in Lancaster to Potosi Point. The river flows near numerous dripping cliff formations. 42.814746, -90.834051.

GREEN COUNTY: Browntown Oak Forest State Natural Area, within Cadiz Springs Recreation Area $, Browntown. Old-growth oaks dominate the site. 42.586683, -89.760159.

GREEN COUNTY: York Prairie State Natural Area, Blanchardville. Native and restored prairies dominate the landscape. 42.841128, -89.788725.

GREEN COUNTY: Muralt Bluff Prairie State Natural Area, Albany. One of the premier dry prairies in the state. 42.704513, -89.493553.

GREEN LAKE COUNTY: Puchyan Prairie State Natural Area, Green Lake. Wet prairie and an oak savanna island are protected here. 43.881399, -89.026943.

IOWA COUNTY: Pecatonica River Woods State Natural Area, Mifflin. An oak woodland with rare species. 42.841791, -90.336993.

IOWA COUNTY: Military Ridge Prairie Heritage Area, Blue Mounds. Extensive native and restored prairie lands. 42.949151, -89.866984.

IOWA COUNTY: Trout Creek Fishery Area, Ridgeway. Trout streams, steep woods, and cliffs are features. 43.071027, -89.965754.

IRON COUNTY: Carpenter Creek Woods, Saxon. Old hemlock and cedars are protected as high conservation value on county forest land. 46.558306, -90.449261.

IRON COUNTY: Lake Evelyn State Natural Area, Oma. A wild lake with surrounding bog and uplands. 46.272405, -90.075447.

IRON COUNTY: Island Lake Hemlocks State Natural Area, Knight. A primitive trail leads through a virgin stand of hemlock hardwoods. 46.282440, -90.311160.

IRON COUNTY: Bass Lake Preserve State Natural Area, Lac du Flambeau. A wild lake in a wilderness setting, including bog and mature forest. 45.999185, -90.036802.

JACKSON COUNTY: Bauer Brockway Barrens State Natural Area, Brockway. Stunted jack pine and scrubby oaks dominate this barrens site. 44.298218, -90.750850.

JEFFERSON COUNTY: Red Cedar Lake State Natural Area, Cambridge. A shallow water lake filled with abundant aquatic vegetation is the primary feature. 42.983962, -88.974026.

JUNEAU COUNTY: Cranberry Creek Mound Group State Natural Area, Armenia. Archaeological features dominate the site, but plenty of barrens exist to explore. 44.166014, -90.056274.

JUNEAU COUNTY: Juneau County Forest, Sprague. Floodplain forest along the Yellow River is an immersion challenge. 44.142140, -90.109789.

KENOSHA COUNTY: New Munster Wildlife Area, Burlington. Boggy conditions and low, wet woods provide physical challenges. 42.551240, -88.236515.

KENOSHA COUNTY: Fox River Park, Burlington. Primitive woods along the Fox River are ripe for adventure. 42.540293, -88.176412.

KEWAUNEE COUNTY: Hunner Preserve, Denmark. A forty-acre woodlot open for discovery. 44.327609, -87.636022.

LA CROSSE COUNTY: New Amsterdam Grasslands, Holland. This site is a grassland bird refuge north of Holmen. 43.984570, -91.300676.

LAFAYETTE COUNTY: Hardscrabble Prairie State Natural Area, Hazel Green. Native and restored prairies are found throughout this old mine site. 42.527461, -90.421442.

LAFAYETTE COUNTY: Belmont Mound Woods, Belmont. Enjoy the spring wildflower display on a walk through the woods. 42.769526, -90.352204.

LANGLADE COUNTY: Hogelee Spring Fishery Area, Evergreen. Spring ponds and adjacent white cedar swamps. 45.148997, -88.929410.

LANGLADE COUNTY: Evergreen River Fishery Area, Wolf River. This dense forest along the Evergreen River invites curious adventurers. 45.130583, -88.800916.

LANGLADE COUNTY: Hunting River Paddle, Elcho. Paddle upstream to visit the Hunting River Alders SNA. 45.394450, -89.135784.

LANGLADE COUNTY: Flora Spring Pond State Natural Area, Evergreen. Trek overland through managed county forest land to the pond. 45.200532, -88.833703.

LINCOLN COUNTY: Prairie River Fishery Area, Dudley. Experience what northern rivers looked like before European settlers arrived. 45.343545, -89.466028.

MANITOWOC COUNTY: Fischer Creek Recreation Area, Cleveland. Steep bluffs along the shore of Lake Michigan with views of migrating waterfowl. 43.939821, -87.721349.

MANITOWOC COUNTY: Rahr Memorial School Forest, Two Rivers. Just north of Point Beach, the forest contains ridge and swale communities. 44.237147, -87.517952.

MARATHON COUNTY: Brokaw County Park, Wausau. A forest tract with primitive trails is the primary feature. 45.028889, -89.652243.

MARINETTE COUNTY: Seagull Bar, Marinette. A long sand spit with beach and dunes extending well into Green Bay. 45.086956, -87.587626.

MARINETTE COUNTY: Lake Noquebay Wildlife Area, Lake. Extensive wetlands on the east shore of the lake. 45.258085, -87.842007.

MARINETTE COUNTY: Town Corner Cedars State Natural Area, Athelstane. This wildlife management site has a dense cedar swamp surrounding a bog lake. 45.540187, -88.081773.

MARINETTE COUNTY: Athelstane Barrens, Athelstane. A portion of the Marinette County Forest is dedicated to maintaining pine barrens. 45.449484, -88.126984.

MARINETTE COUNTY: Amberg Wildlife Area, Amberg. Cedar swamps and pine barrens are the dominant features. 45.478138, -88.056013.

MARINETTE COUNTY: Miscauno Cedar Swamp State Natural Area, Beecher. The extensive cedar swamp with outstanding floral displays is the primary feature. 45.586243, -87.961728.

MARINETTE COUNTY: Marinette County Beech Forest State Natural Area, Athelstane. Old-growth mesic forest is found on this 40-acre tract. 45.446788, -88.328094.

MARINETTE COUNTY: Grand Island State Natural Area, Niagra. Access is by watercraft only to this island with a natural origin of red and white pine. 45.672876, -87.803003.

MARQUETTE COUNTY: Page Creek Marsh State Natural Area, Packwaukee. A mosaic of wetlands with upland savannas is featured. 43.764335, -89.424890.

MARQUETTE COUNTY: Lawrence Creek Fish and Wildlife Area, Lawrence. Abundant springs emanating from sandy oak savanna hillsides are highlights. 43.894511, -89.592281.

MARQUETTE COUNTY: Caves Creek Fishery Area, Westfield. A large spring pond and oak barrens uplands dominate the site. 43.937605, -89.539659.

MENOMINEE COUNTY: Nearly the entire county is an immersion opportunity, but only for tribal members or those with specific tribal permission.

MILWAUKEE COUNTY: Franklin Savanna, Franklin. Giant bur oaks dominate the savanna restoration. 42.858028, -88.046165.

MONROE COUNTY: Eureka Maple Woods State Natural Area, Portland. Abundant wildflowers dominate the site. 43.738387, -90.866012.

MONROE COUNTY: Sand Creek Stream Protection Area, Little Falls. Sandy barrens and small waterfalls. 44.071330, -90.957872.

OCONTO COUNTY: Oconto Preserve, Oconto. This land trust property encompasses 148 acres and lies just west of more public land. 44.894558, -87.858496.

OCONTO COUNTY: Forbes Springs State Natural Area, Lakewood. White cedars surrounding this outstanding spring are found on public land. 45.317073, -88.389080.

ONEIDA COUNTY: Patterson Hemlocks State Natural Area, Lac du Flambeau. Old-growth hemlocks dominate this site. 45.897438, -89.968601.

ONEIDA COUNTY: Upper Kaubashine State Natural Area, Hazelhurst. Boggy meadows and dry-mesic forests with access over county forest land. 45.792159, -89.787262.

ONEIDA COUNTY: Germain Hemlocks State Natural Area, Harshaw. Old-growth hemlock preserve named for the former head of the SNA Program. 45.725553, -89.606641.

ONEIDA COUNTY: Holmboe Conifer Forest, Rhinelander. Old-growth hemlocks and white pines along the Pelican River. 45.627259, -89.426268.

OUTAGAMIE COUNTY: Heath Van Handel Memorial Forest, Appleton. Primitive trails lead through this wooded tract. 44.329912, -88.510077.

OUTAGAMIE COUNTY: Casaloma Conservancy, Appleton. Urban woods are open for exploration. 44.285116, -88.473651.

OZAUKEE COUNTY: Hawthorne Hills County Park, Saukville. Primitive trails and woods near a lake. 43.452817, -87.976756.

OZAUKEE COUNTY: Birchwood Hills Nature Preserve, Port Washington. Woods and grasslands traversed by primitive trails. 43.408700, -87.865060.

OZAUKEE COUNTY: Sauk Creek Nature Preserve, Port Washington. Primitive trails and a stream are highlights of this preserve. 43.394833, -87.882454.

OZAUKEE COUNTY: River Forest Nature Preserve, Mequon. Protected forest land along the Milwaukee River. 43.236167, -87.938043.

OZAUKEE COUNTY: Pleasant Valley Nature Park, Grafton. Trails through grassland and shrubs are features. 43.352249, -87.975226.

PEPIN COUNTY: Lake Pepin Wildlife Area, Stockholm. Wooded bluffs and patches of native prairie are highlights. 44.476403, -92.242378

PIERCE COUNTY: Rush River Delta State Natural Area, Maiden Rock. The delta of Rush River extends well into Lake Pepin. 44.570333, -92.329118.

PIERCE COUNTY: Trenton Bluff State Natural Area, Hager City. Outstanding prairie with many Great Plains species present. 44.616386, -92.562245.

PIERCE COUNTY: Morgan Coulee Prairie State Natural Area, Maiden Rock. Fifty-four acres of exceptional prairie. 44.611895, -92.311855.

PIERCE COUNTY: Rush River Paddle, Salem. This seldom-used canoe route goes through incredible scenery 44.665563, -92.327508.

POLK COUNTY: Apple River Demonstration Forest, Apple River. From the Highway 8 bridge across Apple River, walk south into the county land, then state forest land. 45.395749, -92.364403.

POLK COUNTY: D.D. Kennedy County Park, Amery. Ninety-nine acres of prairie and woods with no hunting. 45.378544, -92.459112.

PORTAGE COUNTY: Emmons Creek Barrens State Natural Area, Waupaca. Pine-oak barrens near Emmons Creek highlight this immersion site. 44.304867, -89.234517.

PORTAGE COUNTY: New Hope Pines State Natural Area, New Hope. Old-growth white and red pine dominate the site. 44.574299, -89.263886.

PRICE COUNTY: Spring Creek Wildlife Area, Phillips. Springs, wet meadows, and young forests are highlights. 45.593934, -90.471095.

PRICE COUNTY: Memorial Grove Hemlocks State Natural Area, Fifield. Old-growth hemlock stands, and a veterans memorial is highlighted. 45.891018, -90.055610.

RICHLAND COUNTY: Burlington School Forest, Burlington. Wooded 106 acres just west of the Bong Recreation Area. 42.630294, -88.188413.

RICHLAND COUNTY: Willow Creek Fishery Area, Ithaca. Scattered woods and wet prairie are found along the trout stream. 43.377463, -90.259673.

RICHLAND COUNTY: Melancthon Creek Fishery Area, Henrietta. Wet meadows are along the stream, but the hills have rich wildflowers. 43.542466, -90.355256.

ROCK COUNTY: Androne Woods, Beloit. Forty acres of woods with trails are the highlights. 42.555441, -89.139342.

ROCK COUNTY: Spring Creek Reserve, Beloit. Nearly 70 acres of prairie restoration. 42.525777, -89.095243.

RUSK COUNTY: Ten Mile Creek Wildlife Area, Rusk. Immersion values include stream, sedge, meadow, and ponds. 45.325912, -91.539701.

SAUK COUNTY: Sauk County Forest, Lone Rock. A combination of planted pines and native jack pine-oak barrens. 43.188844, -90.173030.

SAUK COUNTY: McGilvra Woods State Natural Area, North Freedom. Immerse yourself in rich mesic woods with abundant spring wildflowers. 43.451134, -89.818227.

SAUK COUNTY: Fairfield Marsh Waterfowl Production Area, Greenfield. Extensive marsh and wetlands are found near the Baraboo River. 43.474301, -89.656254.

SAWYER COUNTY: Osgood Springs, Lenroot. An outstanding spring system with challenging access over county forest land. 46.081834, -91.380622.

SHAWANO COUNTY: Jung Hemlock-Beech Forest State Natural Area, Herman. Eighty-acre tract of virgin old-growth forest. 44.811187, -88.770473.

SHEBOYGAN COUNTY: Nichols Creek Wildlife Area, Cascade. Numerous springs and old-growth cedars dominate this tract. 43.680081, -88.039775.

SHEBOYGAN COUNTY: Amsterdam Dunes Preservation Area, Cedar Grove. Immersion visitors should limit their excursion to winter or summer. Hawk banding. 43.557639, -87.793135.

SHEBOYGAN COUNTY: Willow Creek Preserve, Sheboygan. An urban nature area open for exploration. 43.745240, -87.744613.

ST. CROIX COUNTY: Oakridge Lake Wildlife Area, New Richmond. A sizeable productive prairie pothole and oak woods are available for exploration. 45.180505, -92.489772.

TAYLOR COUNTY: Kuse Farm Nature Preserve, Medford. Great spot for the very young to get a taste of nature. 45.148429, -90.365113.

TREMPEALEAU COUNTY: Chimney Rock Wildlife Area, Eleva. This site contains an oak savanna and scattered sedge meadows. 44.491254, -91.461804.

TREMPEALEAU COUNTY: Vosse Coulee Wildlife Area, Taylor. Extensive wetlands with patches of native wet prairie are found here. 44.342535, -91.170951.

TREMPEALEAU COUNTY: Osseo School Forest, Sumner. Walk the Buffalo River Trail to the school forest pines. 44.577494, -91.246739.

VERNON COUNTY: Eagle Eye State Natural Area, Harmony. Bluff lands and rare plant species. 43.591490, -91.028933.

VERNON COUNTY: Romance Woods Preserve. A 1.5-mile trail leads into the woods. 43.57323, -91.12171.

VERNON COUNTY: Tunnelville Cliffs State Natural Area, La Farge. Steep wooded areas and wetlands occupy this site. 43.564081, -90.674985.

VILAS COUNTY: Camp Lake and Pines State Natural Area, Lac du Flambeau. The site features a very clear lake with unusual aquatic plants and the natural origin red pines. 46.002781, -89.728401.

VILAS COUNTY: Lake Alva-Birch Hemlock State Natural Area, Plum Lake. Hike overland to this wild lake with shoreline yellow birch and hemlock. 46.083408, -89.483979.

VILAS COUNTY: Van Vliet Hemlocks State Natural Area, Presque Isle. A primitive trail leads through old-growth hemlocks. 46.198817, -89.751744.

WALWORTH COUNTY: Turtle Creek Wildlife Area, Darien. This wildlife area has shrubby wetlands along a stream with many rare species. 42.620133, -88.786001.

WALWORTH COUNTY: Peterkin Pond Wildlife Area, Bloomfield. This prairie pothole has abundant shallow marsh species. 42.528215, -88.408188.

WAUKESHA COUNTY: Beaver Dam Lake Waterfowl Production Area, Eagle. The site has restored prairie and an extensive prairie pothole lake. 42.926679, -88.530947.

WAUPACA COUNTY: Radley Creek Fishery Area, Dayton. The primary amenities are a large spring pond and the hillside oak savanna. 44.280752, -89.169281.

WAUPACA COUNTY: Myklebust Lake State Natural Area, Scandinavia. A deep spring-fed lake and surrounding savanna woods are features. 44.491682, -89.123394.

WAUPACA COUNTY: Whitcomb Creek Remnant Fishery Area, Helvetia. Springs emanating from a white cedar swamp highlight the immersion values here. 44.591029, -89.066574.

WAUPACA COUNTY: Tellock's Hill Woods State Natural Area, Union. This small woodlot has outstanding spring wildflower displays. 44.556731, -88.860800.

WAUPACA COUNTY: Jackson Creek Woods State Natural Area, Harrison. This hardwood tract has excellent spring wildflowers. 44.671564, -89.163310.

WAUPACA COUNTY: Mud Lake Bog State Natural Area, Big Falls. A bog surrounded by rich woods is the primary feature of this site. 44.639420, -89.102123.

WAUSHARA COUNTY: Wilcox Waterfowl Production Area, Wautoma. Restored grasslands and shallow marshes are the primary features. 44.031605, -89.267331.

WAUSHARA COUNTY: Plainfield Tunnel Channel Lakes State Natural Area, Oasis. Shallow, highly fluctuating water-level lakes. 44.206775, -89.468009.

WOOD COUNTY: Paul J. Olson Wildlife Area, Milladore. This grassland site is part of the Greater Prairie-Chicken Management Area.

WOOD COUNTY: Marshfield School Forest, Lindsey. Explore 320 acres of wooded school forest land. 44.555952, -90.287638.

WOOD COUNTY: Little Bear Hemlocks State Natural Area, Eau Pleine. This hemlock-hardwood woodlot has old-growth trees. 44.606353, -89.719589.

Photo Credits

Page 12: Apostles Islands: Photo courtesy National Park Service.

Page 14: Birchwood Lakes: Photo ©Randy Hoffman.

Page 16: Shutterstock

Page 18: Shutterstock

Page 20: Shutterstock

Page 22: Shutterstock

Page 24: Flambeau River State Forest, Lake of the Pines campsite photo by © Randy Hoffman.

Page 26: Flambeau River Paddle, Flambeau River photo by © Randy Hoffman.

Page 28: Governor Knowles State Forest, bunchberry photo by © Randy Hoffman.

Page 30: Harrison Hills pond photo by © Randy Hoffman.

Page 32: Shutterstock

Page 34: Shutterstock

Page 36: Northern Highland State Forest & Turtle Flambeau, Common Loon photo by John Picken courtesy Creative Commons License CC 2.0.

Page 38: Shutterstock

Page 40: Shutterstock

Page 42: Shutterstock

Page 44: St. Croix River Paddle, photo of St. Croix River by © Randy Hoffman.

Page 48: Chequamegon-Nicolet National Forest Bayfield-Ashland Natural Areas, Morgan Falls photo by permission © Linda Parker.

Page 50: Chequamegon-Nicolet National Forest Bayfield Wilderness Areas photo by permission © Linda Parker.

Page 52: Chequamegon-Nicolet National Forest East Vilas Wilderness Areas photo by permission © Linda Parker.

Page 54: Shutterstock

Page 55: Shutterstock

Page 58: Chequamegon-Nicolet National Forest Moquah Barrens photo by permission © Linda Parker.

Page 62: Chequamegon-Nicolet National Forest Price-Vilas Natural Areas photo by permission © Linda Parker.

Page 64: Chequamegon-Nicolet National Forest Sawyer-Ashland Natural Areas photo by permission © Linda Parker.

Page 66: Chequamegon-Nicolet National Forest Taylor County Natural Areas large tree photo by permission © Linda Parker.

Page 70: Sutterstock

Page 72: Black River State Forest: Photo ©Randy Hoffman.

Page 74: Chippewa Moraine, Townline Lake photo by © Randy Hoffman.

Page 76: Door Peninsula, Moonlight Bay Bedrock Beach photo © Randy Hoffman.

Page 78: Eau Claire and Clark County Wild Areas, Coon Fork Barrens photo by © Randy Hoffman.

Page 80: Shutterstock

Page 82: Jackson-Wood County Natural Areas, Spaulding Fen photo by © Randy Hoffman.

Page 84: Shutterstock

Page 86: Shutterstock

Page 88: Lower Chippewa River, Photo of Dunnville Barrens by © Randy Hoffman.

Page 90: Shutterstock

Page 92: Meadow Valley Wildlife Area, primitive campsite photo by © Randy Hoffman.

Page 94: Shutterstock

Page 96: Shutterstock

Page 100: Shutterstock

Page 102: Wyalusing State Park, Cerulean Warbler photo by US Fish and Wildlife Service under Wikipedia license cc-by-sa 2.0.

Page 106: Boundary Waters: Canoe pictograph photo by D. Gordon E. Robertson CC BY-SA 3.0.

Page 108: McCormick Wilderness, hiker photo by © Randy Hoffman.

Page 110: Shutterstock

Page 112: Shutterstock

Page 114: Sturgeon River Wilderness Area, photo of Sturgeon Falls by © Randy Hoffman.

Page 116: Shutterstock

East Fork of the Black River photo by © Randy Hoffman.

Page 235: Photo by © Laura Stingley.

Page 256: Accessible trail at the Ridges Sanctuary photo by © Randy Hoffman.

Page 260: Lake Swimming Beach photo by © Laura Stingley.

Page 265: Shutterstock

Page 266: Rock Island camping photo by © Randy Hoffman

Icon Attribution

Adrien Coquet, (April 27, 2019). "Paved/Packed Trail," https://thenounproject.com/icon/path-2587338/.

Barurezeki, (October 4, 2020). "Fishing," https://thenounproject.com/icon/fishing-3931035/.

Deemak Daksina, (November 26, 2018). "Lake," https://thenounproject.com/browse/icons/term/lake/?qv=2183546.

J703, (November 12, 2002). "Waterfall," https://thenounproject.com/icon/waterfall-5354754/.

Kukuh Wachyu Bias, (December 5, 1029). "River," https://thenounproject.com/icon/river-3535459/.

Made, (October 10, 2017). "Beach," https://thenounproject.com/icon/beach-1331649/.

Made, (March 7, 2018). "Camping," https://thenounproject.com/icon/camping-1629609/.

Marc Serre, (February 24, 2016). "Mountain Bike Trail," https://thenounproject.com/icon/mountain-bike-364631/.

Mariia Nisiforova, (September 2, 2015). "Hiking," https://thenounproject.com/icon/hiking-204712/.

Melvin Ilham Oktaviansyah, (September 4, 2020). "Cliff," https://thenounproject.com/icon/cliff-3906038/.

Tamiko Young, (December 13, 2017). "Snowshoeing," https://thenounproject.com/icon/snowshoeing-1484244/.

Verry Poernomo, (May 20,2020) "Visitor Center," https://thenounproject.com/icon/address-3781313/

Vicons Design, (June 14, 2014). "MTB Off-Road Track," https://thenounproject.com/browse/icons/term/mtb-off-road-track/?qv=55286.

Wireform, (June 13, 2017). "Canoe," https://thenounproject.com/icon/canoe-1107304/.

About the Authors

Retired ecologist, Randy Hoffman, spent his nearly 30-year career with the Wisconsin State Natural Areas Program. His statewide responsibilities provided the opportunity to experience the best nature Wisconsin has to offer. Hoffman's ecological work led to the establishment of more than 300 State Natural Areas. He is the past President of the Wisconsin Society for Ornithology, author of Wisconsin's Natural Communities, When Things Happen, and was the major contributor to Wisconsin's Important Bird Areas. He enjoys nature exploration, birding, writing, and public service. He lives with his wife, JoAnn, in Waunakee, WI.

Cody and Laura Stingley live in DeForest, WI, with their two children. Both are proud graduates of the University of Wisconsin-Stevens Point, where they met and bonded over their shared love of the natural world. When responsibilities pry them away from Wisconsin's magnificent natural areas, Laura works in Internal Operations at an accounting firm and Cody teaches Math and Computer Science at a public high school.

Index

Printed in the United States
by Baker & Taylor Publisher Services